THE PARADOX OF PROGRESSIVE THOUGHT

The Paradox of
PROGRESSIVE
THOUGHT

David W. Noble

University of Minnesota Press, Minneapolis

Library of Congress Catalog Card Number: 58-8765

PUBLISHED IN GREAT BRITAIN, INDIA, AND PAKISTAN BY THE
OXFORD UNIVERSITY PRESS, LONDON, BOMBAY, AND KARACHI
AND IN CANADA BY THOMAS ALLEN, LTD., TORONTO

Revised portions of the following articles by David W. Noble are here reprinted by permission of the copyright holders: "The *New Republic* and the Idea of Progress, 1914–1920," copyright 1951 by Mississippi Valley Historical Association (*Mississippi Valley Historical Review*); "The Paradox of Progressive Thought," copyright 1953 by *American Quarterly*; "Simon Patten: Relativist or Utopian," copyright 1954 by *Antioch Review*; "Herbert Croly and American Progressive Thought," copyright 1954 by *Western Political Quarterly*; "The Religion of Progress in America, 1890–1914," copyright 1955 by New School for Social Research (*Social Research*); "Veblen and Progress: The American Climate of Opinion," copyright 1955 by *Ethics*; and "Carl Becker: Science, Relativism and the Dilemma of Diderot," copyright 1957 by *Ethics*.

Preface

THIS is an essay in interpretation; its method was inspired by Carl Becker's *The Heavenly City of the Eighteenth-Century Philosophers*. It is a book, therefore, about a climate of opinion, specifically the climate of opinion shared by the men included in this book. By implication it becomes clear that I believe it is a climate of opinion shared by others of their generation. I do not believe, however, that this group of attitudes is that of all Americans who lived between 1880 and 1920. Nor do I believe it exhausts the attitudes of those discussed in this book. But it is my conviction that these attitudes are central to the intellectual life of the men involved here and extremely important to the America of their day.

To avoid confusion, I may add that it is my view that the central ideas, which I have chosen to call the climate of opinion of these progressive-minded social philosophers, were not built up concept on concept by any one particular man. Here are ideas which developed among many men during these decades. Each man emphasized particular aspects of what appears to be a common faith, a common set of assumptions about man and the world, held deeply and emotionally in the heart and not alone in the mind. I have, therefore, not tried to trace the influence of one thinker on another, an influence which, indeed, does not exist on this fundamental level of belief.

The climate of opinion described here is part of the liberal tradition of America. Since I question many of the accepted views about the philosophical basis of the liberal tradition, this study has a peculiarly timeless quality; it does not fit into a story which stops in

v

1880 or begins again in 1920. For the historian this is not only regrettable but unpardonable. As a partial excuse, I plead the tentative quality of this study. I, like the reader, will want to find out more about the place of Aristotelian evolution in Western thought. I too want to know more about the continued existence of primitivism in the nineteenth century; the place of moral philosophy as a background of social science; the influence of Emerson, of Hegel, and of Comte; the role of the German university in shaping American attitudes; the place of liberal Christianity as a basic philosophical force in America and much more. And to rectify this situation somewhat, I ask the reader to relate what I have written to two books which may provide some of the perspective which is necessary for every historical analysis. These are Louis Hartz's *The Liberal Tradition in America* and Henry Nash Smith's *Virgin Land*.

For Professor Hartz, the key to an understanding of American liberalism is the social structure of colonial America. Here were to be found middle-class Englishmen armed with the liberalism of John Locke which was designed to free the individual from the traditions and institutions of feudalism. But in America there was no feudalism and the liberal idea of Locke could flourish without opposition. The ideal of the self-sufficient individual rooted in private property could become the one and only American ideal permeating our culture until it was both the American mind and the American soul.

It has been impossible, therefore, in the estimation of Professor Hartz for Americans to define liberty in any other way than the absence of institutional restraint. This is a major principle for the men included in this study. But since there has been no challenge to Locke in America, Professor Hartz also believes that there has been the paradoxical danger of this absolute liberty becoming absolute conformity. If one carries equality under natural law to extremes, one arrives at the necessity of unanimity as equal people agree on equal things. Here again is a major principle held by the men studied in this book.

The perspective to be gained from *Virgin Land* amplifies that of *The Liberal Tradition in America*. In his analysis of the role of

Preface

agrarian myth in American culture, Professor Smith has emphasized two major agrarian traditions or myths. One is Manifest Destiny or the course of the American Empire westward. Breaking from the eighteenth-century English background which stressed an empire based on sea power and trade uniting the Atlantic community, American thinkers wrote of a new empire, a uniquely American Empire which would unfold in the heartland of our mid-continental wilderness in the nineteenth century. Up from savagery would develop, in orderly succession, a series of cultural advances that would culminate in an American civilization unsurpassed in the world, a civilization that would be the light of the world, the beacon of progress for all mankind. Certainly, the social philosophers included in this book shared this assumption of American Manifest Destiny. Indeed, they believed that this destiny was culminating in their generation.

Like Professor Hartz, Henry Nash Smith has found a basic paradox in American agrarian philosophy. For while Americans looked forward to technical progress and complex civilization flourishing in the environment of the American heartland, they also defined the great valley as the Garden of the world where corrupt Europeans might regain an innocence and virtue and become American democrats. The return to savagery, not the growth of civilization, was the true definition of progress. It was in 1893 that America's most famous historian, Frederick Jackson Turner, suggested how the savage environment west of the Appalachians stripped men of the burden of history, the burden of inherited institutions and traditions, the burden, therefore, of evil. The Lockean wish for complete freedom from institutions was achieved and Americans had found utopia in the Garden. But for Turner, as for his comrades in the liberal tradition, the cleansing process of savagery was merely the beginning of a better civilization: a civilization that was necessary and yet would enmesh the freehold farmer, the symbol of Lockean self-sufficiency, in the web of institutions and traditions.

As absolute liberty and absolute unanimity are self-defeating terms in the analysis of Professor Hartz, so the myth of the Garden and the myth of Empire are self-defeating terms for Professor Smith.

And he finds in Turner the symbol of the end of the agrarian tradition, a turning point in American intellectual history, because Turner could not surpass the paradox of which he was conscious.

But this need not be such a critical turning point in the history of ideas. The myth of the Garden was a restatement of the Lockean belief in the goodness of the natural man. Savagery, the essence of innocence which flowered in the Garden, was the mechanism to strip from natural man his corrupting burden of traditions and institutions. The mechanism of salvation seemed lost with the re-establishment of civilization which traditionally was defined in terms of institutions and traditions. But, if civilization were to be redefined as a mechanism that would in itself strip man of this burden, then indeed the Gordian knot of the agrarian paradox might be cut and the Manifest Destiny of the American Empire might include within itself the innocence of the Garden. This is the paradox of progressive thought analyzed in this study. The social philosophers of progressivism blended to their satisfaction civilization and savagery; and in doing so, they also fully accepted the paradox Professor Hartz has found in American liberalism: they could postulate total freedom accompanied by total uniformity as the basis of the completed cooperative commonwealth which would be the Kingdom of God on Earth.

It is a sincere pleasure to acknowledge my indebtedness to friends and colleagues for the help that made this book possible. I wish to thank especially Professors Eric Goldman and E. Harris Harbison of Princeton University; Stow Persons of the State University of Iowa; Merle Curti, under whose direction this study began, and Howard Beale of the University of Wisconsin; and Herbert Heaton of the University of Minnesota. My wife, Lois, gave indispensable editorial assistance at every stage of writing.

I would like to thank also the American Council of Learned Societies and the Universities of Wisconsin and Minnesota for grants which facilitated the research and writing of this study.

DAVID W. NOBLE

October 1957

Table of Contents

THE PARADOX OF PROGRESSIVE THOUGHT

A World without History

As AMERICANS move into the second half of the twentieth century, they do so with an increasing awareness of the revolutionary nature of the world they live in. Change, foremost in the realms of technology and science but also change with deep ramifications in the entire social, economic, political, and intellectual order, is the keynote of the day. As the average man becomes aware of this fact, he reveals a greater interest in the writings of historians who can, perhaps, help provide perspective amid so much that is formless and fleeting. Furthermore, it is not surprising that historians have moved swiftly to meet the challenge of this new responsibility and nowhere is this more true than in a fresh area of historical endeavor, the field of intellectual history. Indeed, the development of intellectual history in the twentieth century may indicate the reaction of historians, themselves, to an era of chaos. It may indicate a desire to cut through confusion and create order within the discipline of history.

It is surprising, however, that many intellectual historians, who have been concerned with delineating the American revolution of the twentieth century as it is reflected in the main currents of thought, have reached a tightly knit consensus as to the nature of the changes in ideas during this period. This consensus is that the revolution properly begins with the impetus given the growth of industry by the Civil War. With ever-increasing acceleration through the 1870s and 1880s, this growth continued until, by the last decade of the nineteenth century, change became revolution. One of the most recent historians to place our major intellectual trends in perspective, Henry Steele Commager, in his book *The American Mind* describes this dramatic moment in these terms:

> The decade of the nineties is the watershed of American history. . . . On the one side lies an America predominantly agricultural; concerned with domestic problems; conforming, intellectually at least, to the political, economic, and moral principles inherited from the seventeenth and eighteenth centuries. . . . On the other side lies the modern America, predominantly urban and industrial; inextricably involved in world economy and politics; troubled with the problems that had long been thought peculiar to the Old World; experiencing profound changes in population, social institutions, and technology; and trying to accommodate its traditional institutions and habits of thought to conditions new and in part alien.[1]

This is the background material which supports the group agreement that there is a sharp division between the thought patterns of pre-1890 America and the America of the twentieth century. This, however, is merely the background. For these historians of ideas, the incisive factors in this almost total transformation in ideas are not the bludgeoning rude forces of social, economic, and political change but other keen-bladed ideas. Here again, Commager succinctly states the general position: "The neat, orderly universe of the Enlightenment — a universe governed by laws whose nature could be discovered by man — was disintegrating under the blows of Darwinian evolution, the new physics and the new biology . . ."[2]

With this collapse of the eighteenth-century world of ideas, a new climate of opinion, that of the twentieth century, arose to take its place. The ideas of 1950 are the logical outcome of the new doctrines which captured the American imagination at the turn of the century. In Commager's estimation ". . . the threescore years that came after 1890 possessed an unequivocal unity . . . the seminal minds of that decade still [in 1950] directed popular thought."[3]

In many ways it is truly remarkable that so many intellectual historians have found the elements of a coherent twentieth-century pattern of thought and society amidst the swirl of two world wars, enormous material growth, astonishing advances in technology, and revolutionary changes in science and also in the face of what seems inevitable — the confusion born of the sharp cleavage between the past and the present. One and perhaps the major reason for this confidence of the historians' control over the materials of history in the twentieth century is a certain assurance that while the institutional world may resist, in its complexity, a marshaling into clear-cut lines of development, the world of ideas does possess great consistency, a consistency which colors other areas, a consistency born of the pervasive scientific influence on our modern climate of opinion. Just what this scientific influence is and what our climate of opinion is were brilliantly outlined a quarter of a century ago by Carl Becker in his analysis of the eighteenth-century Enlightenment. Indeed it was Becker who made the concept of a climate of opinion fashionable as a method of historical analysis. While the focus of his book is the eighteenth century, Becker believed it impossible to comprehend that period without contrasting it with our own.

To bring understanding to the terms climate of opinion and our own climate of opinion, however, Becker first returns to the Middle Ages. Here, in an era so far removed from ours in time, it is possible to see clearly the essentials of a climate of opinion. These are, Becker relates, "instinctively held preconceptions," which control the individual's use of intelligence and logic. The preconceptions of medieval man were that "Existence was . . . a cosmic drama, composed by the master dramatist according to a central theme and on a rational plan. Finished in idea before it was enacted in fact, before the world began written down to the last syllable of recorded time, the drama was unalterable either for good or evil." Such beliefs directed men to bring logic and intelligence "to demonstrate the truth of revealed knowledge, to reconcile diverse and pragmatic experience with the rational pattern of the world as given in faith." [4] The Middle Ages, then, was an era of both faith and reason, in which reason was employed to support faith, and this is the direct antithesis of the climate of opinion of twentieth-century America.

In dramatic contrast to a world of faith and reason, Becker opposes our century which accepts neither faith nor reason, a century which cannot have faith or reason because, under the influence of modern science, we believe only in specific facts. "We start with the irreducible brute fact, and we must take it as we find it, since it is no longer permitted to coax or cajole it, hoping to fit it into some or other category of thought on the assumption that the pattern of the world is a logical one." [5] This is emphatically true because the accumulating facts of scientific research point overwhelmingly to a world without pattern or logic, to a universe of constant flux in which there are no absolutes.

Abandoning then the questions of "Why?" we have also abandoned the disciplines of the Middle Ages — theology, philosophy, and deductive logic. We ask only "What?" and "How?" and our tools of enlightenment have become history, science, and their corollary techniques of observation and measurement. Without essences of fixed natures, we must have recourse to history to identify a thing by relating its process of development and change. Even more, however, we turn to science with its appreciation of the unending realm of brute fact; we turn to science to control these facts and turn them to our immediate use without attempting to understand their ultimate meaning. Our modern climate of opinion is factual rather than rational.

We necessarily look at our world from the point of view of history and from the point of view of science. Viewed historically, it appears to be something in the making, something which can at best be only tentatively understood since it is not yet finished. Viewed scientifically, it appears as something to be accepted, something to be manipulated and mastered, something to adjust ourselves to with the least possible stress.[6]

Then Becker comes to the major purpose of the book, a correction of historical emphasis, which had previously dated in the eighteenth century the moment of substantial replacement of the medieval climate of opinion by the scientific outlook. Such an interpretation, however, Becker argued, had arisen because of a lack of understanding of the way in which men think, a lack of understanding of the power of the implicit assumptions in a climate of opinion. We can read Voltaire and Hume, he continued, and we can sympathize with them because they use terminology which is in many ways modern. We can even understand one side of their arguments — the negative — but we have ignored the positive foundations of their arguments, and it is here, Becker insisted, that they "betray their debt to medieval thought." Consciously, the *philosophes*, as reformers, used the concepts and the terminology of the growing scientific tradition to undermine established institutions and inherited ideas. Unconsciously, they used the weapons of scientific knowledge to make possible the establishment of a world based on concepts inherited from the past. ". . . there is more of Christian philosophy in the writings of the *Philosophes* than has yet been dreamt of in our histories," Becker announced, and "I shall attempt to show that the *Philosophes* demolished the Heavenly City of St. Augustine only to rebuild it with more up-to-date materials." [7]

The simple key which locks off the eighteenth century from our climate of opinion is the continued faith of the *philosophes* that existence is a "cosmic drama, composed by a master dramatist according to a central theme and on a rational plan." The eighteenth-century thinker who rejected historical Christianity continued, however, to share this same faith in the inherent, rational order of the universe. It is true that he used different terms to describe the world, but the underlying optimism of the intellectuals of the Enlightenment rested on the belief in the eternal, immutable, rational structure of their universe. This key then also opens what Becker calls "the little backstairs door that for any age serves as the secret entrance way to knowledge," a door in this case constructed of the words, "nature" and "natural law." God had revealed himself to man, not through the mysteries of established religion, but through the laws of nature. Newtonian philosophy, through the efforts of popularizers, became the common knowledge of the educated classes by the middle of the eighteenth century and it was interpreted to mean that mystery had been banished from the universe, that the universe was rational and intelligible throughout, and that with ease man could bring himself into harmony with its design.

Perhaps the eighteenth-century men had denatured the God of the Middle Ages, but they had deified nature. They also had gained confidence in their ability to conform to the precepts of this spiritually endowed nature. Here Becker joins another great name, John Locke, to that of Newton as a formative influence on the climate of opinion of the Enlightenment. The *philosophes* insisted that histori-cal Christianity obscured rather than revealed God's work, and they also insisted on the fundamental error of Christianity that preached the innate evil of man, which in turn precluded man from rationally observing God's law in nature. Now a psychology, following the precedent of Locke, was elaborated to demonstrate that man is born free from innate ideas and dispositions, and that he is shaped by his environment. It was possible, therefore, to argue that man's institu-tional and intellectual life could be brought into complete harmony with the laws of nature.

This capacity for human reform, according to Becker, was all important to the *philosophes*. It did not matter to them that the world of nature was lawful and reasonable unless man could share this law and reason. For the men of the Enlightenment, Becker wrote, were reformers first and philosophers second. The new scientific outlook, which they admired so greatly, had no intrinsic importance for them; it was meaningful only as it could be utilized in the reform and redemption of the individual and society. In bringing up the batteries of scientific inquiry to shatter the mysteries of Christianity, these men were not concerned with destruction but with construction on a higher and more advanced plane. Meeting the charge of the conservatives and defenders of Christianity that rationalism was undermining the morality of the social order, Diderot replied, "It is not enough to know more than they [the theologians] do: it is necessary to show them that we are better, and that philos-ophy makes more good men than sufficient or efficacious grace." [8] Becker's argument that the liberal thinkers of the eighteenth century were caught in the medieval habit of thought, in the habit of recon-ciling diverse and pragmatic experience with a rational pattern of the world, instead of accepting the facts of scientific knowledge in their irreducible individuality, rests on the reformist character of the Enlightenment philosophy.

The crucial task of their century was to free man from history, to break him loose from the shackles of his inherited institutions and traditions. To accomplish this, the *philosophes* had declared the availability of a standard by which to judge the past: the laws of nature. They had declared the availability of a standard on which to construct the future: the laws of nature. They had affirmed the possibility of shaping man to fit this standard because of his plastic nature. They had assured their contemporaries that man could achieve this total reform according to the laws of nature because he was endowed with the capacity for reason, a reason which could comprehend these necessary laws.

If, however, the eighteenth-century liberal, reformer though he was, was to follow logically the precepts he associated with the science of his day, he soon came face to face with a serious dilemma. He had stressed environmentalism, in order to free man from the innate weaknesses attributed to him by the conservative defenders of the *status quo*. Now he was confronted by another philosophic defense based on the necessity of accepting the *status quo*. If man is the product of his environment, if this is the reflection of nature, are not all the attributes of man equally good? Is not the superstition of history as much the product of nature as the science of the present? Who is to judge which of the environment's products are superior or inferior?

Here, Becker believes, the *philosophes* had to make a strategic retreat from their advanced position on the coldly impersonal quality of nature. They were forced to reconsider the ability of abstract reason to inform man of the distinction between good and bad. The path which this retreat followed, Becker recounts, can best be illuminated by a statement from Jean Jacques Rousseau, "We should distinguish between the variety in human nature and that which is essential to it." This, then, writes Becker, is symbolic and symptomatic of the eclipse of scientific reason in the interest of the eighteenth-century thinkers. To arrive at a necessary standard of goodness, the *philosophes* were returning to a theory of innate ideas which they had previously dismissed in advocating Locke's postulate of the mind as a *tabula rasa*. In the best tradition of medieval realism, they would search to discover what was permanent and universal in mankind as an entity. They had to identify, enumerate, and describe the qualities that were common to all men in order to determine what ideas, customs, and institutions in their own time were out of harmony with the universal natural order. Not reason but the experience of history was to provide the illumination necessary to ascend from the pervasive darkness of the present to the golden threshold of the future.

Becker credits to the Enlightenment, therefore, a renaissance of historical study in the latter part of the eighteenth century. Previous history had to be rejected *in toto* because it had studied facts for the sake of facts. Now men had to survey afresh the records of humanity along the dimensions of time and across the dimensions of space in order to gain the facts that would provide man with self-knowledge, with an appreciation of what was good and natural within the historical tradition and also of what was evil and artificial and unnecessary. Furthermore, Becker asserts that here, too, the *philosophes* took still one more step away from the scientific ideal they had claimed to cherish. In their approach to history, they foreswore a strictly objective, inductive, scientific, comparative method. They were not searching truly for the common traits of historical man; they were producing evidence to support a theory of human nature they had already accepted on faith. Beneath the veneer of science, beneath the tribute to nature, beneath the lip service to history, the eighteenth-century liberal intellectual held a religious faith. It was the basis of his climate of opinion; it was the measure against which all facts must be forced to conform; it was the source of his picture of the qualities of the natural man. It was a creed with four parts:

(1) man is not natively depraved; (2) the end of life is life itself, the good life on earth instead of the beatific life after death; (3) man is capable, guided solely by the light of reason and experience, of perfecting the good life on earth; and (4) the first and essential condition of the good life on earth is the freeing of men's minds from the bonds of ignorance and superstition, and of their bodies from the arbitrary oppression of the constituted social authorities.[9]

In comparing the thirteenth, eighteenth, and twentieth centuries, it was not fundamentally important in Becker's estimation that the thirteenth and eighteenth centuries differed in their concept of heaven. What was important to him was that they both believed in a heaven, based on an a priori faith in that heaven and on a priori faith that heaven's existence could be proved by reason. It was important that the twentieth century had broken irrevocably from this pattern of a priori faith and reason to a totally novel climate of opinion, resting on the full logical implications of history and science, implications which made impossible any faith in a heaven demonstrated by reason whether it be above or of this world.

It was Becker's interpretation that, to a significant degree, the eighteenth century was the last stand of this older pattern of thought. It was true that there was no sudden break between the ancient and the modern. Indeed as he wrote, "It has taken eight centuries to replace the conception of existence as divinely composed and purposeful drama by the conception of existence as a blindly running flux of disintegrating energy. But there are signs that the substitution is now fully accomplished." [10] It was his view that the nineteenth century was one of transition in which the power of the scientific ideal was infinitely reinforced by the prestige of the doctrine of evolution. Even here, however, evolution merely accelerated trends inherent in the logic of scientific doctrine, scientific doctrine that was being written even during the highest point of philosophic devotion to the ideal of the Heavenly City on Earth.

The divided mind of the Enlightenment, the tension which existed between the intellectuals' loyalty to the logic of progressive science and the commitment to a primitivistic natural man, has been the subject of attention of other important scholars who have, however, been more interested in the manner in which the logic of science triumphed over the tenacity of past habits, and who have been concerned with the manner in which eighteenth century science provided the basis for nineteenth- and twentieth-century advances. Ernst Cassirer in his influential book, *The Philosophy of the Enlightenment*, [11] has stressed the revolution which took place within the eighteenth century as thinkers began to abandon the deductive outlook of Descartes. He believes they came under the influence of Newtonian analysis which made no fetish of system for system's sake as Cartesian logic had done. Cassirer is sure that by the second half of the eighteenth century intellectuals were radically shifting their viewpoint of reason from a body of principles and established

truths to a theory that it was a kind of energy which operated func-
tionally. He also believes that nature lost its static qualities in the
minds of thinkers in the latter part of the century and came to be
regarded in terms of diversity and heterogeneity. Combining the
changed characteristics of reason and nature, Cassirer is finally
ready to announce that the most revolutionary aspect of the eighteenth century was the birth of a functional psychology almost completely foreign to its materialistic antecedents.

An American student of the history of philosophy, Charles
Frankel, has written a synthesis of the conflicting views on the nature
of the Enlightenment held by Becker and Cassirer. He attempts to
show the unstable combination of the outdated philosophy of progress stressed by Becker and the encroaching power of newer scientific
doctrines. He writes:

Underlying the ideas of the *philosophes* on progress were thus
two widely divergent interpretations of science, two different notions
of its nature and relationship to older dispensations. The one,
combining elements drawn from Descartes with ideas drawn from
empiricist sources, placed science in a larger metaphysical context,
attempted to establish its validity as an instrument of progress unpro-
visionally by basing it on absolute grounds external to the method of
science itself, and defined progress in terms of the movement toward
fixed moral goals which were also established absolutely; the other
. . . drew its interpretation of science, not from antecedent metaphysical principles, but from the *method* of science itself, and argued
that the use of this method required no external, absolute justification because it was itself self-corrective, and implied, consequently,
that the persisting goal of science need not be anything external to
it, but simply the preservation and extension of the conditions and
methods of inquiry.[12]

Still another authority on the history of ideas has concurred in
this thesis on the manner in which one aspect of eighteenth-century
thought anticipated the future developments of the nineteenth and
twentieth century. Arthur O. Lovejoy, in his important synthesis,
The Great Chain of Being, stressed the birth of a new idea during the
Enlightenment, the idea that "Man is by nature insatiable, and it
is the will of his maker that he should be so." [13] Even before the
romanticism of the nineteenth century then, thinkers had postulated

an active, willing individual who could not be contained within the neat, logical categories of Cartesian philosophy. Building on this beginning, however, the nineteenth-century romantics came to postulate a world of inherent motion because the creator of reality was defined in terms of development: "God himself was temporalized — was indeed, identified with the process by which the whole creation slowly and painfully ascends the scale of possibility." The romantics of the early nineteenth century were stating poetically, therefore, what was to be stated scientifically by the end of the century — that reality is a process of evolution.

Since Becker wrote his essay, historians have described the erosion of the climate of opinion of the *philosophes* as it had flourished in America until the end of the nineteenth century. They have charted the emergence of the new intellectual world of the present. It has been noted that there was a decided reaction against the Newtonian-Lockean complex of ideas by the transcendentalists in the years from 1820 onward. But it has also been recognized that Locke remained the most important single philosophical influence for the average American until the years after the Civil War. Then, with almost overwhelming suddenness, Darwin's theory of evolution entered America and proceeded to overwhelm, with a ferocious efficiency equal to the slogan "the survival of the fittest," both the Lockean and transcendental traditions.

At the end of the old century came the symbolic waning of traditions out of the past. With the dawning of the first days of the fresh new century, the American intellectual emerged, cleansed of the burdens of history, thinking in the clear-cut, functional ways so necessary to the dynamic future ahead; he was cleansed even of those half-modern ideas, half evolutionary and scientific, of the philosophic innovators like Emerson because Emerson's theories "would not truly blend with Darwinism. Transcendentalism was intuitive, not experimental, speculative, not critical; self-evident axioms served as rational premises for logical deduction, not being inductive generalizations based upon observation; and absolutes clashed with evolutionary relativism." [14]

Ringing clear and loud and unashamed in this paragraph of Professor Loewenberg is a tone of approval, approval of the transition he is describing. There can be no doubt in his reader's mind that the intuitive is not equal to the experimental, or the speculative to the experimental, or self-evident axioms to inductive generalizations, or, finally, absolutes to evolutionary relativism. There is a definite feeling of triumph and completion in much of the historical analysis of the coming of the scientific outlook to the American scene. Many of the writers participating in this group endeavor have joined Becker in sensing and approving the unique impact of this intellectual change. "Now the most significant effect of Darwin's discovery," writes one, "was not the triumph of certain specific scientific theories, but a revolutionary change in the very process by which men arrived at their convictions." [15] The reader then waits anxiously with the author through several decades of obstinate refusal by educated Americans, between 1870 and 1900, to accept the finality of this revolution and to surrender totally their allegiance to the mythology of the past because, as the author admits, "Only in the early part of this century did a decided revolt develop against the last defense of the Genteel Tradition expressed in the 'Will to Believe' movement."

The emotional involvement of the reader, however, expressed as anxiety is not serious; it is an anxiety born of enthusiasm, the anxiety of impatience. There is after all a new, a better, world in the process of birth. Man is finally losing the chains of muddled thinking which had handicapped him throughout the entire course of history. Man has at last reached the point of standing alone with unclouded eyes surveying reality as it truly is.

As Becker would say, surely an enthusiasm engendered by such a vision of significant historical culmination is pardonable even when it is doubtful whether enthusiasm has a legitimate place in this ultimate and objective world of experiment, induction, and evolutionary relativism. But on the other hand, even Becker could not help giving the impression that he believed in the superiority of his climate of opinion based on an appreciation of "the mass of irreducible brute facts." He wrote approvingly that "No respectable historian any longer harbors ulterior motives; and one who should surreptitiously introduce the gloss of a transcendent interpretation into the human story would deserve to be called a philosopher and straightway lose his reputation as a scholar."

But was history so meaningless for Becker? Was the gradual rise of the scientific way of thinking over the last eight centuries, giving history a dynamic theme, which had dissolved all patterns of thinking to reach a culmination in the twentieth century, so purely coincidental? Was it coincidental even when Becker gave sanction to this theme and voiced his approval of his own time when he wrote, "The rise of history and of science were but two results of a single impulse, two aspects of the trend of modern thought away from an overdone rationalization of the facts to a more careful and disinterested examination of the facts themselves"?[16] One comes finally then to question whether those who have described the modern climate of opinion are controlled by the all pervasive influence of science, or whether those who have delineated our climate of opinion in these terms have not in some vestigial manner operated in the manner of the *philosophes* who also announced to the world that they had forsaken the nonobjective past to follow the purity of the scientific method.

Inevitably, since historians live in the world as well as describe it, they have come to ask this question. It is a point of critical importance to every sensitive American historian because each lives in a world of liberal, democratic values. And this interpretation of history made by Becker and Commager, Cassirer and Lovejoy, Loewenberg, Frankel, and Ratner has to do with the liberal tradition. In turn, the liberal tradition, as it is embodied in the present generation, is in question because there is now uncertainty in the realm of basic principles. While it has become a commonplace to say that we live in an age of intellectual confusion, the essential truth of that statement unceasingly commands a hearing. It is a truth which liberals can deny only at their peril because theirs is a tradition which justifies itself through its ability to offer society a leadership in ideas.

It is not surprising, therefore, that the last few years have seen the publication of books written in the hope of clarifying the nature of the theoretical dislocation in which liberalism finds itself today.

15

One group includes Morton G. White's *Social Thought in America,* Daniel Aaron's *Men of Good Hope,* and Eric Goldman's *Rendezvous with Destiny.*[17] These are books written by avowed liberals who sympathize but disagree absolutely with the optimism of those who so warmly explored and welcomed the coming of scientism to America. In the estimation of White, Aaron, and Goldman, the mistaken optimism of the historical commentators is the mistaken optimism of the theoreticians who labored so hard to bring about the intellectual revolution of evolutionary relativism at the turn of the century.

These three writers have emphasized a thesis which traces liberal bewilderment to a serious weakness that developed during the era of the American progressive movement in the years 1900–1914 — a weakness stemming from the influx of this same scientific relativism into reform thought during those years. Goldman presents this position in these terms: American liberals were faced at the turn of the century with a severe intellectual problem. Wishing to formulate a philosophy justifying action and reform, they were challenged by a conservative defense of the *status quo,* "a steel chain of ideas," that denied the freedom of man to control his destiny, that imprisoned free will in a series of absolute principles and laws ranging from the eternal verities of the Constitution to the universal postulates of political economy. But not quite intellectually secure in an age of rapid change, the conservatives sought to buttress their position still further by adding the sanction of science as expressed in Herbert Spencer's deterministic definition of evolution.

In taking up evolution, however, the conservatives made themselves vulnerable to philosophical attack because, as Goldman points out, liberals could now challenge "Conservative Darwinism" with the following questions: "Why not insist on a thoroughgoing evolution and argue that contemporary institutions could and should change rapidly. . . . Why not consider Conservative Darwinism itself nothing more than an ideology that had developed in an environment of political bosses and trust magnates in order to justify that environment? Why not, in short, work out a Reform Darwinism that would dissolve away conservatism's steel chain of ideas while leaving Darwinism itself intact?"[18]

And so, according to Goldman, and also White and Aaron, the essence of the "Reform Darwinism" which characterized the thought of the progressive movement was a relativism that destroyed the conservative absolutes. Within progressivism itself, however, this relativism also proved corrosive to liberal principles. In the years after World War I, liberals discovered that they had accepted a philosophy which could destroy their own principles as well as those of their opponents; they discovered that victory over the conservatives had brought them ironically to the numbing situation of self-doubt; they discovered that "Once your own movement as well as the other fellow's is stripped of the true and the good, once thinking has entered a phase of sweeping relativism, the troubles come."[19]

The value of the scientific revolution of the twentieth century centered on Darwin has become a matter of historical debate. The first reaction of the liberal scholar was approval as he visualized the freedom of the individual to follow verifiable knowledge instead of being chained to inherited myth and tradition. The second reaction of the liberal scholar has been dismay as, in turn, he sees the individual trapped by the relativity and neutrality of evolutionary science without historical principles on which to construct value systems.

There is debate but there is also agreement among the interpreters of the American mind. Science is the controlling theme of the twentieth century whether for good or for ill. Among all uncertainties and confusions this remains as the one absolute giving meaning and continuity. We are all surely creatures of a world sharply broken loose from the past. In a sense, the historians have postulated a twentieth century without history, if one believes a necessary ingredient of history is the continuity of human experience.

There is, however, something strange and paradoxical in the acceptance by the antiscientific liberals of the definition of the modern climate of opinion by the historian who champions the scientific determination of life. Indeed, paradox may well become outrageous

17

when one considers historians debating history in a century where history does not exist.

Carl Becker has become a symbol of that escape from history which he described so well. For those who have been concerned with the theories of the professionals who write academic history, Becker is a representative of what happens when the relativism of evolution is taken too seriously. Becker, it is said, was one of the leaders in bringing subjectivism into American thinking. It was he who sensed that if evolution is the basic truth, then the world man knows is always transitory, without substantial foundation, incapable of clear-cut definition. For practical purposes, therefore, man lives in the world he creates for himself within this larger ongoing world. Out of this acceptance of Darwin, one paradoxically must move beyond science to a belief that man lives in an ideal world of his own making. According to this idealistic philosophy, man lives in a subjective world because he creates it in accordance with his interests and desires; it is a relative world because each man differs in these interests and desires and so creates his own unique image of the world; it is a presentist world because the individual makes it conform to his immediate wishes, and since he cannot know anything of lasting content and truth, all his wishes are oriented to a present situation whose conditions are his only criteria for action.

It is not that Becker taught other historians to question the basic truth of their writings that is of critical importance; rather it is the ramifications of this theory for all of society. In his presidential address to the American Historical Association, Becker had declared that everyman is his own historian.[20] History, he argued, is the memory each man holds of the past; and this memory reflects the interests and needs of the man. In order to carry on the routine of day-by-day living, each day must be put in the perspective of what happened on previous days. The success of daily enterprise depends upon the ability to relate the present to the immediate past.

Furthermore, declared Becker, a knowledge of the past is only one necessity for living in the present. The present must also be placed in the perspective of the future. "Mr. Everyman cannot do what he needs or desires to do without recalling past events; he cannot recall past events without in some subtle fashion relating them to what he needs to do." [21] And so, he continued, history is the imaginative and artificial extension of the personal experience of the individual. For men, blended together in society, there will be something like a common personal experience. Collectively, from their present interests, men will search back in the past for knowledge that enriches and enlarges their present perspective. History is relative to the interests of the individual and society; men will remember those things that they want to remember, they will discover those things which they want to discover.

This inescapable situation, Becker concluded, defines the task of the professional historian. Since he cannot know the past, the historian must become the servant of his society, to write for society the history it wants written.

We do not impose our version of the human story on Mr. Everyman; in the end it is rather Mr. Everyman who imposes his version on us. . . . Our proper function is not to repeat the past but to make use of it, to correct and rationalize for common use Mr. Everyman's mythological adaptation of what actually happened. We are surely under bond to be as honest and as intelligent as human frailty permits; but the secret of our success in the long run is in conforming to the temper of Mr. Everyman, which we seem to guide only because we are so sure eventually to follow it.[22]

Looking at it in any light, one cannot escape the bald message of Becker's address that might makes right, that the historian must write his history to conform to that side which has the most votes or the most guns. Here, then, is the kind of irrefutable truth carried in the charge of writers like Goldman, White, and Aaron that science has triumphed, bringing about the acceptance of an evolutionary philosophy which, in turn, has undermined all certainties so that, necessarily, in an age without principles might replaces right. Science equals evolution equals relativism equals uncertainty equals chaos — this is the equation which explains the peculiarly historyless society in which we live.

But does Becker really fit this formula and does the formula explain the course of intellectual events after 1890? Instead there is significant evidence that this neat formula is too neat — too abstract — to describe the roughness of a world that cannot escape history with all its attendant complexities. In the first place, Carl Becker was a man, a human being, not an intellectual cipher following blindly and innocently wherever theory would lead him. As a human being, he was keenly aware of the dilemma he faced as a moral man writing as an immoral historian. His awareness of this dilemma also re-emphasizes the fact that his thinking about science and the theory of history was done outside the issues of Darwinian evolution.

For those who have hurried to delineate Becker as a pioneer of novel twentieth-century relativistic concepts, it is well to compare this presidential address with Becker's other most famous writing, *The Heavenly City of the Eighteenth-Century Philosophers*, which appeared almost simultaneously with Mr. Everyman. There is a certain superficial resemblance between the two which obscures the vital differences in attitude of Becker when he wrote each. Strangely enough, the author of *The Heavenly City* did not follow evolution to the conclusion of subjective relativism found in "Everyman His Own Historian." Instead Becker related in this book the thesis that science had finally lifted man out of the subjectivism implicit in all history before the twentieth century. Science had made it possible for men to live in an absolute world of ascertainable facts, whereas, in the past, humanity had always followed the guidance of ephemeral myths.

It was Becker who had admiringly seen all modern history as the inevitable triumph of science when he wrote, "The rise of history and of science were but two results of a single impulse, two aspects of the trend of modern thought away from an overdone rationalization of the facts to a more careful and disinterested examination of the facts themselves." [23] Here is the glaring contradiction. In "Everyman His Own Historian," he had insisted that the present generation is anything but disinterested; he had bluntly stated that all men rationalized all facts. Yet, at the same time, Becker was offering this thesis of the triumph of modern science in the twentieth century which had caused all of us to accept facts as they truly were and not as we wanted them to be. To reconcile the two Carl Beckers, to understand the reason for this seeming contradiction, one must follow Becker back to the formative years of his intellectual attitude.

In 1915, Becker published an article, "The Dilemma of Diderot," in the *Philosophical Review*. With that gentle irony which was to characterize his later writing, the American historian chose to demonstrate the kind of tensions that existed in a thinker of a previous century when his moral values and scientific theories came into conflict. There is little of the human drama which marked Diderot's dilemma in the coldly academic questions Becker first asked in order to lead his readers toward his purpose, the revelation of the inner Diderot.

It was a matter of some little curiosity, he suggested, to answer satisfactorily the question of why Diderot stopped publishing at the very height of his intellectual powers and at the height of his prestige among the French intellectuals of the eighteenth century. Then, precisely, Becker focused the search for an answer to this seemingly innocent question on the *philosophe*'s motives in writing, on his conception of his task as a creative philosopher. While it was true, Becker affirmed, that the Frenchman had demonstrated amazing versatility in his books, which covered natural science, mathematics, drama, political science, and literary criticism, still these works all revolved around a single interest, all in a way were but variations on a single theme: the nature of religion and philosophy. True enough that he expressed contempt for contemporary philosophy and religion, but it was only because "he desired above all things to put in their place a new metaphysics and a new religion, a metaphysics rationally defensible and a religion morally sound." Diderot, Becker emphasizes and re-emphasizes, was devoted to virtue and morality, not merely in terms of theory, but especially in the realm of practice. The *philosophe* hated the established religion and philosophy of the day because he believed these traditions encouraged immorality. He denied their right to exist so that he could replace their false and imperious standards with a better system of morality: a system resting on the firm basis of right reason. For Diderot, the final test

21

for his philosophy of reason was a pragmatic one; it must make "more good men than sufficient or efficacious grace."

Year after year, Diderot poured the corrosive acid of science into his manifold writings in order to undermine the metaphysical foundations of traditional religion and philosophical theory. Successfully, in his own estimation, he destroyed the intellectual position of his greatest enemy, the established church. The world, he proclaimed, is only as science describes it. The universal values of the church, the original sinful nature of man, the miracles — all these find no verification in an empirical approach to reality which recognizes only the material and immediate qualities of things. We can know only specific, concrete facts, Diderot insisted, and, therefore, no man can successfully demonstrate the nonempirical values of the *ancien regime.*

But here, Becker wrote, here was the dilemma which inhibited Diderot in publishing his writing at the peak of his intellectual power. Honest man that he was, Diderot, after the first flush of his attack on his enemies, had come to ask himself what morality could be established on the authority of a scientific position of materialism and empiricism. After all, if man is not shaped by spiritual forces, if he does not have a permanent nature, if, indeed, he is merely one material object in a world of many concrete, specific, material objects, all without inherent value, then how can man define what morality is? Human life, as part of physical nature, shared the neutral aspects of nature. Human life could be described by the scientific method, but it could not be judged.

What could Diderot do? He believed that man could know only what science told him and yet science could not teach man what was moral. The philosophy of science of the Enlightenment, judged by Diderot's pragmatic test that it must produce more good men than established religion had done, quite clearly had failed. Diderot, sympathized Becker, was faced with the appalling fact that "The identification of man and nature, and the conception of both as the necessary product of uniform natural law, had done nothing more after all than to put blind force in the place of God, and by eliminating purpose from the world leave men face to face with the *reductio ad absurdum* that 'whatever is is right.' " [24]

This acute understanding of one intellectual for another across the barriers of more than a century of time was to provide the basis for Becker's masterpiece of historical writing a decade later: *The Heavenly City of the Eighteenth-Century Philosophers.* It was in this book that he elaborated brilliantly and ironically on the themes of his pioneering article on Diderot. It is a book which when placed in relation to his writings before World War I clearly demonstrates the inner struggles of Carl Becker, for whom the dilemma of Diderot became inescapably the dilemma of Carl Becker. It was this inner emotional conflict which undoubtedly made possible his understanding of the eighteenth century. It was also this conflict which led Becker to that subjectivist interpretation of history which he came to reject in the years immediately before his death.

There can be no doubt that by 1915 Becker realized that the dilemma of Diderot was also his. Writing in the *American Journal of Sociology* in 1913, at the moment of the political climax of American progressivism, he proposed that history and historical writing should be used consciously for the betterment of mankind.[25] This was the American historian paralleling Diderot in his desire for a more virtuous and moral world, in his belief that knowledge must pass the pragmatic test of making men better. He had called his article "Some Aspects of the Influence of Social Problems and Ideas upon the Study and Writing of History." He wrote it with the express purpose of enlisting the historical profession in the ongoing battle for progress. He also wrote it to help destroy the intellectual position of those who would use history to defend the *status quo.*

Outlining the reasons for historians to desert the conservatives for the progressive camp, Becker began his case with a refutation of von Ranke. Equating Ranke with conservative historians, Becker summed up the German historian's concepts in this manner: History is a science comparable in method and aim to the natural sciences because it also deals with concrete, specific, verifiable facts. The historian operates with an objective and detached attitude in handling such facts and re-creates an exact image of that area of the past in which he is conducting research. But, wrote Becker, does the historian really do this? Can he do this? Is the record of tangible and isolated facts really the history of a people? Of course not, Becker insisted; rather, the history of a people is the record of its collective life. It is the record of its traditions, values, and ideas, which are held together in synthesis. "If society," he pointed out, "is something more than its external manifestations, an adequate description of it must seek to relate those manifestations which, in their concrete setting, seem to have no connection with each other." [26]

Since history deals essentially with the re-creation of a nontangible world, Becker continued, it is clear that the method of physical science cannot be used as the model for historical research. The scientific method provides no guides for a synthetic understanding of the life of the past, and for the historian "this means that the importance of the fact can no longer be judged by the fact itself." But, then, how could a fact be judged, how could historians find meaning in the past, how could they create syntheses of former societies? Becker's answer was that facts must "be judged by some standard of value derived from a conception of what it is that constitutes social progress." A belief in progress would provide the thread of continuity about which syntheses of past societies could be created. The historian would be able to group the external facts of the past around the great controlling theme of progress, and he would then be able to point out the meaningful aspects of all past society.

So much for the theory involved in upsetting the Ranke position. Becker then made it clear why the erroneous parallel from natural science had been made and why men had been so willing to accept its truth. The fetish of physical science, Becker recounted, reflected the general pessimism of mid-nineteenth-century Europe. Having given up the hope of human betterment, men escaped from the responsibility of moral life to the neutralism of science. Now, however, Becker affirmed, "Philosophy, which natural science, in the heyday and flush of its tawdry intolerance, so carefully interred forty years ago, had come to life again, and its first conscious act has been to announce, in metaphysical and political form, a definition of time which frees the will from deterministic shackles." [27]

It has come to life, he continued, because men have now rejected the pervasive pessimism of 1850; they have entered a new mood. "During the last two decades there has been a revival of faith in the possibility of social regeneration, a revival, one might almost say, of the optimistic spirit of the eighteenth century." This new definition of time, which provides the foundation for the renewal of optimism, Becker declared, involves the concept that man is free to judge the past, to discriminate between those elements which are useful to him and therefore to "appropriate out of the past something which may serve that ideal of social progress which is the sum and substance of our modern faith." [28] Man, wrote Becker, is free to create a future that will fit his present needs and desires because he is really not a product of the past but only of his immediate environment. There was no circumscribing past for man but a plastic, flexible one that he really creates when he consciously searches the past for those facts most useful for an intelligent control of the future.

Becker had issued his call to arms for historians to search through history for the facts to create those universal standards by which progress could be judged. But if there were no past other than the one known by science, a past of unrelated, valueless facts, or if there were only the past of tradition and values which was the creation of the mind of the present, then where was one to search for those objective standards by which facts could be judged and by which progress could be defined? Buoyed up by his faith in progress, Becker could ignore this logical problem in 1913. His article on Diderot in 1915, however, demonstrates that he was already moving toward his understanding of the Enlightenment. And the ability to compare his ideas with those of the *philosophes* destroyed Becker's bland faith in progress.

Separated by the gulf of time and national traditions, the similarities of Diderot and all *philosophes* to himself must, nevertheless, have been painfully apparent. The *philosophes* were moral men interested in reform, so were Becker and many of his contemporaries. The *philosophes* had said that the only facts men can know are those which are concrete and tangible and uncovered by the scientific method. They had said that the traditions of their day were unsupported by scientific evidence and that men were, therefore, free to make new traditions on the basis of scientific knowledge. Becker agreed that men can know isolated facts through science. He agreed that men were free from the past and could create their own future. But Becker had written that his generation believed that science, because of its inability to know anything but facts, could not be used in the creation of new value standards. Becker had argued that a philosophy, a belief in progress, must replace the Enlightenment's faith in science as the source of values.

Now, however, he had discovered that an important *philosophe*, Diderot, had not believed that science could provide positive social values — that a pure scientific naturalism must lead to a world without values. Still Becker was aware that the men of the Enlightenment generally had not followed Diderot into despair. Why hadn't they? Was it because they, like Carl Becker, had substituted a belief in progress for science as a source of values? Was it because they too had turned to history to find the facts of progress? Was it because they were creating history out of their own desires? At the end of his essay on Diderot, Becker suggested that his answer to these questions was yes.

In answering in the affirmative, Becker had made Diderot's dilemma his own. He had also gained the insight into the eighteenth-century mind which made possible his masterpiece, *The Heavenly City of the Eighteenth-Century Philosophers*. Another question, however, now awaits the interpreter of Becker. Why did he so warmly acclaim the triumph of science in this book, the science that had undermined the possibility of a world of real values, the science which seemed to lead inexorably to that awful proposition that might makes right?

In the opening chapter of *The Heavenly City*, Becker had established his criteria for a climate of opinion, and he had drawn the contrast between the reason and faith of the thirteenth century and the cold objectivity of the twentieth century. Having rejected any

26

absolutes of divine origin, modern man has, for all practical purposes, rejected all absolutes. This, in turn, has facilitated modern life because men need no longer try to reconcile experience with rational patterns that do not truly exist. Instead of trying to understand the world, the modern man merely tries to measure and master it, and this permits him to utilize to its utmost the one absolute left in a world of constant flux and change — the brute fact. Science, not faith or reason or philosophy, is the controlling concept of the twentieth century. Science gives knowledge of specific facts, facts that are "primary," "stubborn," and irreducible.

Dramatically, this unqualified thesis, expounded by Becker in 1932, is a direct contradiction of his analysis of the climate of opinion in 1913 as being controlled by philosophy in revolt against science. Indeed, his description of the cold objectivity of a naturalistic and scientific attitude seems to sum up completely the kind of neutralism, the world without values, that he earlier attacked so vehemently in von Ranke and his followers. It is clear that Becker was now asserting that science and the scientific method had inexorably enlarged their place in human understanding from the time when they were first really appreciated at the end of the Middle Ages to their final and complete predominance in the twentieth century. It is also clear, Becker now postulated, that this development was progressive in that it had led men to a healthier life. "The rise of history and of science," he would repeat, "were but two results of a single impulse. Two aspects of the trend of modern thought away from an overdone rationalization of the facts to a more careful and disinterested examination of the facts themselves."

The moral lesson, he implied, was this: All social systems based on reason or faith or philosophy were false and dangerous because they obscured and distorted the factual world man lived in. A truly healthy society was that of the twentieth century in which men had outgrown this attempt to force an artificial structure on the natural physical environment. Modern man lived the really moral life, conforming to the absolutes of the tangible brute facts which science could discover and manipulate instead of conforming to ephemeral and misleading so-called moral laws which were the creation of imagination and which expressed merely the interests and attitudes of each swiftly passing generation. In short, Becker so defined the modern climate of opinion as to deny that the dilemma of Diderot was his. He did this by denying that man needed moral standards and values beyond the morality of accommodation to the brute facts revealed by the scientific method.

The absolute as brute fact, the objectivity of a neutral science, were in a way Becker's only escape from Diderot's dilemma after he had answered the question of why the *philosophes* had not followed Diderot into pessimism. Becker had discovered that his conscious philosophic revolt against science, his conscious faith in progress, during the years before 1914, paralleled an unconscious movement in the thinking of the Enlightenment. He was, therefore, in a position to see that his attempted escape from the limitations of the scientific method was part of an endless cycle of behavior throughout the ages in which men had tried to rationalize the facts of science to their inherited preconceptions. He was in a position to see the irony of men searching in a past of their own creation for facts to verify the conclusions that were the products of the immediate environment. The tension between a scientific attitude and a climate of opinion embodying major presuppositions inherited from the Middle Ages is the major theme of *The Heavenly City*. Becker, who had identified himself with the Enlightenment in 1913, set out in 1932 to demonstrate that the eighteenth century was much closer to the thirteenth in attitude than that twentieth century which had come of age after World War I.

Men, suggested Becker, will always thus live in unreal worlds which have no solid foundation in truth when they do not follow the scientific method to its logical extreme. In retrospect, this was the error of Becker and his progressive contemporaries before 1914. More sophisticated than the Enlightenment thinkers, they had open-ly confessed that science could not create positive values. But no more sophisticated than the *philosophes*, they followed the same Goddess of Progress and believed that man could find universally verifiable standards for progress in a past that he created himself. Suddenly, it had become obvious to Becker that when man knows only specific nonvaluational facts through science and creates his own subjective definition of progress through his personal creation of a history that does have values, there is no real progress.

Becker could confess that before 1914 he too was creating a Heavenly City that had no basis in real fact. And he discovered, between 1913 and 1915, that morality was to be found neither in science nor in progress. He had to accept the problem of Diderot that although science destroyed values and could not replace them, there was, nevertheless, no other way of knowing truth for an honest man to accept. As a moral man, Becker had to confess that all man's moral creations reflect ephemeral, immediate desires; that the values of the Enlightenment and the values of American progressivism reflected the attitudes of sharply circumscribed environmental situations and could have no universal validity; they could not demonstrate progress. He had to confess that his revolt against science was based on subjective desire and that science did provide the only source of absolute knowledge even though it could not sanction morality.

As a moral man, Becker had to confess that his scientific theories undermined the possibility of a moral world because a belief in the validity of only specific, tangible facts destroyed the possibility of proving the validity of moral statements; that further, a belief in the solidity only of physical facts implied that all man's moral theories were the imaginative products of transitory environments and that moral laws could never be proved valid because they were not valid. As a moral man, Becker had to confess this unless he broke morality free from its traditional definition as reflecting spiritual values and identified it with the scientific tradition.

If morality were defined as man's accommodation to the brute fact of scientific revelation, then one could be free from the endless subjectivism of historical morality, then one could judge with absolute certainty whether a man was moral; then one could demonstrate if there were progress. The moral man would be the man who rejected the attempt to build subjective theories of values and standards, who tried to live only as his knowledge of facts directed him. Progress could be defined as the movement of society away from control by myths of temporary environments to the certainty of adherence to objective factual knowledge.

This, after all, was what Becker had written in the first chapter of *The Heavenly City*. The difference between the modern climate of opinion and all others was that modern man, for the first time in history, was not attempting to reconcile his scientific knowledge with ideas about the world spun out of his own mind. From the first appreciation of the ability of science to deal effectively with the concrete environment eight centuries before, the unarguable authority of science, with its inescapable facts, had been undermining man's traditional predilection for subverting facts to nonfactual assumptions about the world. Now the inevitable, irresistible power of science and brute facts had freed man from this kind of confused and contradictory life. The dilemma of Diderot had turned out to be no dilemma at all. Within proper perspective, it was not true that science could not replace the traditional values it had undermined. It was true that it could not replace them with comparable values. But Diderot should have realized the highest progress of man was conformity not to values but to facts. Diderot was wrong then in believing that science would lead to a valueless world in which might makes right.

Yet the ironic, the qualified optimism of the earlier part of *The Heavenly City* begins to give way toward the end to something like pessimism. Men have the scientific method, Becker affirmed, and yet was their belief in it really because of its inherent value or because the structure of their immediate environment had fortuitously brought about an appreciation of science? Was it not possible that this climate of opinion like all climates of opinion was based on nonrational environmental factors which changed and would change the climate of opinion?

This increasingly pervasive note of pessimism that the world of objective facts could not be retained by men whose attitudes were shaped by an inevitably shifting environment was given open and frank expression by Becker in his "Everyman His Own Historian." Here Becker admitted that men cannot live without values, that they must have a richer environment than the antiseptically sterile one of science, and that this richer environment is produced out of man's subjective imagination working within the context of ephemeral social structures. Once more, as in 1915, he was reduced to the belief that man had a means of absolute knowledge, science, which was not applicable to his social world. He had to admit once more that men live in a moral world, a subjectively moral world. He had to concur finally with Diderot that the knowledge of science cannot create an objectively moral world. Finally, he had to share totally with Diderot the *reductio ad absurdum* of this position that in the moral world, therefore, might makes right.

Without question, Becker had arrived at that numbing, debilitating stage of self-doubt so vigorously described by Goldman, White, and Aaron. Just as unquestionably, however, he had reached this point without the fundamental influence of a concept of Darwinian evolution. Becker was stripped of history, he stood naked and afraid in a century hopelessly cut off from the supporting warmth of the past. Yet it is every bit as true to say that he stood within history, that his intellectual problems developed from this involvement with history. Becker was not the victim of evolutionary theory, he was the victim of his own understanding of his place in history. He was not lonely because evolution had lifted him out of the past, he was lonely because his loss of faith in progress had destroyed all history.

It cannot be accurately asserted that Becker had ever become oriented to the philosophy of Darwinian evolution. In his progressive years before 1914, he had taken up evolution as a means to an end. Confronted with the "steel chain of ideas" forged from a theory of the unchanging principles of a static science, he used evolution as the dissolving agent to prove the freedom of the individual to follow progress. In his own self-analysis, he demonstrated how all aspects of his belief revolved around a faith in progress which came straight out of the eighteenth century. He and his generation had relived the experience of the *philosophes* in searching history for the natural man who could define the standards of progress.

Certainly, there were obvious differences between the American liberals of 1914 and the liberals of the Enlightenment. The eighteenth century had naively insisted that a science of fixed and un-changing law was the guarantee of reform, but they compromised this with their environmentalism and historical rationalism. For the American thinker like Becker confronted with the conservative em-ployment of this concept of science, environmentalism and histori-cism were all important to establish a philosophy of human creativity based on freedom from restraint by physical law. But these theoreti-cal ramifications from Darwin were superstructure, which twentieth-century sophistication imposed on the philosophy of the Enlight-enment.

Underneath all, Becker believed that he and his contemporaries shared the faith in a rational world developing irresistably along the course of progress. It was not evolution but historical comparison which brought Becker to relativism because it was his sense of the parallel between his attitude on progress and that of men like Diderot which convinced him of the mythological quality of a doctrine of necessary progress. The relativism of Becker was not the product of a gradual deepening of evolutionary theory over the nineteenth century, which instructed him in an orderly and logical fashion, which prepared him to live in a world without permanent values. Becker reached relativism suddenly and dramatically as his faith in progress disintegrated before his eyes. His was a deeply emotional as well as intellectual experience. He did not choose to live with relativism, nor was he educated to it; he was left with it when his world so unbelievably disappeared.

The key idea that defines Becker's intellectual biography is not evolution, then, but progress. It is a belief in progress which explains his grouping of ideas on science and philosophy before 1914, and it is the lack of this belief which explains the attitudes and ideas taken up by Becker after 1914. In a very real sense, in spite of deep insight and sophistication in the twentieth-century world of ideas, Becker never got beyond the world of Diderot. His triumph is Diderot's and his dilemma is also that of Diderot. Therein is a para-dox which transcends that of the historians who write of the history-less twentieth century. Consciously, the mature Becker felt the loss of the past; the outside observer, however, must conclude that the real problem of Carl Becker was that he could not escape the past and that he could no longer define it in terms of personal desire — the terms of inexorable progress.

Is this, then, the true history of the dramatic breakdown of liberal morale after 1914? The liberal generation did not lose all of the past through abstract education in the implications of Darwinian evolution, but rather it lost a past, a past of inevitable progress imposed on history by a blind faith in progress — so that it can be argued that relativism came not by the route of philosophy, but the end of a belief which had previously ordered the world.

Indeed, as Carl Becker wrote of the "revival of faith in the possibility of social regeneration," a group of enthusiastic reformers had gathered together to give to the America of 1914 the *New Republic*; modestly enough, the magazine would precede for a short time the total reality. With bitter irony, also, the editors would confess in 1920 that there was little coincidence between their journal and the new era which emerged from World War I.

The Heavenly City of the New Republic

No one has the confidence to date precisely even such a definite and circumscribed movement as American progressivism. One must be content to place its birth in the last decade of the nineteenth century and mark its death sometime after 1914 but before 1920. All will agree, however, that the founding of the *New Republic* coincided with the culmination of the enthusiasm which was such an integral part of progressivism. The result of the strange marriage of wealth and reformist zeal, which has symbolized so much of American liberalism — the *New Republic* owed its physical being to the Willard Straights, representative of the American business community. Mrs. Straight was the former Dorothy Whitney, raised to believe in social service; Willard Straight had faith in the American mission to enlighten the world and had become important in financial circles after beginning his career in China. Together, they sensed their responsibility to employ their economic wealth in the liberal education of American opinion, and they chose Herbert Croly to edit a journal of opinion which they would support. Croly was selected and given complete editorial freedom because his *The Promise of American Life*, published in 1909, had convinced the Straights that he was the proper man to break through public complacency and convert the people to progressive ideas.[1]

Indeed, Croly had catapulted to the forefront of the intellectual ferment of the day on the strength of this book, which had challenged the entire tradition of American social, economic, and political thinking and had stressed the need for positive national planning

34

to replace the heritage of drift and complacency. Acting swiftly, Croly selected his editorial staff, whose most influential members were the precocious Walter Lippmann and the liberal economist Walter Weyl. Some wondered at the possibility of harmony in a group which seemingly diverged in their thinking. But one who came to scoff, stayed to admire; it was the socialist John Reed, who wrote that the editors "were one in their 'poised and aggressive attack' on 'this damned shambles of a country which is finally admitting it has bugs.' " [2]

One wonders even more at another seeming divergence of the *New Republic* group: the divergence between the brave title of the magazine implying a new epoch in history, the emphatic statement of Reed that the editors were ready to make a poised and aggressive attack, the description of their progressive philosophy by the editors themselves that "The underlying notion of modern radicalism [is] to substitute a conscious social control for accident and confusion," [3] and the strangely contrary editorial policy on which the magazine was launched, a policy of nonpartisan activity, a policy of refusing to state problems in terms of black and white, a policy of starting "little insurrections" in the minds of readers.

There was indeed something of complacency about the editorial policy of the magazine during the fall of 1914. This was a complacency which must have proved maddening to certain adherents of the liberal faith. On the one hand, it was announced that progressives could not accept President Wilson as a leader because of his extreme partisanship and his conservative belief in *laissez faire*. On the other hand, progressives were warned that they could no longer follow the leadership of Theodore Roosevelt, since he seemed to be abandoning the liberal forces he had led out of the Republican party. It was not surprising, therefore, that certain frustrated liberals, who had anticipated a positive program from the *New Republic* and received merely the pious message of the necessity of distrusting all current liberal leadership, broke into severe criticism. Amos Pinchot was one of the most bitter. With biting sarcasm, he praised the *New Republic* as a magazine magnificently shallow, superficial, and impotently erudite. "Though the *New Republic* does not take sides on the fundamental issues on the larger struggle between privilege and democracy," he wrote, it bravely "does stand for reforms which are incidentally connected in a more or less fringe-like relation with the real conflict." No one could deny, continued Pinchot, that the editors did stand for humanitarianism, for concentration on incidentals and symptoms, and, above all, for safety first.[4]

For those like Pinchot, there was a glaring contradiction between the editorial philosophy that the essence of liberalism was conscious and rational control of the process of history by man, and the editorial policy of nonpartisan criticism of the American scene. The editors talked of mastery but they acted in terms of drift. This was the case for the accusers. How would the defendant answer? How was it possible to reconcile mastery and conscious control with nonpartisanship? How was it possible to reconcile a belief in the necessity of a total revolution of society with an editorial concentration of limited, albeit important, reforms?

Many of the implicit assumptions of the *New Republic* editors become explicit in a reading of their rebuttal of Pinchot's charges. The dualisms, the contradictions of policy, blend into a wider synthesis. The trouble with Pinchot, announced the editors, was that he had become the prisoner of a kind of socialist orthodoxy and thought that progress must come from conflict, specifically class conflict. Such doctrinaires had not grasped the totality of the revolution going on around them, a revolution that included all people, a revolution whose goal was harmony, a revolution that must come, therefore, from all the people. Because this revolution must be equated with life itself, it must go forward as life, tentatively, experimentally, by trial and error, and, above all, by the education of all the people; and the people would gain the necessary education through information on specific reforms. Illuminated by journals like the *New Republic* on such issues as the eight-hour day, collective bargaining, abolition of child labor, and morality in politics and business, the whole of society would move peacefully toward a socialized and moralized democracy.[5]

In a clear-cut fashion, the editors revealed their belief in the necessary and spontaneous regeneration of society; they believed in the inevitability of progress. If, then, the goal of this progress was a total social harmony, the nonpartisan policy of the *New Republic* was nothing if not logical. The magazine had asserted its belief in the future dissolution of political parties in a society without basic conflict. Its chief editor had defined liberalism as "an attitude of mind which seeks to bring understanding to bear upon action, which prevails in social life less through the functioning of liberal institutions than through the activity of an alert, aggressive, and disinterested public opinion." [6] Yes, the *New Republic* believed in a policy of rational planning and control of the future, though not by a small group of leaders, not by a faction or a class, but rather by consolidated and self-conscious society in its entirety.

For the moment, it was true, the *New Republic* had to pursue a course that was passive and inactive. The total transformation of the present society of conflict and selfishness and irrationality into a new order of harmony and cooperation and rationality had to come from within the people, if it was to be really meaningful and complete. The educational policy of the *New Republic*, modest as it seemed, was actually creating an atmosphere which would speed this spontaneous regeneration of mankind. Meanwhile, the liberal had to wait, wait without impatience, because the pages of the *New Republic* exuded confidence that the change would come soon.

At the same time, the editors faced an even greater test in making understood the relation of their liberal philosophy to an entirely new problem, a new area of experience for this generation of Americans — a world at war. Coinciding with the establishment of the magazine in the summer of 1914 were a series of confused and tragic events in Europe which had culminated in a war that had swept up half the civilized world. It was a war that most Americans, caught up in a faith in progress, had deemed impossible. Now it was actuality; now it had to be taken into account. Indeed, the *New Republic* had no chance to evade its brute existence because editorial belief in progress had universal implications. It was not only American society which was moving toward a state of integrated harmony but also world society. The editors had immediately made it clear that they considered America's traditional policy of isolation untenable in the future, not only for geographic reasons, but because the existing national organizations had to recognize the growing international community and accept as their moral responsibility the work of extending its bonds. Conscious social control, the basic pattern of thought of the *New Republic* on domestic affairs, was also to be transposed to the field of foreign affairs; and it was a responsibility which must accept the possibility of using war as one of its tools.

Therefore, justification of force in a moral cause was thus stated:

A nation does not commit the great sin when it fights. It commits the great sin when it fights for a bad cause. . . . Peace is one of those good causes on behalf of which fighting continues to be a necessity. . . . Pacifism must, then, be sharply distinguished from passivism. The newer ideal of peace, whether in domestic or foreign policy, has to be actively and intentionally promoted. . . . Passivism merely makes it easy for militarism. It repeats in the larger realm of international politics the error which the advocates of *laissez-faire* used to make in domestic politics. . . . A modern nation which wants the world to live in peace should not be content to keep the peace itself. It must be willing and ready, whenever a clear case can be made out against a disturber of the peace, to join with other nations in taking up arms against the malefactor.[7]

Here is most of the political and moral position that was to provide the foundation for the *New Republic*'s future editorial policy on foreign affairs. Activism, internationalism, conscious control, cooperation, and the use of just force — all were expressed. The basis of the philosophy of the editors as it concerned domestic affairs was equated with foreign affairs. The fundamental desire to express a positive policy and to control the drift of events was put forth. But now great dilemmas intruded. With whom should the United States cooperate? How was control to be exercised?

Control and mastery depended in international relations, as at home, on the growth of an integrated community of opinion devoted to the righteous development of social harmony. The history of American progressivism in the last decade provided the hope that such a community was being formed here. But where in an angry and hate-filled Europe were there comparable signs of progress?

The *New Republic*

The first issues of the magazine had shown great confusion on the subject of war guilt. Contributors from abroad had written of the imperialism on both sides. Weyl and Lippmann were writing books, which stressed the equal division of imperialistic guilt. For the moment, therefore, the editors were forced to put aside their plans for positive action as they faced the fact that "Neither one side nor the other may claim exclusively to represent the interests of a better international order; and this consideration relieves the friends of peace from any obligation to participate in the struggle as a whole." [8]

Editorial policy, day by day, through the opening months of 1915, however, betrayed a growing separation between the minds and hearts of the editors. With each passing week of the new year, greater sympathy for England and France crept into the pages of the *New Republic*. Increasingly, a hostility toward Germany became apparent. Sooner or later, the editorial of July 10th could have been expected; it was the sinking of the *Lusitania* which set the date. Boldly the editors argued against current proposals to place an embargo on arms — an embargo which might prevent future tragedies like the *Lusitania*. Instead, it was declared by the now openly pro-English and pro-French *New Republic*:

By forbidding the export of arms and munitions, the United States would be aiding and abetting the Germans in bringing to a successful conclusion a deliberate conspiracy against the peace of the world. . . . The government of the United States must continue its profession of technical neutrality, but American public opinion should not deceive itself with the pretense.[9]

Having moved beyond their original analysis, which had postulated a Germany not totally guilty and an England not completely innocent, the editors were restrained, nevertheless, from accepting the Allied cause of 1915 as the nucleus of a new world community. Now it was the other participants fighting on England's side which precluded this possibility. "The original allies may have come together to curb German aggression, but the late accessions to the Alliance, such as Japan and probably Italy, are themselves intentional aggressors. The outlook is ominous." [10]

Still the editors had become convinced of the purity of England

and France. While America could not cooperate with these powers at the moment, because of the unfortunate alliances they had made, the men of the *New Republic* were free to speculate about the future. If the world were to be remade, if nationalistic anarchy were to give way to internationalistic harmony, these powers, which contained liberal elements, along with liberal America had to be the nucleus of this brave new world order. This was especially true because of a new strategic concept which began to find expression on the pages of the *New Republic*: sea power and the Atlantic community. The international thesis of the *New Republic* centered around the fact that the political basis for international cooperation was to be a league of nations. This league would of necessity center at first around the Atlantic Ocean, because this was the area where liberalism was at the moment the strongest. The cooperation of liberal England, which controlled to such a great extent the sea lanes of the Atlantic, was thus indispensable. Over and over again, the following thought pattern was repeated in editorials from July 1915 to November 1916:

An increasing understanding between Great Britain and the United States would constitute a necessary condition of any League of Peace, and if it could develop into an alliance, it might become by virtue of an unassailable maritime supremacy the substance and chief support of such a League.

And six months later:

. . . on a system of reciprocal guarantees might be built a solid entente of the Western democracies. An entente of the British Empire, the French Republic, and Pan America would create the largest area of unified liberalism that the world has ever known. . . . [It] would be a nucleus of world organization.[11]

Frustration, intense and growing, coloring the magazine's foreign policy during most of 1916, is apparent and understandable. The *New Republic* desired and expected a better world order. Editorials had made it clear that the men behind the magazine believed that in many ways the war had made the world scene more fluid, providing an increased possibility of sudden change; and this change must be for the better. The editors had even found liberal nations that should cooperate with the United States in ensuring this change for the better. Yet these liberal nations, England and France, were aided in their struggle by friends who were not liberal, who were not regenerate, who could not aid in world development. Once more the *New Republic*, which so wanted mastery, was reduced to drift. It must wait and hope that somehow the Allied effort against Germany would reach a higher moral level, that somehow the war on the Allied side would spontaneously become a crusade for world liberalism, that somehow the war would become the final battle for world harmony, that somehow the world was approaching Armageddon and would struggle for the right.

This frustration, born of anticipation of the course of progress the world must ultimately follow but on which course it was moving with agonizing slowness, also began to find expression in the *New Republic*'s attitude toward domestic affairs in the fall of 1915. After all, the *New Republic* had a year of publication behind it and yet the new republic, the new America, had still not emerged in spite of the educational influence professed by the magazine. Definite signs of impatience appeared on the editorial page. Could not something more be done to hasten the spontaneous regeneration of the American people?

There was a positive answer to this question and it was connected with the problem of the war; Wilson had begun to take steps toward preparedness for possible armed conflict. Seen in the right perspective, this new policy of the government might well facilitate the forced speeding up of the process of progress. Preparedness for war in the twentieth century could only mean a coincident preparedness for peace. To prepare for modern war meant a total organization of society; it meant the end of *laissez faire*. Property, business, labor, and all aspects of society would have to be integrated into a harmonious whole.[12]

While there was cause for optimism in the new attitude of the government, the *New Republic* remained troubled about the political structure of the nation. A theoretical belief in the ultimate end of the political parties could not be used as an excuse for avoiding responsibility in the coming presidential campaign of 1916. However, it was evident that the editors' thinking was shaped by several assumptions about the two parties: One was that the Republican party represented in its progressive wing the closest approach to the nonpartisan nature of the future partyless society. Another was that the Republicans were traditionally the party of government intervention in the economy, intervention that would be basic to the future cooperative society. Right up to the conventions, the editors defined the Republicans as "the party of action which sought to promote the national welfare, not by leaving things alone, but by using the powers and resources of the national government to carry out an economic and political program," and speculated that there were men like Theodore Roosevelt in the party who were "willing to unify and socialize the railroads, and the means of communication, to regulate rigorously basic industries like steel and coal mining . . . willing to recognize labor as a national institution . . . willing to go behind all this and create a workable, modern, scientific, federalized system of education." [13]

When the nominations were made, when the platforms were written, the *New Republic* frankly admitted its inability to find a position it might support. Even for those who were able to see fruitful seeds of the future in the chaos of the present, the Republican platform and Hughes could not be identified with a forward movement to the cooperative commonwealth. Indeed, the *New Republic*'s legacy of bitter disappointment in the leadership of Theodore Roosevelt was related to the Republican party. The Progressive party, growing out of Republicanism, had provided the evidence of the passing of the traditional two-party system and then its leader Roosevelt had led it into disaster and oblivion. Sadly, the *New Republic* had pronounced this epitaph: "Progressivism proved itself to be hero worship masquerading as principle." In turn, the hero leader had also revealed himself as lacking in principle, had revealed himself as "someone who takes on the color of those who surround."

Almost forcibly repelled by their first love, the editors found no solace in the leadership and platform of the other party, the Democratic. Traditionally, it was the party of *laissez faire*; its leader,

The *New Republic*

Wilson, had restated this tradition in his New Freedom. Once again the *New Republic* seemed fated to remain outside the political activity of the nation. Once more it must advise a policy of patient waiting for the expected and inevitable dawn:

Constructive American radicalism must bide its time until there is organized a new and better political instrument of social policy than either of the two existing major parties can be. In the meantime, it can preserve its independence, seek indefatigably for new light and try to communicate to others such light and faith as it has.[14]

The rumblings of developing fissures in the smooth surface of such a façade of patience, however, could no longer be ignored. Too long, too long had the magazine waited for the American people to live up to that hopeful title of New Republic. Where was the spontaneous regeneration on which so much of the philosophy of the *New Republic* had been predicated? Suddenly, those middle-class radicals, the editors, came to use the term "middle class" in derogatory ways. One could be patient about regeneration if one knew it was inevitable, but what if there were a danger, a mortal danger, in any delay that postponed the coming of utopia? Previously, the editors had been content to urge the forward progress of the country through the inspiration of promised rewards; now they turned to fear and threats as a motivating force.

The same fluid social situation which is making possible the reintegration of society on the highest possible level can also lead to the destruction of civilization, they warned. Under the impact of industrialism, the relative homogeneity of America was being fragmented. Such a dissolution of old habits, traditions, and institutions was the necessary prerequisite for progress, but the collapse of the old order had removed the foundations on which man had stood. He had to go up or down. Assuming progress, the *New Republic* had been certain of the upward trend, now it was not so sure. Something must be done and done quickly if the future was to be won. Breaking from their own tradition, the editors began to speculate on the need for class organizations to encourage the further movement of democracy. "Only by the organization of powerful independent minorities," they wrote, "can the middle-class political system be jolted out of its stubborn and torpid complacency." [15]

It was easier, however, for the editors, who had pronounced over and over against the class bias of socialism and who forecast a future classless society, to become involved in the middle-class politics of the presidential campaign. Needing desperately some assurance of the future, they began to find it in Wilson. It was not perhaps too difficult to find elements of domestic strength in a man who, it was now clear, was so sound on foreign affairs. Their praise of Wilson's ideas on international relations had been growing since the beginning of 1916, and on the occasion of Wilson's unequivocal approval of a league of peace made at a dinner of the League to Enforce Peace, editorial sanction reached a high point. They predicted that his speech might well make a decisive turning point in the history of the world — the end of America's deepest tradition, isolation. Historians might well write in the future that Wilson had lived in a time of supreme opportunity and had the vision to grasp the meaning of it and the courage to declare it, that on the central issue of modern life he had chosen the noble part.

With thoughts like these, it was not difficult for the *New Republic* to confess an erroneous judgment, it was not hard to go back to the early accomplishments of Wilson's first administration, which had been branded superficial, and discover a Hamiltonian planner where the Jeffersonian individualist had once stood. By September the *New Republic* found solace in the fact that while the Progressive party was dead, its principles were enshrined in the Democratic party. Wilson had revealed "how far he has departed from the Democratic tradition of national irresponsibility in domestic policy and national isolation in foreign policy." He had revealed how far "The old individualistic partisan Democrat, with a political philosophy derived from the Virginia Bill of Rights, is developing into a modern social Democrat . . ." [16] It was Wilson who had lifted up the banner of progressivism from where it had been dropped in the dust by Theodore Roosevelt. Wilson, for the *New Republic*, had become "a better purveyor of progressive principles than Mr. Roosevelt."

There was a reasonable expectation that the magazine would

exult in the victory of their champion who had renewed their faith in the progressive destiny of the American nation. To the contrary, however, the men of the *New Republic* gave little space to Wilson's victory in the cold fall of 1916. Amidst an inescapable feeling of strained anxiety, the editors let it be known that they could not afford to celebrate the fortunes of domestic politics. If they had feared earlier that the sands of domestic progress were running thin, they now faced a greater fear that the world of international affairs had gotten out of control.

With a certain creeping sense of dismay during most of 1916, the editors were forced to admit that the Allies demonstrated no signs of regeneration. Sharing a certain viewpoint with their new hero, Wilson, the editors had pinpointed the importance of the *Sussex* notes. An ultimatum had been made to Germany. The choice of war or peace was in German hands. Yet America had no assurance that a war against Germany would result in a league of peace. No commitments had been made by the Allies. Like Wilson himself, the *New Republic* grew rather desperate by the fall of 1916. Somehow the issue must be forced, somehow the Allies must be brought into coordination with the American desire for a peace without vindictiveness, a peace of equals building for the future.

Urgency gave way to frustration, and frustration to anger. Never had the *New Republic* written so harshly of the Allies as it did in the fall of 1916. Now Wilson must coerce the Allies into accepting the generous American plan of peace. He must make the Allies declare their war aims: "The time has come, if not for a settlement, at least for a show-down. . . . The *New Republic* is unable to understand how else this knowledge could be obtained and how, in its default, the American government could enter the war with any assurance of accomplishing the declared objects of its national policy." [17]

Certainly this was a curious confession of an almost irrepressible kind of anxiousness to participate in the war and thus control the course of history in the direction that the *New Republic* knew led to progress. It was a state of mind that might well interfere with a skeptical view of onrushing affairs. And the *New Republic* was caught up in such a flood of events that editorial policy spun dizzily.

45

Were the Allies winning the War? Was Germany winning? Would Wilson be able to gather belligerents around a peace table? Would he deliver a moral ultimatum to the Allies? Within this wild swirl, the leitmotiv of frustration with the Allies, especially England, continued to strengthen. It would be so easy for the Allies to reform themselves, it would be so easy for America to join with the purified Allies to establish a just and lasting peace on the basis of international cooperation. It would be so easy. Still, the editors had to admit, bitterly admit, through the middle of the December of 1916, that "After January 1st the Allies began to wage a war the object of which was no longer primarily to protect themselves against German attack or to secure the rights of small nations, but to alter in their favor the European balance of power." [18]

The *New Republic* stood momentarily appraising the Allies with a critical eye. Then, somehow, a new pattern of events swiftly brought about a complete metamorphosis. Germany had made a peace offer. Wilson, who had been planning a note on war aims, felt afraid the note would seem to support the German move, but he decided he must act. In the note was included much that the *New Republic* stood for: a plea for the security of all nations based on the cooperative effort of a league. Nothing could have been more in line with the editors' wishes. Wilson's image in the eyes of these editors grew in stature and greatness. Wilson had become a real leader; he had formulated a positive international policy. Was it too much to hope that he could implement this policy? Had the day come when it was possible to fulfill the *New Republic*'s belief that "What the United States needed to bring about was a positive and responsible adjustment to the European system in place of the existing negative and irresponsible adjustment"? Had the day come when Wilson could answer this question — "before this country could commit itself to the Allies, it needed to know how in the event of victory they proposed to accomplish the declared object of organizing international security"? [19]

Yes, the *New Republic* was sure that day was dawning when the Allied reply to Wilson's note was analyzed on the editorial page. A masterpiece of diplomacy, the editors termed it. Glowingly, they recounted how the Allies had sent "a brilliantly ambiguous, a triumphantly equivocal document." Lightheartedly, they announced that "The off-hand interpretation, of course, is that of the *Daily Graphic*." The Allies would demand Trentino and Trieste for Italy, the break up of Austria and Hungary into many tiny states. All this to the knowing sophisticate was so much propaganda to please the conservatives. Several things demonstrated "that the authors of the note were willing to throw phrases to the extremists," but the phrases hardly meant what the extremists said they meant. The men of the *New Republic* prided themselves on their ability to see the loopholes. To men always logical, if Lloyd George promised victory in 1917, he must mean a compromise, not a crushing peace. There were other loopholes. Alsace Lorraine was left the possibility of division; Italy was not absolutely promised Trieste; local autonomy must have been meant for the Austrian minorities — "that, too, could be regarded as liberation from foreign domination." For the *New Republic*, the Allies had "renewed democratic allegiance to their cause." [20]

Then the thermometer of editorial enthusiasm reached a new high the next week with an analysis of Wilson's speech before the Senate, a speech which followed the *New Republic* philosophy of peace without victory and the promotion of world democracy by a league of cooperative nations.

It was with joy in their hearts and the road to the better world appearing before their eyes that the editors entered the month of February. Doubts about the Allies were almost gone. Wilson was giving powerful leadership toward internationalism. The situation was ripe for a decisive frame of mind when the renewal of the submarine campaign came. A supplementary headline to the February 3rd issue, dated February 1st, read: "The crisis — without delay diplomatic relations must be broken. . . . The terms and conditions of our entrance into the war should be discussed and announced." [21] There were no doubts in the minds of the *New Republic* editors; this was war. They were happy because this was not just war; it was the crusade — the crusade which would precipitate the nation and the world into utopia. There was a thankful acceptance by the editors that at last frustration was ended and fulfillment was at hand.

Candidly, the *New Republic* confessed its place in the united ranks which would follow Wilson in the war to end all wars:

For two and a half years we have been an uneasy people. Those who thought at all about our future were discouraged and ashamed . . . This uneasiness has been the one helpful element in the national spirit. It was a discontent aching for leadership which would sweep small-mindedness before it. . . . In the President's address were stated the terms on which we could . . . pledge ourselves to the organization of the world.[22]

No, this was not war, this was the making of the good society. The conditions of war had greatly accelerated the transition the world was undergoing; they had greatly increased the fluidity of society; they had made man's environment plastic and capable of being remolded into a new and better form. Mankind, standing on the edge of something approaching the millenium, could not help seizing the opportunity.

The league of peace exists sooner than any of us dared to hope. . . . The liberal peoples of the world are united in a common cause. . . . The cause of the Allies is now unmistakably the cause of liberalism and the hope of an enduring peace. Democracy is infectious — the entrance of the Russian and American democracies is sure to be a stimulus to democracy everywhere, and it is now as certain as anything human can be that the war . . . will dissolve into democratic revolution the world over.[23]

Democracy was to be triumphant everywhere because the war had made it triumphant here in America. All the slow agonizing waiting for the American community to integrate itself spontaneously into a cooperative commonwealth was ended. It was true that regeneration had not come from within, but the discipline of war had delivered the conservatives into the hands of the radicals. The people were now totally united, totally integrated by the purpose, not of war, but of creating a lasting peace. It was beyond doubt that the spirit of the nation was now "far more nearly the morale of a cooperative commonwealth than of a nation in arms." The same logic, of course, applied to the world situation. The war, because of the entrance of the Russian and American democracies, had ceased to be a national struggle for power. Here, too, the conservatives had placed themselves in the hands of the radicals and allowed the war to become "a gigantic experiment in internationalism." [24]

In the fullness of their confidence, the editors described a number of points, which were to be followed by the government as it moved to institutionalize the cooperative commonwealth that now existed in the spirits of the citizens. There would be the nationalization of all important economic resources; the government regulation of output, prices, profits, and labor conditions; the conscription of income to pay for the war; the treatment of labor as a national institution; the increase of government support for education and research; the subordination of the military to political leadership; and the retention of a completely free climate of political, economic, and social discussion. In the realm of foreign relations there would be the policy of peace without victory. There would be the welding of the Allies into an organization dedicated to the creation of a peace between equals and the retention of that peace by an integrated international community of cooperative commonwealths. [25]

All of this planning for the future course of the war took place in the spring of 1917 before America began to participate actively. Then it became America's war. Then the world began to crack beneath the editors' feet. The people, the press, and the government were all breathing unexpected fire and brimstone. Minority opinion was suppressed. Government propaganda was focused on hate and not on a just peace. The crushing blow was the discovery that the discussion of peace terms was now called treason and that such magazines as the *Outlook* termed the *New Republic* "a seditious and disloyal sheet" that gave "aid and comfort to the enemy."

Briefly, the editors fought back in their editorials; then, suddenly, they abandoned almost all discussion of the domestic scene and concentrated attention on advice as to how the war should be prosecuted. The editors had not surrendered their program or their principles, but their philosophy restrained them from fighting for these views. Progress depended upon the acceptance by the people of the *New Republic*'s vision of the new order. Unless the editors were prepared to abandon their concept of progress, they were forced into a quiescent waiting for a rebirth of enlightenment.

During 1918 the editors were once more reduced to a policy of drift, but somehow they retained a faith that things would grow better. As November approached, this optimism became more fragile and desperate. How could the peace turn out well when the Allies had refused to accept the liberal peace aims of Wilson? Then, miraculously, out of the November elections, Wilson emerged triumphantly with Allied acceptance of his Fourteen Points. Exultantly, the editors wrote: "Every ancient right of princes or castes or classes to dispose of the wills of other men is on the table for liquidation. At this instant of history, democracy is supreme." [26] As they wrote these lines, the editors may have momentarily believed them. They were lines that were fitted to signify the end of a war fought to remake the world in the pattern of humanitarian democracy.

But as Wilson sailed for France, their now shrinking faith in progress could no longer sustain the editors. Wilson was the key to the whole program of world organization. The *New Republic* had placed all its trust in him to push its program through. The November election had revealed that the American people did not understand this program. Wilson, by his failure to build war propaganda around the aim of a world organization, was to blame. He had allowed George Creel to concentrate American passions on the war as hate. He had not worked with liberal forces in the Allied countries. As this indictment grew coherent in the editors' minds, the platform of their hopes correspondingly sank because Wilson, alone, had been that platform. The editors, however, could not admit that the war would end in failure; something would be salvaged. And so they spent the winter of 1918–1919 fighting the Republican foes of internationalism.

When the Treaty of Versailles was published, however, the *New Republic*'s vision of world progress was finally shattered. Even during the dark days of 1917 and 1918 the magazine's psychology had been that of fighting against dangerous enemies of progress. Now the *New Republic*, founded to lead in the vanguard of progress, was compelled to fight reaction; for Versailles meant reaction to the editors. It was a treaty built solidly on the tradition of European national selfishness. The editors could not allow Wilson to give international sanction to something so vicious. Still internationalists, the editors spent the summer and fall of 1919 in attempting to defeat Wilson and the League.

With the physical collapse of Wilson, however, the excited energy of the editors waned. For the first time since 1917 they had the opportunity to survey America and to look into their own souls. What they saw was something entirely new, something that conformed in no way with the vision of the new era held by them in 1914.

One irrepressible question comes to mind when the history of the *New Republic* for the years 1914 to 1920 is reviewed: Why did the editors commit themselves to a belief in a realized utopia in the opening months of 1917? To such a question there is also one obvious answer: They had faith in progress and expected progressive forces to triumph in America and throughout the world. This, in turn, is an answer which in its abstract generality brings the questioner no closer to the dynamic human aspects of the problem. The vast majority of Americans in pre-World War I America believed in progress, and this same vast majority hoped intensely that the war would eventuate in the triumph of righteous and democratic and, therefore, progressive forces.

One wants to know, however, why specifically and concretely the men of the *New Republic* in the confused days of January 1917 accepted as fact the controlling influence of Woodrow Wilson over the international affairs of the Atlantic community; why these supposedly skeptical, intelligent, informed men were willing to accept as accomplished a sudden transformation or regeneration of the Allies; and why these men who knew so well the attitudes of the American political parties and of the middle class, which was the basis of politics, were certain that the pressures of a war effort would transform these admittedly tradition-bound groups over night into a bright, shining, and novel homogeneous cooperative commonwealth.

Perhaps these are insoluble questions and most certainly so in their total ramifications. Yet there may be tentative answers which do make possible an understanding of the naive optimism of the *New Republic* during the stirring early days of the year 1917. By going behind the broad acceptance of progress to the specific assumptions on the nature of man and society and history on which this over-all belief rested, by utilizing what Becker called the analytical tool of the climate of opinion to come to grips with those factors that were implicitly accepted by the editors, an explanation of the policy of the magazine may be developed.

A major clue, perhaps the critical one, to the set of presuppositions on which the editors operated is the far from hidden frustration increasingly evidenced in the pages of the magazine during 1915 and 1916. Clearly, the *New Republic* had been founded on more than a faith in the progressive course of history moving gradually and inevitably onward and upward. Springing from almost every weekly edition was a driving enthusiasm reflecting a certainty that a sharp break in the historical process had been made — that the tempo of historical change had been so greatly accelerated, that a comparison with past change must be made in qualitative not in quantitative terms. Now in 1914, here in 1914, a new era was being ushered in, a new era in which civilization would be defined as having different and higher characteristics than were found in past history. A basic presupposition of the *New Republic* editors, therefore, was the ability of man in society to free himself from the historical process. There was a reality above the relativity of history which man could reach. The editors, like the *philosophes* of the Enlightenment, held to a philosophy which was ahistorical.

Since they believed that man could escape the past, in logical terms, they must also believe that man could transcend the society of which he was a part, transcend its institutions and traditions to become part of a new and better social world. This preconception had found more explicit expression in the magazine than the ahistorical position. Again and again, the magazine had carried analyses of the manner in which industrialism had disrupted historical society. Strong emphasis had been directed to the social plasticity that flowed from the industrial revolution. Indeed by the end of 1915, the *New Republic* had publicly voiced its alarm that a progressive reformulation of society had to take place soon if total social dissolution and chaos were to be avoided. Inescapably, one reaches the conclusion that, again like the *philosophes*, the editors of the *New Republic* believed the individual could escape his immediate social environment to bring his personality into coordination with higher standards.

Furthermore, what was the presupposition of the nature of the future good society on which the confidence of the *New Republic* rested as on a solid rock? The *New Republic* knew the coming cooperative commonwealth was to be comparable to a utopia. Since it was to be a society different from all past societies, it could draw no parallels, no conclusions from that direction. Unable to base its confidence on the historical forms of society, the *New Republic's* only alternative was to be sure of the quality of the characteristics of the individual, universal characteristics that could be defined and discovered outside historical society.

When these assumptions are brought together, their similarity to the intellectual pattern of the *philosophes*, that philosophy on which the Heavenly City on Earth had rested, becomes evident. Once again in history, men had clung to past traditions with such allegiance that technical ideas, especially the ideas of science, had been manipulated to conform to and buttress that tradition. In the case of the *New Republic* this was at least a major enterprise. From the opening issue in 1914, the editors had made it clear to their readers that the magazine stood in the very forefront of the ongoing intellectual revolution that had its inception in the magic name of Darwin. Directly and succinctly, the *New Republic* had revealed its enthusiastic acceptance of the implications of Darwinian evolution coupled with advances in the social sciences: that the physical and social worlds are in constant flux, flux that is not teleological in nature; that the social world is not under the control of physical forces; that man is formed by his historical society and has no characteristics that transcend this temporary social environment; that when society changes, man too must change; that the value system of any given historical society must be based on the needs of the particular society alone. Surely the *New Republic* was a perfect product of an age that had but two intellectual principles: historicism and organicism. It accepted man as part of an organically connected society, which must be recognized as a seamless whole. It accepted this seamless whole as part of a seamless web of history that was the sole explanation and determinant of a momentary present.

Like the men of the Enlightenment, the men of the *New Republic* lived in two worlds of ideas. Like their historical predecessors, they had smoothed apparent contradictions into functioning coordinates —functioning, that is, until implacable history after 1917 had snapped the relationships between these strange intellectual allies. With this final cleavage we are left with more fascinating questions such as, If the *New Republic* deceived itself on the nature of its participation in novel theoretical trends, did it deceive its contemporaries? The answer is, of course, yes. The *New Republic* was damned for being too modern, too pragmatic, too relativistic, and too much caught up in historicism. The yes is further reinforced by a subsequent acceptance during the 1920s and 1930s of the *New Republic* of 1914 as the journal of the fresh current of pragmatism in pre-World War I America. All of which suggests that since the strange dualisms of the *New Republic* remained hidden from their contemporaries, they must have had the perfect disguise of appearing as the natural and normal intellectual pattern of the day. The *New Republic* must have been representative of a wider climate of opinion.

Logically, then, the questions must be pushed further. What are the outlines of this climate of opinion? When did it take shape? What are some of the historical patterns from the past around which it was formed? Perhaps some of the material with which to formulate answers to these questions can be found in the intellectual career of the *New Republic*'s chief editor, Herbert Croly, who had become one of the foremost political philosophers of progressivism before the fateful days of 1914.

Herbert Croly THE PROGRESSIVE ROAD TO POLITICAL UTOPIA

AT FIRST glance, it appears something of a paradox to inquire into the intellectual background of Herbert Croly for clues that will illuminate the climate of opinion which allowed the *New Republic* to consider itself and to be known as a journal of pragmatism. Eric Goldman, in one of the most recent studies of the American liberal tradition, has interpreted Croly as a unique and isolated contributor to that tradition. He writes,

Herbert Croly's thinking, far more than the ideas of most progressives, was heavily influenced by European patterns . . . His severe intellectualism and inordinate shyness cut him off from progressives who swept each other over ideological difficulties in a tide of emotion. These facts tended to make Croly write about American progressives the way foreign ambassadors often talk about American baseball games. He was there, he wanted to be part of it all, but he remained an outsider who could not help wondering at some of the antics he saw.[1]

Goldman based this conclusion on the peculiar home environment in which Croly was raised. His parents, who plunged actively into the intellectual life of New York City, were British immigrants; and while their tremendous involvement with public affairs in America necessarily eroded their foreignness, this fact was greatly mitigated by their personalities and their theoretical philosophical position. Indeed, they judged America in their own terms and attempted to mold it to fit their value system. This, in turn, was based on a passionate belief in the principles of Auguste Comte, the French philosopher, who desired to build a spiritually integrated cooperative commonwealth for all mankind around the social laws uncovered by scientific research. David and Jane Croly disciplined Herbert, therefore, within a faith which would isolate him from the contemporary American scene.[2]

Furthermore, when the young Croly, off to college at Harvard, rebelled against his parents and Comte, he was caught in a position in which it was difficult to come to grips with the everyday currents of American thought. At home he had been taught that the message of Comte was the necessity of working for the welfare of mankind, and he had been trained in Comte's method of achieving this goal. Now he rejected Comte's technical social philosophy, but he retained the moral impulse for social welfare. Becoming more serious about this task of human regeneration in his last years at Harvard, Croly searched for a new understanding, for a new framework within which to express his purpose, and his search took him more and more to the discipline of academic philosophy, which continued at this time to express explicitly European traditions. His home experience, his social isolation, his academic training — all divorced him from the America of the late nineteenth century.

But the record of the *New Republic* from its inception is unmistakable; it was accepted as the journal of American liberalism, and Croly was most certainly the major element of the *New Republic*. Somehow and somewhere, between 1890 and 1914, Croly established a rapport with the American liberal tradition. The reception of his book, *The Promise of American Life*, in 1909, as the most solid contribution to the political theory of the progressive movement, suggests the extent to which he succeeded in making himself understood to his contemporaries. Nevertheless, there is a quality to the book which justifies Goldman's statement that his intellectual background was such that he was not swept up by the tide of emotion that caused other progressives to oversimplify the intellectual problems which liberalism faced in 1909. Certainly it is a book that demonstrates an appreciation of the complexities of the day and of the complex program necessary to deal with them. Certainly it is a book that continues to demonstrate Croly's involvement with the European philosophic tradition.

The central concern of *The Promise*, however, was contemporary America as it was entering the twentieth century, an America in crisis. America, wrote Croly, had been founded by men who believed in progress. These men had assumed that the American nation as a political organization would provide the secure framework within which individuals could advance their economic interests. But the founding fathers had not defined progress merely in terms of a rising standard of living; rather they had viewed the economic factor as merely a prerequisite for individual moral and social progress, which was the true definition of progress. Now, declared Croly, the citizen of 1900 was faced with the inescapable fact that the traditional promise of American life, progress, was not only seriously threatened, but that at the moment there was no real progress at all. There was still an expanding economy; there was increasing national wealth. There was not, however, a healthful distribution of this wealth. Economic growth was not serving to increase the moral and social qualities of the nation. Somehow the economic developments of the last half century, designated as the industrial revolution, were undermining the conditions on which progress had rested without creating new conditions for future progress.[3]

Croly wrote with a tone of grimness, this was a crisis; the American future was threatened. Yet he did not write in desperation. If industrialism had destroyed a beneficent historical pattern, if it had not replaced it with one equal in worth, still the facts of the industrial situation did not preclude a revival of the process of progress. This novel historical situation demanded that Americans consciously take control of impersonal economic forces and shape them into a pattern that would result in progress.

Here was the purpose of Croly's book, here was his message to his contemporaries: In order to save American democracy, with its traditional promise of progress, the people would have to break from their traditional views of progress. To redeem their traditional values, they would have to replace the traditional techniques which had supported those values. Such a rejection of past habits, Croly realized, would be difficult. Nevertheless, it had to be made if democracy was to survive, and he believed it could be made if the people recognized this need. In this process of recognition, they would have to understand the conditions that had helped create the traditional views of the way in which progress operated. First of all, the initial political theory of the new country was influenced by the conflict with England. Americans had come to define democracy as individualism, as freedom from restraint; they had come to believe that the isolated individual, free to exercise his self-interest, was the basis of political society. Second, they accepted as sound theory the concept that the activity of each individual pursuing his self-interest would automatically produce progress.[4]

The possibility of holding this almost anarchic political philosophy and the parallel theory of progress, which postulated a pre-established harmony between the satisfaction of private needs and morally desirable social results, depended upon the facts of the American environment. Set off from Europe by a formidable ocean barrier, face to face with a bountiful frontier which seemed to promise endless opportunities to all individuals, Americans could be complacent, they could be fatalistic about a constantly better tomorrow. They could afford to shirk the serious philosophic problems surrounding their definition of individualism as equal opportunity for all men to rise in society without removing the ladder to success by the consolidation of their own success. History, by isolating Americans and by granting them material conditions which guaranteed a certain rough homogeneity based on equal individual rights and privileges, conspired against Americans becoming self-conscious about the process of progress.

Now history, operating through the dynamic forces of industrial growth, had drastically altered this situation. Barriers of time and space had been removed and Americans were put back into the web of world events. The insatiable appetite of the new corporations had suddenly flung agents across the continent to consolidate in one generation what had seemed endless economic resources for individual opportunity. More important still, the institutional structure of industrialism was obliterating with fantastic speed the previous habit patterns of American behavior. The substantial individual freedom, the fundamental equality of the average American, was no longer a reality. Industry massed men into complex groups, it demanded that they become specialists geared to the differentiated needs of large ongoing institutions. In short, industry had brought about conditions that demanded an exceedingly fine division of labor, and this had shattered the rough homogeneity of the frontier with its working units of equal individuals.

Since this new world of social integration was so foreign to the principles of the founding fathers of the nation, inevitably there was a wide area of confusion when men continued to try to use the older concepts to define the new institutional patterns. Inevitably, too, the men most closely related to the expanding corporations began to think and act differently from their fathers. In doing so, they were forced to break from established codes of morality, law, and political practices. The corporation head required certain novel practices from political organization. He was unable to achieve these legally because of the limitations of traditional political thought and technique, but his specialized economic needs encouraged the development of specialized politicians who operated outside the established constitutional practices of local and national government. This politician was the political boss of the post-Civil War era who granted to the new industrialist those favors he could not otherwise obtain from our outdated political forms.[5]

All this pointed, Croly firmly declared, to the fact that our history was now intimately related to industry; that industry because it was a living, growing historical force could not be destroyed; that, indeed, industry, because it provided the material means for a rising standard of living, should not be destroyed. This, Croly continued, was the very weakness of his contemporary reformers. They were men who were afraid of the way industry had threatened the American tradition of untrammeled individualism; they were men who wanted to turn back the clock and return to the simple and relatively equal economic conditions of the Jeffersonian age. In refusing to recognize the permanence of the industrial revolution, reformers had, therefore, circumscribed their ability to correct the vicious

59

wrongs that had accompanied industrialism, and they had made themselves vulnerable to the doctrines of those conservatives who denied the possibilities of correcting the abuses of the present economic and political situation.[6]

Croly, however, was prepared to accept industrialism, to outline its evils, and to refute its apologists. Most obviously, industrialism had brought about glaring inequalities in social conditions and economic and political power. This, in turn, had led to political corruption as the rich few had used their power for special advantage. Inequality and corruption, coupled with the all-pervading specialization of the economy and society, meant but one thing: the loss of that homogeneity which had given substance to our democracy by giving practical reality to its beliefs in individualism and equality. America was breaking up into mutually suspicious class groups or congeries of selfishly motivated individuals.

In such a situation of social chaos, with great and unchecked power adhering to certain men, individualism could only mean the destruction of other men. Striking back at the new economic barons, the masses, in the name of equality, were apt also to destroy individualism. Croly concluded then that America was in desperate need of a new outlook, a new intellectual synthesis. This synthesis must accept industrialism while being true to the traditional American values of individualism and equality. It should also continue to fit those values into the promise of American life — unending progress: economic, political, and finally spiritual progress. The starting point of the synthesis was the realization that the lost instinctive homogeneity of the people could be replaced with a conscious social ideal.

Here Croly came into conflict with the conservative defense of the *status quo* which denied man's ability consciously to change his present environment. Most of this philosophy of inactivity he ascribed to the very liberal tradition on which the country had been founded. The liberals, Croly elaborated, had delivered themselves into the hands of the conservatives by defining the individual in terms of abstract and exaggerated isolation from society. They had stated that the self-interest of the isolated individual was the basis of political society; they had postulated the inevitability of progress working without human guidance. Now when the conditions of industrialism were destroying the substance of equalitarian individualism and blocking moral and spiritual progress, the liberals, who wanted to alter this situation, were faced with a conservative defense of the *status quo* that was based on liberal doctrine. This defense of the present chaos was summed up in the philosophy of Herbert Spencer, who argued that any attempt by society to manipulate economic and social life would deny the values of a completely independent individual. Conscious reform must repress uninhibited individual freedom, and it was the liberals who had defined this as the highest value of our culture.

Furthermore, Spencerian doctrine, built around the current interest in evolution, postulated the other liberal thesis that evolution or progress was the product of extrahuman sources. Specifically, Spencer declared that evolution was the result of certain inexorable physical laws, and the individual, to find happiness, must conform to these laws by adjusting to their present expression in the immediate environment. Beyond the fact that it violated the value of individualism, reform was clearly impossible, because man had no power to adjust his social environment, which reflected the material process of inexorable evolution.

But, since the solution of the crisis of industrialism demanded social reform, Americans must gain perspective to criticize effectively and to destroy the "steel chain" of Spencer's ideas. Such perspective was to be gained from a re-education of the average citizen to a more realistic definition of democracy based on a more accurate understanding of the nature of man and of society. Americans might save themselves by substituting conscious social cohesion for anarchic individualism, Croly wrote, because the individual was not a natural fact but a creation of the society of which he was a part. Then Americans might also save themselves because creative society was not subject to the control of natural law as Spencer had insisted, but instead was a moral fact. Its progress depended not on the course of physical evolution but on the conscious efforts of its members.[7]

Croly had now to explain to his contemporaries, however, why the individual as a social creation had not demonstrated a sense of

social consciousness, why there was now this crisis of social disintegration. For Croly the answer to this question was that man had a
dual nature, and in one aspect, he was selfishly motivated as both
American liberals and conservatives had argued. The selfish man
was not the whole man, however; man reached his highest individuality by controlling this lower self and by achieving a sense of social
consciousness and social responsibility. Americans had never made
this effort because they had not been taught that this higher self
existed or that a meaningful society existed.

Here confusion marks Croly's thought. He was arguing that man
was social and that he was created by a social environment. Croly
was intimating, therefore, that society was a constant factor in
history. Yet he was also stating that society was a moral fact, created
by man's conscious effort. He was declaring that Americans had not
overcome their selfishness in the past, because they had not lived in a
social environment that could develop the true potential of personality.

Inescapably one is then led to a second dualism implicit in Croly's
thinking. There is not only the dualism between the altruistic and
selfish individual. There is also a more profound dualism between
the ideal society that will make man good and his immediate chaotic
social environment. Croly was not telling his contemporaries to
transcend their social environment; he was telling potentially social
men to transcend an imperfect society to become complete individuals in an as yet unformed ideal social structure. A great deal of
moral effort and a great deal of self-discipline was therefore necessary to achieve the better society; and for the moment, Croly believed the approach to this ideal could be accomplished in only one
way. The individual must consciously blend himself into a whole
by becoming loyal to his nation.[8]

Pragmatically, Croly argued, social democracy, as opposed to
individualistic democracy, would develop as men found a common
bond represented in the national state. He declared the organization
of society within the formal structure of the nation state was essential
both for democracy and for its ideal of progress. Democracy, he was
sure, could not be defined in terms of machinery, but only as the

expression of the sovereign will of the people toward the pursuit of an ideal purpose. It was this will that was the basis of morality and reason. This will, moreover, was not a natural fact; it was a difficult achievement, which must be created out of the selfish and atomistic aspect of human nature through the blending of individual wills into a community — a community based on the feeling of cooperation derived from a common loyalty to an all-inclusive ideal. It was the ideal of the modern nation that would give, through its forms and institutions, the substance that was needed to provide the bonds of loyalty necessary to the formation of a community and its concomitant sovereign will. This bond, this loyalty to the nation would indeed provide the progressive principle because

it also serves as a ferment quite as much as a bond. It bids the loyal national servants to fashion their fellow-countrymen into more of a nation; and the attempt to perform this bidding constitutes a very powerful and wholesome source of political development. It constitutes, indeed, a source of political development which is of decisive importance for a satisfactory theory of political and social progress, because a people which becomes more of a nation has a tendency to become for that very reason more of a democracy.[9]

Challenging what he felt was the traditional liberal distrust of nationalism, Croly elaborated a theory of man's place in history to demonstrate the necessary connection of nationalism and democracy. While it was true that he had affirmed human freedom against the immutable material laws of Spencer's version of evolution, Croly now added that he did not believe that men were completely free to act as they pleased. Because their natures were created by society and since society was a historical phenomenon with roots in the past, it followed that society and its members were conditioned by past experience. Man had freedom to alter his society but only within the limitations of his historical context. In modern history, social traditions had found focus in the nation state.

While Croly believed that the very existence of the concept of a nation implied democracy, that "The tendency of its normal action is continually . . . to diminish the distance between the ideal of human brotherhood, and the political, economic, and social conditions, under which at any one time men manage to live together," still as a historical product the nation-state carried over with it many undemocratic practices of the past. But this was true only in Europe where nations must "offer faithful allegiance to a network of somewhat arbitrary institutions, social forms, and intellectual habits." It was most emphatically not true in America, because our country had been created as a democracy committed to the ideal of progress. "The American democracy," Croly affirmed, therefore, "can trust its interest to the national interest, because American national cohesion is dependent, not only upon certain forms of historical association, but upon fidelity to a democratic principle. . . . American patriotism . . . combines loyalty to historical tradition and precedent with the imaginative projection of an ideal national Promise." [10] In breaking from the traditional technical concepts of democracy and progress, Americans were actually becoming more closely attuned to the fundamental democratic and progressive ideals of their tradition.

Generous democrat that he was, Croly nevertheless was prepared to follow out the logical implications of these rather drastic philosophic changes necessary to defeat the crisis and chaos of the day. If the sense of a moral social unity through loyalty to the nation is difficult to achieve because of the inherent selfishness of man, it must follow that "An individual's education consists primarily in the discipline which he undergoes to fit him both for fruitful association with his fellows and for his own special work." If this is true, then only a few will achieve it at first and therefore

The common citizen can become something of a saint and something of a hero, not by growing to heroic proportions in his own person, but by the sincere and enthusiastic imitation of heroes and saints, and whether or not he will ever come to such imitation will depend upon the ability of his exceptional fellow-countrymen to offer him acceptable examples of heroism and saintliness.[11]

Still further, accepting the seriousness of the social crisis, these "heroes of the struggle must maintain their achievements and at times even promote their objects by compulsion. . . . Like all sacred causes, it must be propagated by the Word and by that right arm of the Word, which is the Sword." [12]

Herbert Croly

Perhaps the very vehemence of this affirmation of militant nationalism and leadership by something like supermen betrays the tremendous inner tension which existed between Croly's adherence to the eighteenth-century religion of humanity, expressed in his faith in the ultimate perfectibility of all men, the necessity of man's constant rejection of the past in order to pursue progress, and the technical philosophical means that Croly felt constrained to advocate for the salvation of American democracy. Above all, Croly believed that a community must be reconstructed out of the current social chaos. But the only philosophic justification he could offer for such a community seems to stem from his knowledge of Hegelian political philosophy.

There is something of a real parallel between the central points of Croly's political theory and those connected with Hegelian conservatism: (1) The unformed individual comes as an inferior to an already established group of social institutions. (2) This unformed individual is not capable of acting on a civilized or cooperative plane by himself; he can reach such a plane only through the mediation of the state. (3) The individual can perceive the pattern of development which has resulted in the creation of the national state and thus can form an absolute code of ethics, but he cannot go outside the historical pattern of established institutions to acquire standards with which to criticize or to alter this pattern; he can look only to the past, not to the future. (4) Finally, the education of men, given these other principles, must be a training that will bring them to respect authority, for only through such subordination to the existing social conditions can man's spiritual self escape from the eternal conflict with the selfish, physical self.[13]

The sensitive Croly who wished to exalt the creative freedom of the individual had spun a web of logic that effectively circumscribed just such freedom. For the moment, he had to make this sacrifice in the name of his contemporaries because he hoped to check social disintegration, but the blatant disparity between the ideal and the method undoubtedly spurred the insatiably curious Croly to look deeper into social theory for a concept of social integration that would better express his ideal of freedom and progress. If only the

65

community were not an artificial creation, then the individual would not have to be so strictly disciplined. If only the individual were not forced to suppress a lower personal element, then he would not have to be forced to sacrifice freedom for constraint.

Croly was saved from this dilemma as he came into contact with the writings of American social psychologists, sociologists, and philosophers. Since the 1890s, many of these men had been breaking from the tradition of both Spencer and Hegel. They had been postulating this crucial thesis, that society was the natural environment of man, that man's nature was innately social so that there was no need to mediate between the individual and society through a kind of authoritarian state. Sometime in the years between 1909 when the *Promise* was published and 1914 when his second book, *Progressive Democracy*, appeared, Croly became acquainted with these technical aspects of the American intellectual environment.[14] These ideas formed a leaven which altered his political philosophy so completely that *Progressive Democracy* escaped the limitations of Hegelian authoritarianism.

Nevertheless, it was the same Croly because the writer of the first book had constantly attempted to transcend the limitations of his concepts. This impatience with himself was revealed on an even more profound level than the psychological or sociological points concerning the community and the individual. Beneath the involved logic-chopping of proving that progress and tradition were compatible, that freedom and subordination were synonymous, can be felt all the fire and intensity of a religious prophet who stands waiting to solve every problem through an all-powerful, yet simple, act of faith. It was this Croly who had written at the end of *The Promise*, "The task of individual and social regeneration must remain incomplete and impoverished, until the conviction and feeling of human brotherhood enters into possession of the human spirit." [15]

Here was an element of Croly's thought more important than sociological detail, yet it, more than psychological and sociological theories on the nature of man and society, was restricted by Croly's kind of Hegelian historicism; more restricted because of its greater emotional intensity attached to the yearning for human freedom.

Croly was writing about total individual and social regeneration, about a perfect sense of brotherhood shared by all men. This was total religious utopianism, and it makes one wonder about the nature of some of the basic concepts he had used in *The Promise*. Of fundamental importance to Croly as a reformer was the need to give Americans a standard by which they could judge and transcend their present confused society, which was no society at all. He had, therefore, written in somewhat Hegelian terms that actually American society was a historical organism with a national tradition of progress. People could appeal to this historical national mission as the standard by which to condemn the chaos of 1900. They could conform to a social tradition against the ephemeral present. Similarly, they could argue that the individual must be social in order to be a real personality and that this goal was to be achieved by conformity to the nation which embodied tradition.

Like Hegel, Croly postulated that conformity to a national tradition would bring progress because he seemed to believe in some basic spiritual force pushing the nation on toward fuller expression of this spirit, which, in Croly's case, meant greater democracy. But Hegel claimed that this spiritual force should be defined only in the institutions of the present and that man fulfills himself, therefore, by accommodating himself to the present. But this, after all, was merely an idealistic way of denying man's creative freedom as Spencer had done in a materialistic manner. Croly was postulating a perfect society and a perfect individual who would need neither constraint nor discipline. He had a standard in mind to judge and criticize and then transcend not only chaotic contemporary society but also national tradition. The religious Croly had faith in a perfect metaphysical society and individual which would find expression through a metaphysical history that must eventuate in progress.

Within his dependence on a kind of social authoritarianism, there was no room for such transcendence. He did not, he could not discuss in *The Promise* any mechanism, any method by which the individual would triumph over or even correct historical tradition to reach swiftly a religious utopia. The mature Croly, the American Croly, becoming more steeped each day in the living traditions of his culture, came into contact with philosophical theories of transcendence which helped to overcome his own philosophical determinism. Happily, this transcendentalism was to be found in the writing of the same social philosophers who were outdating Hegelian concepts on the nature of man and society. *Progressive Democracy*, therefore, expressed also a new-found transcendental mechanism for expressing Croly's belief that there was an ideal society and individual and history beyond the real world, which could, however, be achieved in this world by the creation of a religious utopia; and that these ideal forms justified the individual's rejection of his immediate society and of the historical traditions of his society.

Croly's escape from the limitations of a Hegelian-like historicism did not depend entirely on his re-education in the principles of sociological and psychological analysis or of a philosophic expression of transcendentalism; in the final analysis, his conversion to a new faith in human freedom was based on a religious conversion — by the American people. The underlying assumption of *Progressive Democracy* was that "the conviction and the feeling of human brotherhood" had entered into possession of the American spirit. Miraculously, Croly wrote, the old ideas and traditions of irresponsible individualism had vanished with all the swiftness and finality of the passing of their last two great exponents in America, William McKinley and Mark Hanna. These men were the end of an epoch. Suddenly American life had entered a novel and critical phase. "A movement of public opinion, which believes itself to be and calls itself essentially progressive, has become the dominant formative influence in American political life." [16]

The essence of this progressivism was a belief in the necessity of social orientation toward the future, not the past. Its key words were freedom and experimentation instead of discipline and conformity. Its philosophical justification was the postulate that life was growth. Its political philosophy was the total rejection of the American constitutional tradition in order to bring into being a complete democracy.

The American constitutional tradition was a curtailment of democracy because the will of the people was made subservient to the mechanism of a legal system. Within the context of colonial experience, the founding fathers were suspicious of power and of human nature. Interested in individual rights that conflicted with society as expressed by the British Empire, they exalted these rights into untouchable absolutes embodied in a higher law. Surrounding this law and protecting it from possible corruption by majority action, they established a government of checks and balances. "The active government was divided, weakened, confined and deprived of integrity and effective responsibility, in order that a pre-established and authoritative Law might be exalted, confirmed and placed beyond the reach of danger." And this form of absolutism provided the bulwark for the present conservatives who argued that "the continued subordination of the democracy to a specific formulation of the Law . . . will make for popular moral integrity and improvement." [17]

But all this talk about absolute constitutional principles, Croly affirmed, was the result of an ignorance of human history. History was life and life was growth and development — constant, ceaseless, irresistible growth and development. The conditions of a healthy life must be conditions which encouraged the expansion of living forces. The passage of human history, Croly continued, might be likened to the journey of a band of travelers following an illuminating star toward an ideal environment. The beginning of the journey was based on instinct not reason. As they journeyed on, the travelers became conscious of their journey and they learned ways to facilitate their passage. But at times they were tempted to substitute the expedients of the moment for the purpose of the journey. They set up immediate knowledge and values as goals rather than as tools by which to pursue the final ideal. This error was encouraged by the loss of the sense of instinctive solidarity which marked man's early history. Knowledge, which facilitated progress, tended to make men into antisocial individualists. Now the fragmentation of the human community, with its concomitant confusion of means as ends, was being overcome as men came together through the elevating and binding influence of the new religion of solidarity and democracy. It was this faith which would prove an incomparably better tool on the road to progress than had reason. "The assurance which American progressivism is gradually acquiring, and of whose necessity it is finally becoming conscious, is merely an expression of faith — faith in the peculiar value and possible reality of its own enterprise, faith in the power of faith." [18]

Faith was the transcendental mechanism that Croly was searching for to raise the individual above society and tradition — faith in the ideal society, in the ideal human nature, in the ideal history that was progress. This was all a spiritual premise above and beyond the real world, and it would never exist unless man had faith in it. Once he did, he was truly free from the limiting control of the laws of the physical environment and the traditions of the social environment. He was free because he could create his social world to conform to these ideals. "Individuals and societies are not natural facts. They are wilful processes — moral creations," Croly wrote and he added, therefore, that "The success of a thorough-going democracy is not to be prophesied. It is to be created." All theories of determinism, whether social or physical, were absolutely wrong. Freely, because they had come to share a religious faith in progress toward an integrated community, a socialized democracy, men were choosing to establish just this ideal. They had come to realize that knowledge was only a helpful tool to be used to this end. Knowledge was pragmatic in nature, not absolute.[19]

Croly had now risen above his previous historical determinism on the strength of a kind of transcendental idealism related to an apparent democratic religious revival among the American people. He championed the complete freedom of man to follow the ideals of this religion and to make it a part of his mundane life. He had renounced any debt the individual might have to his present social environment. The ideal of society and the socialized individual had nothing to do with present society. Now, however, Croly moved to qualify this view and to introduce a curious, complicating social positivism into his position. The religious ideal of social solidarity, Croly affirmed, is not "unenlightened and blind. On the contrary, it is associated with an increasingly better understanding of the nature and meaning of the essentially social process." [20]

Such an affirmation that his religious ideal reflected the workings of a very material social evolution could help Americans understand why the crisis of social disintegration was being so easily overcome by a religious revival. Such an understanding of the social process could also help Croly to repudiate point by point his adherence to a Hegelian-like political philosophy. It was the social psychologists, according to Croly, who had finally demonstrated the truly social nature of man and had made possible a revaluation in social philosophy. A knowledge of these writers had allowed Croly to change his conception of society.

Replacing his earlier view that society must be created through the form of the national state, he postulated society as a natural phenomenon. Coupled with this view of society was a new analysis of the relation of the individual to society. Previously, he had believed that man drew his meaning and dignity from society, but that the individual came unformed to the existent society; thus he had stated the necessity of individual subordination to the society. Now, however, while continuing to believe that the social environment was crucial, he wrote that society and the individual were mutual in their relationships — neither could exist without the other. In this view, man could not come unformed to society because he was from birth a part of society. These two changes freed Croly from the restraints on the individual which were essential when it was necessary to bind individuals together to form society, and it freed the individual to play an active role in the development and change of society, since he was now, by nature, a functioning part of that society and no longer merely a member through loyalty to given institutions.[21]

All of these basic principles of *Progressive Democracy* — the sociological concept of the natural character of society, the reciprocal relationship of the individual and society, the philosophical premises of the evolutionary nature of society, and the subordinate relationship of science to faith — were blended into an integrated philosophy of progress by the conception of education that informed this second book. In *The Promise*, Croly had believed that "an individual's education consists primarily in the discipline which he

71

undergoes." Now he quoted John Dewey's theory of education with approval when he wrote, "The wisest of modern educators has declared that 'the only way to prepare for social life is to engage in social life.'" The theory of human nature based on the hypothesis that character was created by social participation, that education embraced the totality of man's life, and that the wider and more flexible the environment, the higher the type of individual produced, made it possible for Croly to jettison completely the awkward thesis of progress through the leadership and discipline of an elite.

As against the keynote of discipline and imitation in *The Promise*, freedom and participation became the theme of *Progressive Democracy*. Man as a social animal, as a part of a natural community, would progress toward perfectibility as he became a responsible and creative member of the community. Bound together by a new religious feeling, Americans were coming to have faith in themselves, in the community; they were making man and his social environment sacred. Because of his social nature, because of this religious spirit based on the recognition of the sanctity of human brotherhood, because of his creative control over the future, man must be free to expand his potentialities, to build the good life, to push the human race along the road of progress, to reach perfectibility.

In serving as a means to accomplish this better world, politics had a dual role. Its primary task was "first, last and always to promote political education" and, second, to develop a vigorous social program that would aid in the concrete development of the community and its individual members. In facing the first problem, that of education, Croly had made it clear that the great obstacle to be overcome was not the irresponsible individualism he had singled out in *The Promise*, but the belief in the immutability of the Constitution. The community and its individuals in an evolutionary world must be free to develop, to adjust, to experiment. Progressive democracy, he affirmed "depends upon the truth of its claim that the emancipation of the democracy from continued allegiance to any specific formulation of the Law, and its increasing ability to act upon its collective purposes, is far more likely to contribute to the moral stamina and the collective enlightenment of the people."

Therefore, he continued, the best organization of "political power is not to confine its exercise within the limits defined by certain rules, but frankly to accept the danger of violence and reorganize the state so that popular reasonableness will be developed from within rather than imposed from without." [22]

The secondary task of politics, that of a social program, Croly related directly to the problem of education and individual development. The social program would be the democratic substitute for the law and it would gain permanence and allegiance from the community, because it would be derived from the democratic faith and ideal. The social program also became the concrete means for the spiritual regeneration of the community: "The loyal devotion to an ideal of social righteousness will not as the mere result of its own affirmative power bring into being social righteousness. The ideal must be embodied in a temporary program. The program must be realized by legislative and administrative action." [23] Croly's state, therefore, had to fulfill two functions: "It must be a genuine expression of the popular preference, and it must be adapted to the efficient accomplishment of its immediate purpose."

As in *The Promise*, Croly realized that immediate reconstruction of the national government was impossible, although he urged his contemporaries to act as swiftly as possible to alter the Constitution. Meanwhile state governments were to be used as laboratories for political experimentation; especially because it was on the state level that legalism had revealed its utter bankruptcy. It should, therefore, be possible to go at once to the power behind the law, the people, and create truly popular state governments.

At each step of his reformulation of the forms of the state governments, Croly made his readers aware that technique was intimately connected to a larger moral reconstruction of society; at each step moral and religious premises provided the foundation for politics. When Croly accepted the concept of a natural community and when he became convinced that a social spirit was sweeping across America, he dropped the defense of class divisions, which he had made in *The Promise*, and came to stress in *Progressive Democracy* the raising of all men to a level of participation in society. What

Croly visualized, then, in the not too far-distant future was a society essentially without conflicting classes and whose one class had standards that were, in the main, middle class. Since he was thinking in terms of a cooperative community bound together by a spirit of human brotherhood, it was logical for Croly to write, "Just in so far as a group of really democratic political institutions are created, the foundations of the two-party system are undermined. The two parties seek to accomplish for a democratic electorate certain purposes which such an electorate ought to accomplish for itself." [24] As the coming community would be classless, so it would be partyless and Croly's new proposals of political forms were based on this premise.

Executive leadership, therefore, became a crucial point. The executive was to be the representative of public opinion. He would be similar in this respect to the prime minister of England except that, in the new partyless democracy, he would represent merely the majority opinion and not a party. Indeed, he would be primarily a lawgiver and maker and not an executive. His cabinet would participate in the legislature and work for the executive's program. The legislature could veto the executive's program in which case the executive would appeal to the people for a direct vote on the proposed program. If their vote were favorable, the legislature must also accede; if the vote were unfavorable, there would be an election for a new executive. Croly visualized the role which the legislature would play in the new social order as chiefly that of a maker of public opinion. Since there would be no parties, the legislature would be elected by the varying interest groups in society. As a forum for discussion, this legislature of interests would be instrumental in the formation of constantly changing majorities. [25]

While Croly's ideas on the roles of the executive and the legislature under the proposed new system were striking, even more important, perhaps, were those on the administrative agencies of the new government — ideas which reflected his belief in the union of faith and pragmatic knowledge as reason. While the executive and the legislature were occupied with the more fluid and experimental aspects of the social program, it was the administrative corps, performing the role formerly preserved for the law, that would give stability and continuity to the state. These administrators would not, however, be the custodians of particular laws but of the social purpose of the democratic community. Their administration could be defined as encompassing two tasks. The first was action; the second was the acquisition of knowledge. In both cases the tool used would be the scientific method. Alternating its personnel between the points of action in the field and the planning councils, the administration would work pragmatically for the welfare of all. Through the use of scientific knowledge of society as it existed at the present, they could plan with precision for progressive change. But always Croly made it clear that pragmatic science concerned means and not ends: "The goal is sacred," he reiterated, only "The program is fluid." [26]

These words sharply emphasize the complex nature of Croly's final philosophy of progress with its fusion of religion and science held together in tension. For the basic premise of this liberal philosophy was religious and because it was, Croly felt certain that he had proved the individual's freedom from the chains of any thesis of predestination. Bitterly, the American journalist had criticized Herbert Spencer and the concept of materialistic determinism. Impatiently, he demonstrated that man's life was meaningful only within a social context beyond the control of physical laws. Just as emphatically he had turned on the socialist creed which, to his mind, postulated the control of the future of man and society by laws of social materialism. Here was Spencer, only in a more sophisticated guise.

Man was free from physical or social materialism because he was spiritual, and because he had the capacity to transcend his environment through faith to gain insight into the future that he would help build. This was where Croly so consciously rejected his previous dependence on a Hegelian-type idealism. In *The Promise* he had urged his fellow Americans to transcend their immediate society by coming into adjustment with the real tradition, the true ideal of their national destiny. He had urged on them the concept of the inevitable development of the purpose of their nation. He had implied, therefore, borrowing precedent from Hegel, a spiritual force that was present within social forms. This was idealistic monism, however, and offered the individual no freedom but to conform to its march through history.

Now, his religion, with its element of transcendence, had moved far from this postulate. Inescapably, Croly was suggesting a kind of dualism. Man lived in a factual social world. His freedom was based on his ability to appeal from this environment to an ideal situation. His creativity came from the necessity of his activity to transform his real world according to the pattern of the ideal. Indeed it was Croly's exhilarating affirmation that, without the mediation of individual effort, the material environment would never approach the ideal because the ideal was not present within the real as Hegel had declared.

Croly's religion of progress then was this joyous declaration of man's responsibility and creativity, and yet he gave his readers the added assurance that the individual was working to further a cause whose success was inevitable. Curiously, perhaps, the individual in his freedom from the bonds of incomplete and irrelevant social structure was gaining the strength of absolute standards. Beyond even this, there is the further implication in *Progressive Democracy* that history demonstrated the steady conquest of the material world by spirit, that the history of man had also been the progress of man. In a definite contradiction, Croly, who had written of man's escape from the history of time to the history of ideal progress, from real society to perfect society, from incomplete individualism to the completely integrated individualism of utopia, also announced that this imperfect history did demonstrate progress, and that society and the individual reflected progress. Arguing in a circle, Croly said man was social in nature and part of a sustaining society but that man must transcend his society in order to reform it to ideal standards. Yet, scanning history, he could affirm that society was increasingly approaching the ideal and, indeed, this approach enabled the individual more sensitively to visualize the final ideal.

Here was his scientific proof of faith. Social science could demonstrate the two major tenets of the progressive faith: that man was social and that society was cooperative in nature. On the secular level, social science could therefore reinforce man's desire to reach ideal social integration. Science could encourage man to use faith to achieve what was innately part of his nature.

This too then provided the rational explanation of why, out of the desperate chaos of 1900, there had come the sudden saving emergence of the progressive faith. Social evolution had brought man's emotional nature closer to the ideal of total social integration. Social science had taught man that the true structure of his society and personality was the same as the true tenets of the progressive faith. Faith had then lifted him beyond the imperfections and inadequacies of the immediate to make the final leap toward the ideal.

This curious combination of transcendental idealism, of a dualism of spirit and matter with man as their mediator, this faith in freedom and creativity and positivistic social science and progressive social evolution, this faith in faith — this is the Americanization of Herbert Croly. It explains the success of the *New Republic* under his direction in 1914 as the reflection of the hopes of American intellectual liberalism. The curious combination of philosophic tidbits held together by an abiding faith in ineradicable freedom was already tightly contrived and deep-flowing tradition by the time Croly found it in the years after 1909. The purity of his translation of it in *Progressive Democracy* undoubtedly results from its central place in the writings of the American social psychologists that Croly must have found so rewarding in these years. Such academic social theorists as James Mark Baldwin and Charles H. Cooley express with utmost clarity all of these themes which seem to have no right under the same philosophical roof; they illuminate one more step toward the discovery of the climate of opinion of progress shared by Carl Becker and Herbert Croly and the *New Republic* on the eve of 1914 and Armageddon.

James Mark Baldwin THE SOCIAL PSYCHOLOGY OF THE NATURAL MAN

THERE is artistic as well as intellectual unity between Croly and the American who first gave a complete scientific rationalization to the theses of *Progressive Democracy*. James Mark Baldwin stands as one of the great pioneering figures of American social psychology.[1] It was a role of which he was acutely conscious, and he filled it in the best Victorian conception of a moral hero. His writings had all the artfully contrived dignity that a turgid and elaborate prose could give to them, with an added stolid stature based on the proud conviction that they contained the culminating thesis on human nature. They drew on the best of all that had ever been written on the subject and then synthesized them with the genius of the author himself.

It is small wonder that historians of social psychology have described Baldwin's importance in terms of his role in transmitting European ideas to America. Here was the mechanical synthesizer carefully blending in precise fashion the ideas of the giants in this developing branch of psychology. This is the fame of Baldwin, this was the basis of his success in the 1890s when he dazzled the American academic world. From Comte he borrowed the concept of applying positive scientific methods to the study of man and the belief that human relations could be regulated by science. From Spencer he added the evolutionary concept that man must be studied as part of a developing environment. Most fundamental was his emphasis of the philosophical idealism of Hegel. One student of psychology has stressed the point by writing that "the 'objective mind' of Hegel's system is the true antecedent of all theories which pass beyond the individual and see in the mind a reality which is not separated from other minds." [2] And he demonstrates that the basis of Baldwin's work in social psychology was just this belief that the individual could not be described as an entity without reference to a larger grouping, society, which was the creator of the individual and therefore the reality from which the individual drew his identity. Finally Baldwin brought back from Germany the inspiration of his teacher, Wilhelm Wundt, to bring laboratory research into the field of social psychology.

This is Baldwin the pioneer. He is an innovator in American thought because he symbolizes the break of American intellectuals from the technical ideas of the ahistorical individualism of the Enlightenment which had served so long as the basis for discussions about human nature. From now on, American social philosophy would be solidly based on the assumptions that man is only a product of his society, and that society in turn can be only understood in terms of its place in the ever-changing process of history. This is also Baldwin the borrower. The heaviness of his prose, the involved logic-chopping of his sentences serve to remind us that his purpose was to transmit other men's ideas, European ideas, to his American contemporaries. Perhaps there is even an artistic usefulness in his kind of writing. It was respectable writing and one knows an idea by the words it wears. There could be nothing radical and un-American about the calmly weighted, the judiciously sifted, the impartially balanced scientific doctrines taken from men who by themselves might be unacceptable.

Yet Baldwin was a radical; beneath the heaviness of his pages there does run a constant theme with life and verve and intense purpose. Baldwin was supposedly a scientist, not a reformer, yet there were heroes and villains in his pages. Baldwin was a mechanical borrower, an uninvolved scientific sifting machine, yet the borrowings were always those which demonstrated free will and the coming of the classless, middle-class utopia. There was moral purpose, then, behind the scientific innocence of the question he posed in the 1890s as the critical one for social psychology to answer: Is man a socialized individual self or an individualized social self? This was the question for the new science to investigate and to answer. Almost as he asked it, however, Baldwin could answer it. "We have quite given up the old abstraction of an anti-social self, an individualistic and egoistic person. . . . On the contrary, social psychology shows that the 'self' of the individual's 'self consciousness' is in its materials and processes of formation, thoroughly social in its origin." [3]

If Baldwin could convince his contemporaries that this statement was true, he would overthrow the traditional American attitude on human nature, "the point of view of historical individualism," and he would then open up the possibilities for fruitful research and writing on the subject of human nature now correctly viewed from its social background. One can repeat this sentence with modifications at the end and come closer to the real Baldwin: If only he could convince his contemporaries that this statement was true, he would overthrow the traditional American attitude of human nature, "the point of view of historical individualism," and he would then open up the possibilities of social reform based on collectivism.

To accomplish this conversion of his generation to the truth, Baldwin had to destroy its allegiance to Herbert Spencer, who dominated American social philosophy. Herbert Spencer was not a social scientist, he was a social philosopher. He was not the advocate of evolution as the basis for social thinking, rather he called on evolution to buttress historical individualism. Underneath his affirmation of being modern he clung to the structuralistic and atomistic themes of the outdated association psychology which blocked both the progress of the science of psychology and the progress of mankind.

Simply stated, Spencer wrote against the social nature and the freedom of man. For Baldwin the ridiculous implications of his writings were that the individual was absolutely controlled by a monistic materialism. Each man lived not in society and its history but lived as a biological atom controlled by natural laws. The English engineer-philosopher therefore emphatically insisted on the futility of all attempts to remake man and society.

James Mark Baldwin

This was a defense of the *status quo* which denied the dignity of man. Above all Baldwin had to demonstrate the inadequacy of this materialistic viewpoint so that his fellow Americans could remake their society. And so he cried out: "What is there to eclipse the vision of the poet, the inventor, the seer, that he should not see over the heads of his generation, and raise his voice for that which, to all men else, lies behind the veil? The social philosophy . . . of Spencer cannot answer these questions." [4]

Now Baldwin moved decisively to smash Spencer, not by appealing to other social philosophers like Hegel or Comte, but by borrowing directly from a greater authority on evolution than Spencer, the scientist Charles Darwin. After 1859 no philosophy could take a position, with any hope of convincing cultural leadership, that did not assert its harmony with science. This was the secret of Spencer's success as a philosopher; the most important scientific doctrine of the age of biological evolution buttressed his arguments. Or did it? Here was Baldwin's opening; here was the key to his whole philosophical system. If Darwin proved human free will rather than determinism, Spencer would be pushed aside and conscious reform and progress could be attained.

Again and again the American social psychologist insisted that his ideas were not based on Hegel or Comte or Spencer. "My favorite doctrines," he proclaimed, ". . . have been consciously inspired by the theory of natural selection." Baldwin had accepted even the terminology of the enemy. The American conservative, who denied the possibility of reform, used Spencer's definition of natural selection as survival of the fittest to sustain his argument. All literate Americans then, conservative and liberal, were acquainted with the term and with its antireform implications: social anarchy was necessary for progress; atomic individualism had its complete justification. But that was just the point, Baldwin argued, natural selection proved human solidarity and collectivism; it proved man's independence from the physical world.

It has been established, Baldwin began persuasively, that the definitive human psychological trait is plasticity of the mind. While Lamarck and Spencer are wrong in contending that there is direct

81

biological transmission of mental education or experience, plasticity is a congenital character and can be transmitted through biological inheritance if it is useful in the struggle for survival. Since there is evidence that the plasticity of the human mind is increasing, one must assume logically that it is a useful trait in this struggle.

The next point was to define the usefulness of this increased learning capacity. Such definition was straightforward: Able to learn more and more, the individual made increasing use of the past experience of his species which was transmitted to him through social heredity, the traditional structure of his society.

Individuals who were part of the best integrated social groups would have the greatest chance of survival because they had the richest store of experience to draw on. Human plasticity, it followed, was only useful in group situations. As evolution proceeded, the individuals who were the most social in outlook would be the ones to survive. Gregariousness, like plasticity, was a congenital trait and it could be passed on by biological inheritance. Gradually the individual who could not adjust to the group, who therefore could not make use of the social tradition available for the development of his mind, would die out.

As evolution continued, the biological traits of plasticity and gregariousness were progressively lifting man out of the control of physical law and making him quasi autonomous within his social tradition or history. Within his society, the traits of highest utility for man, those of survival of the fittest, were not egoism or individualism but conscious cooperation and unity. In answer to the Spencers and Huxleys who did not find social ethics in the Darwinian concept of evolution, Baldwin could affirm, "It is the extension of the application of natural selection to groups, rather than its direct application to individuals, that has given birth to morals," and "Utility for the group *presupposes self-control and altruism in the individual.*" [5]

Baldwin continued to roll up the Spencerian flank. The chief biological traits of man were plasticity and gregariousness, and their development lifted man out of the control of biological law; they made man an ethical, social, and historical animal free from the arbitrary rule of nature. And this was only half the true meaning of Darwin. Once the central importance of plasticity and gregariousness were understood, then all man's habits of thinking would be revolutionized. Evolution means change — uncharted change. Once the mechanism of natural selection had started man on the road of social life, it became irrelevant. "Natural selection is itself a negative principle," Baldwin had affirmed, "variation remains the point of direct and emphatic importance. In it the intrinsic vital processes must exhibit themselves." Evolution was not the materialistic mechanism of Spencer but the chance for novelty, for human purpose which Darwin had really suggested. Darwinism meant that ". . . absolutely new and unheard-of phases of reality may 'arise and shine' at any moment in any natural series of events — constituting new 'genetic modes.' " [6]

Baldwin does represent a tremendous upheaval in American thought as he rewrote a theory of evolution away from Spencerian doctrine. He is part of the twentieth-century world whose intellectual father was Charles Darwin and whose only possible technical philosophy was one of instrumentalism. Darwin had broken the eighteenth-century view of a static world of fixed law — a world peopled with equally abstract and unchanging individuals. Now human nature must be related to an environment of constant change and growth. The individual could not be understood by deductive insight within a finished, ideal context; he must be studied by scientific, experimental observation within the details of mundane, fluid evolution. If man was always in the process of adjusting to novel situations, then intelligence was an instrument which facilitated his survival in his evolving world; it was the instrument of his freedom to create the world he needed for the present moment.

This was Baldwin's essay into the twentieth century. He had the vision of a better world to be created; he had the need for new ideas to use against present opponents so that mankind might see more clearly the better world and the way in which it could be built. But his better world was not taken from the future; its blueprint was to be discovered in the past.

Baldwin began, then, a long march back to the earliest history of mankind. He defended this turnabout by denying the extreme novelty of his philosophy of instrumentalism. Evolution had freed men from the ephemeral past, not from the ideal past. Evolution had given us the power to shape the plastic world according to the precedent of the ideal world. We were free and we were unfree. Some philosophers of the day like William James had been carried away by the idea of freedom and novelty and had defined the world as composed merely of its immediately apparent aspects. This was the unbalanced statement of William James' pragmatism which expounded absolute human freedom.

Immediately, he recoiled from the possibility that readers would confuse his doctrine with the philosophy of William James. Such a pragmatism was not freedom; merely to act was not to be free — it was the exercise of license. The truly free act was creative and man could not create in a world which was without objective meaning and value. James had reduced man to the level of the animal who lives in an amoral world; in reacting against the sterility of the Enlightenment world view, he had gone too far. While he was right in that the world could "no longer [be] thought of as a piece of mosaic work put together by a skillful artificer," still, Baldwin emphasized, it must be conceived "as a whole, as a cosmos, of law-abiding and progressive change." [7]

Man's freedom, his ability to use his intelligence creatively to bring about changes in his immediate environment, took on dignity and meaning when they were related to the effort to bring about a more lawful universe. Man was free and creative because he was serving an absolute spiritual principle, not because he was above physical law as James would have it. Man was free because he could see how he must use natural law to aid in the progressive unfolding of the greater spiritual purpose that governed the world: "It is not a teleology of the human type, operating individually and tentatively against nature, that our philosophy must recognize; but mind in the larger sense of a principle whose mode of operation is in and through the reign of natural law." [8] Instrumentalism was a philosophic method within a philosophy of technical idealism. Darwin was a

84

weapon to destroy Spencer, not the final intellectual guide. Evolution as interpreted by Baldwin was a traditional philosophy, a philosophy of preordained change. He defined evolution as progress because man was able to discover at the beginning of history the pattern of evolution and predict its final culmination in utopia.

Perhaps this concept was easy for Baldwin because, unlike Croly, he was brought up in several of the major streams of American intellectual life in the nineteenth century. Although his family had moved south for reasons of health, he was reared in a strict New England moral atmosphere, and he continued his devotion to Calvinism by preparing for the Presbyterian ministry at the Princeton Theological Seminary. But other influences stimulated his interest in psychology and set him on the road to his eventual career. Above all, Princeton brought him into contact with President James McCosh, a vigorous theologian-philosopher, who was not daunted by the seeming threat Darwin's theories posed for revealed religion. Instead it was McCosh's firm conviction that evolutionary theory was in no way dangerous for those who viewed the world as God's creation. Furthermore, working from the common-sense school of Scottish philosophy, McCosh was enthusiastic about the trend to study psychology by empirical methods. Truly, he believed science could be accommodated to faith.[9]

It is this youthful training, this initial commitment to a scholarly tradition stretching back to the eighteenth century, which is one key to Baldwin's technical philosophy. He had used Darwin to prove the biological basis of man's social nature and to underwrite the quality of variation and possibility in evolution as against Spencer's theory of rigid causation. In emphasizing evolution as a novel concept at the end of the nineteenth century, one forgets that evolutionary ideas are almost as old as Western civilization. Indeed, one historian of the social sciences has suggested to what a large degree the eighteenth-century pioneers of modern social science were influenced by evolutionary theories that were essentially Aristotelian in nature.[10] One of the basic problems for ancient Greek thinkers, F. J. Teggart has written, centered around the question "How did things originate?" These men were interested in explaining the present in terms of the past and therefore developed the study of genealogy, which became in time the historical method for the Greeks.

Central to this genealogical-historical method was the idea of teleology. As used by Aristotle, this method postulated that the way to study nature depended on the visualization of its end or purpose. All movement, then, is directed toward some end and becomes intelligible only when that end has been discovered. To continue this line of reasoning, the end or purpose of each particular is the realization of its highest potentialities. In this philosophy the aim of science is to discover what is normal in the history of each object, to discover the path of movement from its origin to the fulfillment of its purpose and potentiality. There is no interest in the isolated, fortuitous fact.

Furthermore, according to Teggart, this Aristotelian position became linked in eighteenth-century social science with the idea of progress. The heritage of this union is the belief that progress is natural and that the purpose of social analysis is not to discover the conditions under which advancement takes place, but to determine those obstacles which have interrupted the natural course of development. Baldwin was educated at Princeton in the tradition of the moral philosophers and social scientists of the eighteenth century like Adam Ferguson, who has been called the father of modern sociology and yet who was committed to this Aristotelian theory of progress. It should be added that Ferguson's generation, like Baldwin's, was in reaction against the belief in materialistic determinism. Like Baldwin, Ferguson affirmed that progress could be described by science, but he too insisted on the role of free will and a final spiritual force behind physical law.[11]

For Ferguson, science was the study of laws that govern the natural world and man. There were two types of law, physical and moral, the one concerned with the relations of cause and effect, the other dealing with what is good and just. There was a vital connection between these two types of law. While it could be said that moral law applied first to what man should do, rather than what he does do, it was rooted, however, in man's social nature and it could become permanent natural law. Man, then, for Ferguson, had the capacity for growth and must work to perfect his potentiality. The function of moral philosophy, and one might read here Baldwin's social psychology, was the discovery and description of the kinds of perfection for which mankind should strive. This approach to perfection, to be defined as progress, could be predicted by moral philosophy because of the uniform nature and capacity of man. Man was a social animal whose social inclinations were derived from a moral sense that was amalgamated with human reason; and it was the social character of man that ensured the constant growth of man as his culture became progressively richer.

Ferguson defined social progress not only as increasingly richer tradition but as the parallel development of society with the qualities of the individual. Professor Gladys Bryson has described his theory of dual growth in this manner:

Now the life of man in societies is analogous to the life-span of the individual; man in his original condition of society is comparable to a baby, and the progression in the forms of society that man has gone through has no more made him a different creature than does adolescence change a child into a creature of a different species. There has in both cases simply been growth and progress of a natural kind.[12]

Still further, Ferguson forecast the kind of analysis that Baldwin and Croly used to transform the historicism of the nineteenth-century conservatives into a theory of conscious progress. This theory of natural growth constituted a vigorous denial of the primitivist concept that the natural state of human society was man's earliest one. All parts of man's history were as natural as any other part. The early nineteenth-century conservatives had rejected the liberalism of the Enlightenment which had declared that men could judge the justice of contemporary society against the ethics of man's natural state. Man was made by his society, wrote the conservatives; whatever society he was a part of was natural; justice, therefore, could only be defined by the justice which existed at the moment.

But Ferguson demanded the use of moral philosophy to discover what was the potential achievement of man. Baldwin and his American contemporaries were to echo this demand, utilizing the offspring of moral philosophy, social science, as a very concrete tool to break the bonds of the past and present so man could be free to follow the future. They agreed with Ferguson that "it is of far more importance to know the condition to which we ourselves should aspire, than that which our ancestors may be supposed to have left." [13] For Baldwin and his fellow liberals, Ferguson had demonstrated the way to say that all stages of human history were equally natural and yet to recognize that each succeeding generation was natural only so far as it fulfilled a potential which was progressive; he had established the way to claim, then, that the customs of each generation were also unnatural and must give way to the next stage of social evolution which man could comprehend through his reason.

Again creating precedent for his twentieth-century successor, Ferguson felt that a world of mechanical social change, understood by social science and cooperated with by man, really offered no free will to man. After positing man's power rationally to understand a rational social development, Ferguson and then Baldwin denied the full adequacy of man to know the concrete steps of history, and they denied that history really could be described as having a rational, mechanical character. Like Baldwin, Ferguson leaned to an ideal interpretation of the world in order that, in a more plastic environment, man could have the freedom that comes of creativity. As Ferguson wrote,

Parts that constitute the system of nature, like the stones of an arch, support and are supported; but their beauty is not of the quiescent kind. The principles of agitation and of life combine their effects in constituting an order of things, which is at once fleeting and permanent. The powers of vegetation and animal life come in aid of mechanical principles; the whole is alive and in action. The scene is perpetually changing; but, in its changes, exhibits an order more striking than could be made to arise from the mere position or description of any forms entirely at rest.[14]

The basic underlying presupposition of Baldwin's philosophy of social science was the Aristotelian conception of evolution. His social psychology was firmly anchored in the moral philosophy of the eighteenth century. But social science had proved to be but a small part of Baldwin's total philosophic position. He wanted to prove that man's nature was such that progress could be rationally predicted, and still more that man was free to create that progress, not passively adjust to it. Baldwin had therefore announced himself a philosophical idealist and had denounced as inadequate for the freedom of man the monistic materialism of Herbert Spencer, the central figure of Anglo-American thought at the end of the nineteenth century. Yet he was aware of the pitfalls that the other major philosophy of the period, Hegelian idealism, held for anyone who wanted to postulate the creative freedom of the individual. Hegelian idealism substituted an idealistic monism for Spencer's physical monism and continued to advise the individual that he found real freedom in conformity to his present environment, which, after all, represented the irresistible forces of progress over which he had no control.

Baldwin broke out of this philosophical impasse by developing a dualistic theory of experience. There was a spiritual purpose that influenced the world, but it did not find direct expression in the physical world as in Hegelian monism; it was not completely immanent in the world as man knew that world. There was a physical world which somehow had an independent existence apart from spirit. It was the purpose of the ideal force ultimately to dominate matter completely, and its growing domination was progress. The individual's freedom came from his necessary role as the mediator between spirit and matter. He was the agent who actually spiritualized his environment. Man could have creative freedom and at the same time follow an absolute purpose if he knew that he was indispensable for that purpose.

So it was that Baldwin came to the detailed writing of social psychology burdened with a most complex task: to blend Darwin and Hegel and Aristotelian evolution into a philosophy of inexorable, intelligent spiritual progress while retaining a creative role of freedom for the individual. It was a task he approached with confidence and assurance. The keystone of this intellectual edifice was his conception of the individual. In refuting Spencer, he claimed to stand for the view of man as an individualized social self. This was his legacy from German idealism. But in using Darwin against Spencer, Baldwin had postulated the gradual socialization of the individual through the biological process of evolution. Thus he had written, "Even in the animal world there is the beginning of a departure from this pure individualism in the direction of natural collectivism." The higher the type of animal, the more gregarious were its activities. In order that civilization, which was defined as cooperation, could come about, "The self-seeking tendencies of the animal must give place to cooperation and sympathy. And the process of selection in order to get the human race started on a career of sociability, must have put a premium on variation which did this." [15]

Everything that he borrowed from Darwin, therefore, pointed to the fact that man was a selfish individual who had been gradually socialized until he had become inherently social. The individual was basic to society, not society basic to the individual. The socialized individual who had emerged from biological evolution into social evolution had within himself the potential of social perfection. Human conscience, Baldwin declared, "is the normal personal self coming into its social heritage of rights and duties and recognizing its place and station." [16]

Bluntly, Baldwin was not prepared to deliver the creative individual from bondage to Spencer and a new bondage, that of Hegelian idealism, which insisted on the individual's subordination to the social whole. Baldwin admitted his debt to German idealism and its traditions; he would not criticize Hegel with the harshness he had used on Spencer. Yet this statement about a "normal personal self coming into its social heritage" was of great strategic importance. It placed the emphasis of social solidarity on the individual, the social individual, and not on the current social structure. In a very real sense, society depended more on the individual than the individual on society.

A decade before Croly, Baldwin was aware of the need to revise Hegel if a philosophy of progress which centered around a fully creative individual were to be held. Somehow he would explain how the individual was innately social and yet distinct; somehow he would demonstrate the reality of an independent individual and a society that was more than the sum of its component individuals. Pointing directly to Hegel, Baldwin declared that the exponents of philosophical idealism "give a relatively full and accurate answer to the question of the matter of social organization; but . . . they fail to describe the imitative process or type of function by which the social matter . . . becomes public, and is so made available for society and for the individual *both at once*." [17] This distinction was a crucial one for the American; from it, he worked out a system of social psychology which replaced point by point the conservative implications of the Hegelian type of political philosophy outlined in the chapter on Croly. It was this kind of social theory which was available to Croly in the first decade of the twentieth century when he moved to escape the restrictions that traditional idealistic philosophy placed on individual freedom.

The first element of this German theory was that the individual came unformed to society and was made human by a group of established institutions. Baldwin agreed, in part, that the individual was created by a social process, but he denied that the individual was then inferior to an institution. While it was true that "social psychology shows that the 'self' of the individual's 'self consciousness' is, in its materials and processes of formation, thoroughly social in its origin," Baldwin asserted, it did not follow that the individual could be conceived of as inferior or passive in his relation to the social body. Man becomes a developed personality through a dialectic of social growth which proceeds through three states: "Projective, subjective, and ejective." At the initial or projective level, the infant understands himself purely in terms of the people who surround him. Next as a child, after imitating the people in his environment, he reaches the subjective level when he reads all the actions of others in terms of his own personal thought. Finally, reaching maturity, he enters the ejective stage where there is a union of the previous projective and subjective levels so that the individual understands his identity with his social group, but understands also that the social group includes him as a participant and depends upon him for its definition.

Therefore, Baldwin continued, if it could be said that society was the natural state of man and was more than the aggregate of the individuals who made it up, it must also be said that there would be no society without its individual members. In underscoring this mutual relationship between the individual and society he was breaking the first and most important restrictive principle which troubled Croly. He was also laying the foundation for a theory which would undermine the other restrictive concepts. This was the rock of all of Baldwin's social psychology: his affirmation that

I do not see . . . how the personality of this child can be expressed in any but social terms; nor how, on the other hand, social terms can get any content of value but from the understanding of the developing individual. This is a circle of definition of course; and that is just my point. On the one hand; we can get no doctrine of society but by getting the psychology of the "socius" with all his natural history; and on the other hand, we can get no true view of the "socius" at any time without describing the social conditions under which he normally lives, with the history of their action and reaction upon him.[18]

The vast importance of this concept, Baldwin added, was that it undercut most of past thought which assumed a dualism, a distinction between man and society. The Spencerian individualists stated that the individual was hampered by any activity of society. Such a notion was meaningless when it was realized that there was no real individual as against society, no real selfishness against altruism, "that man is not two, an ego and an alter, each of which is in active and chronic protest against a third great thing, society." This doctrine of the mutual nature of the individual and society made irrelevant not only Spencer's fear but also one of the bases of that fear: the claim of the philosophical idealists that, in a certain sense, the individual must discipline a lower self in order to reach a higher, more socialized life. For although Hegelianism insisted upon the social nature of true personality, its conservative bias rested upon this belief in the dual nature of man.

Baldwin's theory of mutuality destroyed the second restrictive point which handicapped Croly: the claim that the partly unsocial individual could be saved from his lower nature only through the discipline exercised by the institution of the state. On the contrary,

James Mark Baldwin

Baldwin expressed the belief that man was certain of salvation, if it could be called that, without the mediation of the state. This was true because the imperfections of human nature at the present and in the past were not the result of an inherent and irreducible division in his personality. What could be called the imperfection of man's social qualities up to the immediate moment merely reflected the unfinished nature of the social process. The evil or selfishness in man was not a positive force; it was to be defined as negative, as a lack which would disappear as the true and the total social potential of man, his normal character of complete altruism, unfolded.

This social potential, as Croly phrased it in *Progressive Democracy*, was to flower out, not by discipline, but by the creative self-directed activity of the individual himself. Ethical man and ethical society were spontaneous expressions of the progressive evolution of society. Here was a social psychology that made redundant all discussion of the necessary disciplinary relation of the state to society. The state for Baldwin meant nothing more than the functions of governmental machinery, functions which had little vital significance when compared to the importance of the all-encompassing and all-beneficent society of which the government was merely one specific institution.

Having provided the individual with equality to his society, Baldwin enhanced his dignity by giving him a key role in the development of society. The Hegelian view of the solidarity of society had postulated social progress through the disciplinary action of institutions on the individual. Somehow the absolute that was the source of progress found expression in institutions, which then disciplined the individual to accept the further social advance. Croly had wrestled with this notion that progress was imposed on the individual as he attempted to find within it a place for individual initiative. Baldwin had incorporated in his social psychology a well-developed theory of the creative role of the individual in social progress. While one basic concept of his psychological theory of the socialization of the individual was imitation, Baldwin so qualified it that it became subordinate to its opposite, invention. Accepting the fact that there was a mutual relationship between the individual and society, the

93

logical corollary was that while the individual was dependent for his knowledge on society, society was equally dependent on the individual. Indeed, while integration into the traditional experience, embodied in society through imitation, made man into a real human personality, this relationship in no way explained the further development of society. Society was not motivated spontaneously but was led by its individual members. "All social reform," Baldwin insisted, "is accomplished by individuals who think and act outside the established conventions and traditions." Or as he put it in another way, "Society is the disciplinary agent, the schoolmaster, to the individual's thought, but the pupil outgrows the social school." [19]

Furthermore, Baldwin demonstrated that invention on the part of the individual was becoming ever a more frequent and more easily accomplished act because the course of social evolution had now brought man to a point where each individual must invent, must think for himself.

The history of society, Baldwin postulated, necessarily goes through stages of development: (1) the instinctive or gregarious; (2) the spontaneous or plastic; and (3) the reflective or social proper. The first social stage, the instinctive, finds man completely under the control of natural law; his bond of union is biological. The second stage, the spontaneous, has man above the domination of biological law but he is not yet a self-determining creature. Now his life is guided by habit so that, influenced by imitation which is essentially a mechanical response, society is static. The third stage is the final and highest form of social development. The bonds which tie men together to form their community are not the result of habit and mechanical imitation; cooperation is the result of rational choice. At last society can be defined as completely ethical.[20]

As Baldwin stressed that the culmination of social growth was a society of free agents voluntarily cooperating with each other, he shifted his emphasis from imitation to judgment as the factor of socialization. The individual, as he approached the social intelligence necessary for ethical life, learned less from imitation in his social environment than from judgment. More and more the individual, at this high level, acts as the genius has always acted. While the average man conformed to the established patterns of society, the genius brought crucial variations to these patterns. Understanding his society, working with the material provided by social tradition, the exceptional thinker reworks their content so that progressive novel conceptions are offered to his society. The true genius then leads his contemporaries and never breaks radically from them. They, in turn, must sanction his contributions before they can have positive effect. There is a constant reciprocal relationship between the creative individual and his society. Society impresses social tradition on the individual, who then transcends it, returning to inspire society to follow along the path of his discoveries.[21]

By making all social progress depend upon the creativity of the individual, Baldwin went far to provide the intellectual weapons that Croly needed to break from the restrictive concepts he was caught in when he borrowed from the Hegelian-type philosophy. The denial of the ability of the individual to go outside the accepted values of his time for standards with which to criticize those values was turned around by Baldwin to read that the individual must go beyond the standards of the day if progress was to be achieved. Even more, he so outlined the process of social evolution that the psychological structure of the individual would force him to question his society.

Then because the individual must be free to initiate new social values, the philosophy of education of the American social psychologist forecast Croly's ideas in *Progressive Democracy* and provided the basis for criticizing the philosophy of educational discipline that had informed *The Promise of American Life*. Baldwin's discussion of the place of institutions in the educational experience of man highlights the manner in which his practical theories were directed to the defense of man's freedom to learn by experimentation.

Naturally, Baldwin saw in society itself the most important educational institution for the individual. But within the amorphous unity of society, distinct separate institutions had specific roles in the individual's education. Most fundamental was a joint category that could be called the family-school. This was the institution which was the basic means for the indoctrination of the individual into the ways of society; this was the institution which impressed him with the highest values of sociability binding him with his neighbors.[22]

Against the fruitful positive influence of the family-school, Baldwin contrasted the minor and negative task of the political state. In deep disagreement with the Hegelian outlook on the importance of the state as a source of values, the American social philosopher described its role as that of a policeman to enforce the social relations already worked out by society and impressed on the individual by the family-school. Even as a policeman the state was relatively unimportant because the increasingly socialized individual needed less and less outer discipline to cooperate with his associates in following a course of social altruism.

Furthermore, the highest attribute of man was not conformity but creative freedom. These two institutions of the family-school and the state were utilitarian in that they served to inculcate and underwrite basic conditions for social life. But it was the third great institution, the church, that was closest to the active role the individual played in creating social progress. Nonutilitarian, the church was a product of advanced social evolution. Along with art, the church was a luxury of life because "They do not seek justification in practical utility or direct advantage" but serve to satisfy "the demand of the individual for a full and complete personal life." Seemingly conservative because it was built upon the established morality of society and effectively inculcated in the individual, nevertheless, the church was really radical because it helped to loose the individual from convention; it encouraged him to project his ideals beyond the immediate world and work to make them real. The greatest educational gift of an institution to man, then, was inspiration to go beyond institutions for the values to guide his life.[23]

A concept of freedom had been achieved by Baldwin's social psychology, a concept which could be used by political theorists like Herbert Croly to demonstrate the individual's power over physical law and social tradition. Man was a free intellect using his reason as an instrument to fulfill his wishes. But man was exercising his freedom to approach a sacred goal, that of a perfectly integrated social community; freedom was relative to an ideal purpose. The free individual was creating what amounted to cosmic destiny. There could be but one definition of progress. Man transcended immediate society to measure progress by that universal standard — the normal individual.

It was Baldwin's theory that social and individual development paralleled each other. If one knew what was the normal development of the individual, then one could know what was the normal growth of society. Happily for Baldwin's progressive-minded generation, the professor of social psychology had this information. The process of the personality development of the individual, Baldwin declared, is an ethical one. At birth the child has a self divided into two aspects: a self of habit and a self of accommodation. Neither of these, of course, is an ethical self and they compete with each other in giving the child guidance. Gradually this division is overcome as the personality develops and the child gains a sense of the difference between himself and his society. This makes possible the formation of a third aspect of self, the "socius," that is identified with society. The location of this new self outside the individual leads him to fulfill the laws of society; it is the individual conscience, the self that advises what ought to be done.[24]

The individual becomes fully ethical when he identifies this self, not with immediate society, but with an ideal social situation. When the individual associates his self with the *status quo*, he is on what Baldwin called the rational level of behavior where "We find that the individual's thought or judgment is 'controlled' by the facts he is dealing with, on the one hand, and by the customs, habits, social and disciplinary conventions . . . under which he does his thinking." [25] This control is broken by the sanction of fully ethical personality because the individual now creates an ideal outside of society to which his conscience adheres. Because this is the essence of personality development, society cannot stop the judgment of its members from transcending it, and society must recognize that "*in the ethical realm the individual may rule himself by rules which are in advance of those which society prescribes, and also exact them.*" [26]

Such a process of freedom for the individual was dependent, of course, on the fact that the ethical man was the completely socialized personality who willed total cooperation with his associates. The ethical individual leads his society toward its final and ethical stage beyond the primitive social history of the instinctive and spontaneous levels. When society does reach the parallel position of the total ethical development of the individual, then each of its members "intentionally and voluntarily cooperates with others in pursuit of intelligent ends" and "These intelligent acts of cooperation cannot be considered as due to either physical or social heredity. . . . *They are social novelties.*" [27]

Baldwin wanted the assurance of Aristotelian evolution, but he also wanted the fact of human creativity within this normal process. And so he was using reason to prove that the inevitable development of human potentiality depended upon free activity, which was in turn part of that inexorable process. Auguste Comte was right, he continued, in that society goes through three stages of intellectual growth; but Comte was wrong in viewing positivism as the culmination of this growth. Instead Baldwin rewrote the chart of intellectual evolution in this form.

I. INDIVIDUAL INTERPRETATION

Stages	*Modes*
I. Prelogical	I. Intuitive
II. Logical	Quasi-discursive
III. Hyper-logical	II. Discursive
	Over-discursive
	III. Contemplative

II. RACIAL INTERPRETATION

Stages	*Modes*
I. Prelogical	I. Mystical (Religious)
II. Logical	Mythical
III. Hyper-logical	II. Speculative and Scientific
	Critical
	III. Contemplative [28]

In the first, the prelogical stage of thought, men accept directly their sense perceptions and their feelings as the final criteria of truth; they accept blindly the authority of their society, since they have no means of testing the validity of its values. From this control by the immediate aspects of their life, they are freed by the tools of logic

98

and science, which are the mark of the logical stage of thought. They can now test their experience and the values of society by the criteria of logical consistency and the laws of nature. They strive to find objective meaning.

Apprehension of reality, however, is obtained through the mediation of logic and science, which stand between the knower and the objects he experiences, and this leads men into an unresolved conflict revolving around fact and value. Fact is now the product of mediation, but men still feel that value is an immediate experience. To overcome this conflict it is necessary to go on to a higher stage of thought. "The Positivism of the scientific view of the world is not the last word." Comte's second and third stages of thought, the metaphysical and the positivistic, had to be merged into what Baldwin called the logical and men must pass on to the hyperlogical level of thinking where imagination would free them "from the trammels of thought, from the machinery of mediation." This was the final freeing of the human mind.[29]

Earlier philosophers had fallen short of a resolution of the conflict between fact and value because they had not visualized this highest stage of thought. Men like Spencer had been willing to sacrifice value to follow the logic of the facts as revealed by science. Others like Hegel had been willing to sacrifice fact to follow the logic of value, claiming that an absolute ideal finds expression in the factual world regardless of the contradictory finding of science. Man, however, knows that the natural laws of science are there; he knows he lives in a world whose physical environment is unfinished, changing, imperfect; he knows therefore that this world is not the perfect expression of an absolute ideal. But he also knows that there is value in the world, and that values are expressed by man's will and do control the world, even if imperfectly. Recognizing that the Spencers or Hegels resolved this dualistic split of reality by denying part of experience, pragmatists like William James had tried to deny the existence of objective scientific law or objective values. Reality, wrote James, exists only in each individual's mind.

But, wrote Baldwin, "Does not the real need a point of actuality in which its values may reside? — can the ideal float in a void with-

out presupposing an existing real?" "Any pluralistic theory, therefore, that would have a chance of commending itself to reflection,
would perforce be a relative pluralism, one of the sort that allows
at least the comprehension of the diversity of so-called realities in a
larger unity of some sort." [30]

This is what men will do when they have all arrived at the hyperlogical stage of thought. Technically Baldwin proposed that the
human imagination, in something like an artistic experience, would
unify the world of fact and value. In doing so, the imagination of
man was creating the world. These experiences of the individual
were not isolated and fragmentary. Each experience, he affirmed,
"has its continuous development toward an ideal fulfillment." The
individual then lived in a concrete physical world and also in an
ideal spiritualistic one. He mediated between the two, working
constantly to make the physical conform to the purpose of the
spiritual.[31]

Baldwin's most fundamental assumptions about evolution, then,
were Aristotelian. Nevertheless they were part of a philosophy of
idealism which incorporated an important theory of a dualism between the physical world and a spiritual purpose. These assumptions
can be outlined in four points: (1) Nature is not a mechanism. It is
a developing manifestation of an inner spiritual principle that is
bringing about self-conscious intelligence and moral maturity in
man. (2) But nature is not purely the reflection of Spirit or mind or
God; it is not entirely spiritual; there is matter that must still be
spiritualized. The ideal is then not completely immanent in nature
but is in part transcendent. (3) Evolution, or the spiritualization of
matter, demands the creative effort of individuals. Man is the necessary and active agent of God. (4) Man, therefore, has free will. A
scientific study of nature will reveal the past working of Spirit in
the world but it cannot predict the future without the wilful effort
of man. A direct, transcendent contact with Spirit rather than scientific study will give the inspiration for man's effort to transform
nature in the future. Imagination, not reason, is the key faculty of
man because it alone is creative.

A social science based on Aristotelian evolution and a dualistic metaphysical idealism form two fundamental aspects of the preconceptions of Baldwin the social philosopher. But they do not exhaust Baldwin as an intellectual force in his generation. He was more than a philosopher because ultimately he must be considered as a religious prophet. The culmination of social evolution was a religious society that celebrated the religion of humanity. The creative freedom of the individual was an exercise in religious behavior. Unlike Comte, Baldwin was not openly critical of the religious mysticism which marked the prelogical stage of human thinking. In a way, the imaginative freedom of the hyperlogical era was but a return on a higher level to the emotionally religious behavior of primitive society.

Baldwin had postulated that the human self reaches its final ethical level when it postulates an ideal beyond itself and its society to be the guide for its conscience. Since Baldwin believed that society follows the course of individual development, society, at the point of its culmination as an ethical unit, must have its collective conscience guided by an ideal. Metaphysically this ideal was the spiritual purpose behind evolution; practically it was the perfect community of complete altruism because this was the spiritual goal of this religion of humanity; the ideal of the perfect society would inspire men to bring about its accomplishment more quickly than would the slower forces of impersonal social evolution. In almost the very terms that Croly was using, Baldwin explained the revolutionary leaven of this religion of humanity. He wrote,

It does not follow from this that the group, *as it exists,* is the object of religion. The existing group, the sociological group, is not what the religious ideal denotes, nor what the national aspirations celebrate. . . . The social ideal is symbolized by the group, just as the ideal self or God of the individual is symbolized in the concrete object of veneration. The two ideals are fused in one through the motives under which — as we have seen — personality is at once socialized and idealized. . . . Religion of humanity, then, to be a religion, must mean religion of ideal humanity.[32]

And he added,

We are obliged to conclude then that, instead of disappearing, religion in some form will abide. In the higher union of the motives of personal and social interest in that of religion, there is a return on another plane to the early state of things noted by sociologists in primitive culture, where religion dominated both individual and social life.[33]

Certainly this total position of Baldwin, like that of Croly, was religious, a kind of evangelical reassurance to a troubled world. Underneath the present anarchy, these prophets promised their contemporaries, were laws of progress. Amidst the social wreckage, amidst the myriads of atomic individuals, these laws were creating a new society, a society of perfect cooperation and absolute harmony. "Humanity" then was the place where the lost individual would be saved and "History" was the means for that salvation because "History is the self-realization of the emerging absolute." But while the individual was promised the inevitable outcome of progress in the perfect cooperative commonwealth, this was not a message of quietism. A belief in progress, a spiritual union with the ongoing process was necessary for its consummation; man's mind and soul could receive the proper inspiration and guidance only when he enthusiastically shared the belief in the spiritual power underlying progress. The world was a moral struggle in which man must fight against the evil of the present anarchy, the present negative individualism, and fight for the coming Kingdom of God on Earth with its merging of the individual into the social whole. The communicant in the religion of humanity, the religion of progress, was given the exhilarating message, then, that he was free to create the future because the social reality of which he was a part was above the control of natural law and above the control of what was usually called history — the institutions and traditions of the past — he was free to create a future whose coming, nevertheless, was inevitable and whose rules were absolute.

Charles H. Cooley THE TRANSCENDEN-
TALISM OF SOCIAL SCIENCE

WITH his massive pedantry, his pride in erudition, and his joy in associating himself with the great figures of philosophy, Baldwin is a case study in the dependence of American thought on European culture. Each level of his writing when analyzed is solidly based on the precedents of Western civilization from Aristotle and Plotinus to Hegel and Darwin. Yet there was an unmistakably unique quality in the Baldwin position. He waved the magic wand of Darwinian evolution over leaden historical concepts and created a marvelously golden mixture that had to be American because it glittered and glowed SUCCESS in capital letters. Perhaps, then, Baldwin is the end of the search for the American theory of progress held by the *New Republic*.

Possibly recalling the opening hypothesis of Carl Becker, however, makes it irrelevant to ask the question of originality or even of initial origins. Of course, Baldwin was original in the sense that he put together a unique synthesis of existing postulates. And of course he was American because that unique synthesis included attitudes which were traditional in American thought: the freedom of the individual; the essentially peaceful and cooperative nature of the historical process which was progress; the classless, middle-class nature of the good society; and its spiritual quality. These in turn were not American property except to the degree of emphasis. But emphasis can be crucial in the distinction of one culture from another or one generation from another, and it is this emphasis which is the basis of the climate of opinion of Baldwin and his contemporaries. Given the emotional strength of this attitude, there were many theoretical roads to the conclusions Baldwin had reached; so in the end he was original only in the particular manner in which he constructed his road.

Nothing demonstrates this more clearly than the writings of a fellow pioneer in social psychology: Charles Horton Cooley.[1] In the histories of social psychology it is written that Cooley is more modern than Baldwin. He was a younger man, educated in sociology and psychology in the 1890s; he was a second-generation social scientist building selectively from the materials of the pioneers. For Cooley, then, the whole nineteenth-century apparatus of stages of social evolution and stages of personal evolution, with the concomitant artificial forcing of facts into hardened categories, was outdated and unnecessary. He would study individuals as individuals, as unique personalities each in a unique social environment. With the sophistication of added perspective, he understood better than Baldwin that the inescapable implications of Darwin spelled novelty.

But if Cooley is more sophisticated than Baldwin, it is also true that he is less so. It has been assumed that Cooley rejected the older man's theoretical jargon for scientific reasons. A strong case can be made, however, that the younger Cooley jettisoned this legacy because of his emotional outlook. It was Cooley who could act the role of prophet for the religion so painstakingly worked out with detailed metaphysical and scientific support by Baldwin. Baldwin was by nature a philosopher; Cooley was a preacher; and to preach effectively the gospel of Baldwin, it was absolutely imperative to give it the emotional impact of a simple, straightforward statement. Among social scientists Cooley stands almost alone as a stylist. His writings have both clarity and charm; they are informal and warm; they are not involved and heavy; they are not social science but social preaching. His message carried the impact of personal involvement. The illustrations in the text came back to the author, and as he saved himself, he offered that salvation to his readers.

Charles H. Cooley

The dominant experience of Charles Cooley as he reached the first self-consciousness of youth was the attempt to define himself as an individual. Shy, sensitive, and sickly, he felt overshadowed by a father eminently successful as a jurist. This background was further broadened by the family's New England heritage transplanted to Michigan. He had a conscience which was expressed in a journal that was his companion through life.[2] His was the task of remaining so morally upright and unselfish that he could hope there was not "one in a million of my age who is so well under the control of his will." But this person and this will were not to be judged by the standards of the outside world. Defiantly Cooley added, "A man does right as he follows his conscience." Self-discipline would be the strengthening of reliance on the private self, not the conformity of the public self.

This boy read Emerson and he was reaffirmed in his belief in individual responsibility; he was given renewed confidence that the external world with all its impressive established codes and institutions revolved around the individual. It was not egotism but only responsibility to affirm that "Man is the greatest thing in creation and it is part of his duty to recognize this fact in his every act." From Emerson, too, he learned the more subtle meaning of man's full stature, which was a freedom and creativity that placed mankind above control by reasoned judicial pronouncements, indeed above all attempts to rationalize the world. The rules of society and nature somehow mysteriously depend on the individual man. A rigid reason is not the basis of philosophical principles. "Instinct is the foundation and only criterion for these." [3]

The Charles Cooley who began to search for a career was outwardly diffident then, but inwardly confident, almost brash. As he began the study which ultimately would make him a professional sociologist, he knew that "new thoughts are born, not found. They are born to those who follow the spirit utterly, and follow nothing else." He could now look back and write that his father had compromised with moral principle because he had failed to break from what is customary. The young Cooley was becoming a superbly confident rebel against all that was established in home and society.

But again this was not egotism. Cooley was not becoming an individual through dislike of society. He was becoming an individual so that he might serve society better. He was a rebel who had come to reconstruct not to destroy. As he confided to his journal, "The ideal of my active life is to concern myself with work whose aim is goodness and equity and which has no aim that is selfish." He was also a rebel in deep spiritual communion with a reality beyond the personal self. When he acted as an individual to reform society he would not be alienated from the larger unity to which he must belong. Increasingly, the journals reveal a growing religious sense of identification with an unknown spiritual force, a fact recognized by Cooley himself. "I believe that a vague sense of the whole grows upon me — intangible, not to be scrutinized, yet deep and supporting." [4]

This was exhilarating yet dangerous ground for a thinker who had chosen sociology as the discipline best suited for the reformation of society. Consciously, deliberately, Cooley was a sociologist because he was at heart a reformer. But the specific goal for reform and the specific techniques for reform that he was considering ran counter to the social science philosophy of the American graduate schools of the 1890s, dominated as they were by the rationalism of men like Lester Frank Ward who insisted that sociology was as precise and mechanical as physics because society was controlled by the same kind of predictable laws as was physical nature. Cooley, however, described his own vision of sociology in this way: "I would like to make a connecting link between science and poetry, to show the pressing facts of human life as members of an ideal and beautiful whole." [5] Indeed, during his graduate training, Cooley was assailed by doubts as to whether his poetic instinct could be reconciled with social science. Again and again he asked, "Is my aim aesthetic or scientific? Is it my purpose and the tendency of my character to take up a material, form it into a consistent and shapely whole and present it with the intent that it shall give pleasure; or am I seeking only truth and not beauty, striving to present things in whatever intellectual unity they have and no more?" [6]

Cooley emerged from this period of doubt with the self-assurance that "Is not all larger science aesthetic in its aims?" He could be

Charles H. Cooley

the free, creative inspirational poet discovering the spiritual truths of the universe; he could be Emerson's disciple. He could also be a social scientist dealing with the concrete facts of existence; he could be a scientist because science was subordinate to poetry. He could discover the laws of social development without being controlled by them.

This, too, is the message of his journals. It was not merely a personal, inner struggle to determine whether Charles Cooley as an individual would follow artistic creativity or scientific certainty. As an individual he had to be an artist, as a reformer he knew he had to be a scientist. That was the issue which gave the struggle such urgency. When he wrote in his journal, "The great present need of sociology is a clear and fine outline of the theory of human development," he visualized this knowledge as a weapon to destroy the conformity of society to past tradition. He sensed that he and other exceptional individuals through inner resources could rise above the conventions supported by men like his own judicial father. But the only way to save the hard-headed men of affairs and the unexceptional mass was to demonstrate rationally, with scientific precision, that there were laws of social development which clearly made the conventions of the present obsolete as mankind was carried along the road of progress toward a society infinitely better than that of 1890.

This was the challenge to himself and to his chosen profession, and his response was the creation of a sociology of laws and of freedom. The basic proposition, the cornerstone of this theoretical structure was the underlying spirituality of the universe. Avoiding the technicalities of metaphysics in the manner of Emerson, he would be an instinctive philosophical idealist.

The great reforming sociologist of 1890, Lester Frank Ward, could not be followed because he did not realize this basic spirituality. "Society," wrote Cooley, "of course, is spiritual, but current philosophy does not see this, it sees only the shell." Emphasizing the external, he continued, thinkers like Ward have postulated the same kind of control of society by physical law as is found in the natural world. Given the fact of the spiritual nature of society, however, it followed that "Exact prediction and mechanical control for the social world . . . is a false ideal inconsiderately borrowed from the provinces of physical science. There is no real reason to think that this sort of prediction or control will ever be possible." [7]

The young sociologist could not help admiring Ward because he was the pioneer in the fight against those who defended the *status quo*. Ward had seen the fatal weakness in the conservative defense that appealed to Darwin but rallied around Herbert Spencer. The gospel of Spencerian evolution was that man is part of physical evolution, controlled by natural law, and morality must be adjustment to whatever environment humanity finds current because morality is adjustment to natural law. Spencer, however, admitted that evolution was progress, that the natural laws were carrying men ever forward. Therefore, Ward had asked the inescapable question: Why man's reason, his scientific understanding, could not discover the pattern of progress in the future. He had asked why morality should not be considered as the attempt to lift man out of the present environment to conformity with the more progressive environment.

Writing from the viewpoint of Emerson, however, Cooley declared that Ward had betrayed the dignity of man to almost the same degree as had Spencer. This was not real freedom, this doctrine of Ward. It was of the same quality and character as that of the eighteenth-century liberal *philosophes* against whom Emerson and the transcendentalists had rebelled. Was this freedom that man should escape from conformity to present natural law to conformity to future law? The *philosophes* of the Enlightenment had said yes but the transcendentalists had said no. For Emerson, freedom could only be defined as creativity. Actually, in Cooley's estimation, Ward fell just as far from a true understanding of Darwin as did Spencer. Neither had really escaped from the static view of the world inherited from the past. In American thought, it was the transcendentalists alone who had accurately anticipated the essence of Darwin.

Cooley, therefore, proclaimed his allegiance to the greatest spokesman of modern science, Charles Darwin. Darwin had demonstrated the essential relativity of an evolving world and the necessary relativity of science. This, in turn, guaranteed that there were no rigid physical laws which controlled society and man. It was Darwin, then, who provided the proof of the freedom of man by opening the door for the creative activity of man in a plastic world. There could never be a justification for determinism in physical science because "Science is nothing without an ideal — that is a theory — which it strives to verify and perfect thro facts." Consequently, "all knowledge is subjective in one sense: in the sense, namely, that it is mental, not the external thing, but a construct of the mind." [8]

It was not to Ward, then, that Cooley looked for sociological guidance in his battle against the conservatives. He had to find a tradition that would provide positive alternatives to the dominance of society by physical law and of the individual by utilitarian ethics. And like Baldwin he found this guidance in Germany. Not directly, because Cooley did not study sociology abroad, but indirectly as he literally devoured the books of the German social philosopher, Albert Schaeffle.

Schaeffle transmitted to Cooley the German traditions which so many of the Michigan sociologist's contemporaries were to gain from many different sources. Blending these traditions with Darwin and buttressing them with Emerson, Cooley could demolish Spencer without being trapped by Spencer's metaphysics. Simply stated, for Cooley the German contribution to social knowledge was the understanding of the social environment of man. This meant that man lived not in nature but in society, a society with a past, present, and future; it was society that made the human animal into a civilized man. It was on this necessary social nexus that ethics should rest: ethical behavior must contribute to the welfare of the group.[9]

Here was the solid basis from which to judge Spencer. Looked at from this perspective, his sociology was lacking in human sympathy; it disregarded human personality; it had no insight into the human mind and soul. And this was so because his sociology was biological and individualistic when it should have been historical and social. In one of his first major sociological essays, "The Process of Social Change," published, significantly, in the *Political Science Quarterly* of 1897, Cooley lashed out directly at Spencer's definition of evolution as the survival of the fittest.[10] Such a concept was patently ridiculous, Cooley related, once it was realized that men were not atomic individuals involved in biological competition with each other for the fruits of a physical environment which was their entire world. How far this was from the truth of the situation! Man's meaningful environment was society, not nature. He was reared within a social framework, not as an autonomous creature, but as a cooperative member. His release of natural energy was not in physical competition but in social creativity. This was the true key to human evolution. Society changed not because men competed but because they created. Progress was made, not by the working of physical law upon society, but by the working of individuals within society. Human progress was not the negative elimination of the unfit leaving the strong to survive the battle; rather, human progress was based on the positive ability of men to learn and grow so that all could share in the forward progress in society originated by a few exceptional individuals.

Cooley, at the very beginning of his publishing career, insisted that the creative and free individual was the key figure in human life. This confident affirmation, coupled with Cooley's easy acquisition of German sociological doctrines as alternatives to those of Lester Frank Ward, suggests that he faced no further complicating theoretical problems. The young Cooley, seeking to define himself and his role in society, had championed two doctrines, his personal freedom from external control and his responsibility to free society from external control. Emerson had given him faith in his own creative power. Darwin had suggested the freedom of man from any unchanging laws. Schaeffle had demonstrated the freedom of society from control by an external environment. Sociology was to provide the knowledge of the laws of social development necessary to convince society to leave present conventions, traditions, and institutions behind as outdated, indeed as dead weight hindering the process of progress.

In 1897 Cooley had every theory he wanted, but together they were more than he wanted. As an honest man, was not his idealistic philosophy sheer hypocrisy? Hadn't he returned to the eighteenth century by a more secretive and even more dishonest route than had Ward? It was all very well to say that life, that society, is spiritual; that they are, therefore, not controlled by physical law; that, therefore, man is free to create. But what then when one writes that there are laws of social development? Even if they are spiritual laws of a spiritual society, are they any less limiting on man's creative freedom? Isn't Cooley contrasting present imperfect society with a perfect external model, as would any good *philosophe*? Isn't he telling men that they are free to escape the present to conform to the future? And the philosophical web is still more entangling. If man is made by society, by what criteria can he judge it? The German tradition offers an alternative to the rationalism and individualism of Spencer. But in accepting German theories of social solidarity, can one escape the conservative implications Hegel read into this doctrine? Spencer had erroneously said that morality is acquiescence to the physical environment. Why, however, isn't morality simply acquiescence to the social environment? Why should not the individual, admittedly the product of historical society, conform to that society? Is not the spiritual purpose that is the author of social evolution as limiting as Spencer's material force?

Cooley's negative answer to all of these questions is the formative theme of his first major book, *Human Nature and the Social Order.*[11] Standing shoulder to shoulder with Baldwin, he developed a uniquely American sociology, which would start with the German concept of society as the formative environment for human nature, but which would prove the individual's transcendence of this matrix.

Like his preceptor Baldwin, Cooley began to build his theory on the German insight of the spiritual unity of society. As Cooley translated it, it was the intellectual unity of society — "the imaginations which people have of one another are the solid fact of society." But like his American colleague, he did not define this social entity as a mysterious unity without a functional relationship to its component individuals. Firmly he expressed the organic relation of individual to society and society to individual. "A separate individual is an abstraction unknown to experience, and so likewise is society when regarded as something apart from individuals. The real thing is Human Life, which may be considered either in an individual aspect or in a social." This did not mean for Cooley, however, that society is only the sum of its individuals; the basic reality of social life is the social process which is more than the aggregate of separate personalities. One understands this social process through the genetic study of individuals, the tracing of the story of human personality development from its starting point.

Eliminating the cluttering concepts of recapitulation, growth through stages, and the key role of imitation held by Baldwin, Cooley went straight to the infant, naked, alone, but potentially social. From its earliest days the infant exhibits sociability, and these impulses are brought into contact with other personalities through another tendency, that of communication. Personality and the human mind are developed by a give and take process between the infant and the people in its environment. As these social tendencies are objectified through communication, the child comes to have ideas about the people around him. These ideas, developed out of this reciprocal process, are not isolated phenomena but rather are part of a total web of associations, colored by emotion and sentiment. There is then no absolute separation of individuals from each other or from society since they are society and this society is part of the thinker's mind. Reality, then, is social, it is in the social process which exists in the minds of men. This allowed Cooley to write,

So far as the study of immediate social relations is concerned the personal idea is the real person. That is to say, it is in this alone that one man exists for another, and acts directly upon his mind. My association with you evidently consists in the relation between my idea of you and the rest of my mind.[12]

Given this mutual development of individual and society, there was no fatal division of the human being into ego and alter, there was no need for discipline to suppress inherent selfishness, which did not exist, nor to encourage sociability, which did naturally exist. The normal individual acted both individually and socially.

In a truly organic life the individual is self-conscious and devoted to his own work, but feels himself and that work as part of a large and joyous whole. He is self-assertive, just because he is conscious of being a thread in the great web of events . . .[13]

112

Charles H. Cooley

Within this social web, each generation of men objectified their experience of the ongoing process of life in institutions — institutions which were absolutely essential for the preservation of the traditions so necessary to educate the child into the world of his peers. But the essence of life was progress; constant evolution was the one absolute. Institutions could help socialize the individual, but they could not help him live with the future. It was the individual's responsibility to transcend his society, to live with the future, and to bring society along the road he followed because "Society, like every living, advancing whole, requires a just union of stability and change, uniformity and differentiation." In this view, "Innovation is just as social as conformity" and "New right, or moral progress, always begins in a revolt against institutions." [14]

Cooley knew almost instinctively what Baldwin worked to establish: that society was free from determination by physical law, that it had spontaneous development in history and that the individual was a free and creative part of society. He expressed this philosophy of total freedom with precision and force. Society, directed by its spontaneous individual members, was moving into a future of its own making, evolving its standards and values as each new need or problem was reached. Progress, wrote Cooley, is "essentially tentative . . . we work it out as we go along, and always must . . . it is a process rather than an attainment. The best is forever indefinable; it is growth, renewal, onwardness, hope." Clearly, indisputably, he took evolution seriously as Spencer and even Ward had not.

Furthermore, he would make the most of his insight into the social flux which was man's only environment. The heart of conservatism in America was an economic theory which blandly insisted on the immutability of certain economic laws, the most important of which was the necessity of *laissez faire*. But how could these values be anything but relative, Cooley insisted. They were created to fit a particular institutional situation; they were of the past; they were outdated and outmoded; they must be replaced by new values to fit the present institutional situation. Institutional economics, declared Cooley, must replace static economics when the full meaning of evolution was realized. [15]

This was the glorious, exhilarating message of man's freedom in a completely relative world. Now, however, troubles came for Cooley in the form of the question of what values he and his generation should develop to fit the institutional present of the twentieth century. It was a question Cooley could not ignore. Like Croly, and unlike Baldwin, he was frightened. He had an almost terrifying sense of crisis. He was conscious, as Baldwin had not been, of the impact of the industrial revolution which had "broken down the old groups, based chiefly on locality, family and class," which had brought in a "formless and unchannelled state of things." Industrialism had indeed destroyed civilization as man had known it. It had brutalized the world in setting loose isolated, selfish, competitive individuals to prey on one another in an environment where men were treated as pawns to be manipulated within a cash nexus. No, Cooley could never ignore the problem of values in a relative world if civilization was to be preserved.[16]

There was a necessary, positive side to this fear, however; it was one of the symbols of difference between the philosopher and the religious prophet. If there was the possibility of damnation, there was also the possibility of salvation, and the greater the danger, the greater the thrill of success. Cooley faced his forecast of cataclysm with joyful confidence. As he dissected the values of commercialism to prove their ephemeral qualities, he began to compare them with another set of values. In the final analysis, he did not criticize commercialism in terms of its ability to operate within the framework of the present economic system; he flayed it because it did not embrace the values of universal human nature. Professing that Darwin meant novelty and that he was a Darwinian, Cooley nevertheless stated a theory of natural rights. He recognized that such a position would seem to many readers a revival of the eighteenth-century doctrine of natural right and he denied that relation. The Enlightenment, he wrote, had postulated a group of free individuals, who banded together to create a society and government by contract. "Now in form," he added, "this doctrine is wholly at variance with evolutionary thought. To the latter, society is an organic growth; there is no individual apart from society, no freedom apart from organization . . ."[17] And while Cooley was an evolutionist, he continued,

If it is true that human nature is developed in primary groups which are everywhere much the same, and that there also springs from these a common idealism which institutions strive to express, we have a ground for somewhat the same conclusions as come from a theory of natural freedom . . .[18]

Human nature, he drove on, is social, but while the individual reflects that social environment of which he is a part, there is a form of universal society beneath the relative forms of any conventional culture; there is unity beneath the vast multiplicity of groups and institutions. This unity is in the form of certain universal traits that are found in all societies, and these are based on the primary groups. By primary groups, Cooley meant,

. . . those characterized by intimate face-to-face association and cooperation. They are primary in several senses, but chiefly in that they are fundamental in forming the social nature and ideals of the individual. . . . The most important spheres of this intimate association and cooperation . . . are the family, the play-group of children and the neighborhood or community group of elders. These are practically universal, belonging to all times and all stages of development; and are accordingly a chief basis of what is universal in human nature and human ideals.[19]

These were the universal, timeless groups which developed traits that were universal and timeless in man. Cooley, like Baldwin, had assumed a normal man. He could declare his separation from the eighteenth century in the sense that he repudiated the concept of a self-contained individual who created society. But he could also postulate a natural man, because he presupposed a potentially normal individual who needed a particular and normal social environment to develop that potential. This, however, was only what the *philosophes* had argued in other terms — that man was plastic enough to be shaped by the proper environment to conform to what was natural for him. Cooley had returned to primitivism and an Aristotelian evolution. The standards for modern man were to be found in the original man. Evolution was the perfection of a pre-existing potential. Human nature was those sentiments and impulses that are human in being superior to those of lower animals, and also in the sense that they belong to mankind at large, and not to any particular race or time. It means, particularly, sympathy and the innumerable sentiments into which sympathy enters, such as love . . .[20]

Cooley assumed what Baldwin had demonstrated, that man had emerged from his bondage to physical and psychological law and that he was finally a free agent, capable of perfection through the purity of loving cooperation with his neighbors, capable of achieving the Kingdom of God on Earth. But he assumed that this had happened at the beginning of the history of civilization. He appears so much more modern than Baldwin because he places the final expression of social evolution within everyday life, rather than within the process of mechanical social law. He is much more moving than Baldwin because he relates the religion of humanity to Christianity. The arrival of mankind at the possibility of complete historical salvation, Cooley declared, was symbolized by the appearance of the Christian religion. "The sentiments that Christ taught and illustrated are the strong sentiments, the lasting, the fit, the social, the evolutionary, if you will." These universal traits of human nature have always been operating and so "All modern history may be regarded as chiefly the expansion or organization of ideas that were understood locally at the beginning of the Christian Era." [21]

This is the heart of Cooley's theory of progress. There had been no essential change in human nature since man emerged as a truly social animal, subject only to his innate impulses and social tradition. His only legacy from biological heredity was a plasticity, an extreme teachability. Consequently, Cooley promised his worried contemporaries, "We are so happily contrived that humanity can progress without a change in human nature, through the peculiar constitution we already have." [22] In the primary groups, all the ideals which form the basis of human association emerge: love, truth, loyalty, service, and total moral unity. In the primary groups, there is no evil. Evil can be explained in purely historical terms, and the two basic dilemmas of the men of the eighteenth century who believed in primitivism and progress will disappear. Men have not followed the essential justice of their basic instincts because there has been no unity between the primary groups of the world; there has been no chance for a common mind to grow up around them. Widespread misunderstanding has handicapped social progress.

The second dilemma of primitivistic progress melted away just as easily under the warmth of Cooley's benign optimism. There is no conflict between primitive norms and increasing complexity in social organization. These norms are not individualistic but social; they are the models for any future social growth; the increasing complexity of society meant its inevitable salvation because it was through advancing organization that the values of the primary group would spread throughout the entire human community.

Directly, with the logic of love rather than through metaphysical speculation, Cooley had joined his sophisticated theory of social psychology with the ancient position of primitivism and Aristotelian evolution. His earliest writing was in the field of communication. Mind, he had written, is social. The individual mind enlarges only as it comes into broader contact with the social mind, and the reverse process is also true: the social mind enlarges and becomes enriched only as individual minds are able to fuse with it. Communication, then, is the key to the quality and health of both the individual and social mind. If there is no communication, "The mind does not develop a true human nature."

Now there was the industrial revolution which had solved the problems of mass communication. If industrialism meant crisis, it also meant the possibility of total salvation because it had built the railroads and strung the magic wire of the telegraph and evoked the mass circulation newspaper. "Modern communication fulfills one condition of the 'Kingdom' by bringing all mankind into somewhat familiar intercourse." Knowing that evil was to be defined as "negative rather than positive, as inertia and confusion rather than ill-interest and that selfishness is not something additional to ordinary human nature . . . but rather a lack," Cooley could offer the millennial assurance of an Aristotelian who knew where evolution must eventuate, because "Assuming that the human heart and conscience, restricted only by the difficulties of organization, is the arbiter of what institutions are to become, we may expect the facility of intercourse to be the starting-point of a new era of moral progress." [23]

But was the historical chance of industrialism really Aristotelian evolution? Could Cooley's readers be persuaded that this cataclysm fitted into a more ordered and rational scheme of human development? Cooley also had reassuring answers for these questions which would go far to dispel the elements of danger which even he had admitted surrounded the current crisis. There was a history of meaningless chance, but there was also a history of lawful social development which was progress. Inevitably, inexorably, this "history" controlled history so that the Kingdom of God on Earth must eventuate. Industrialism seemed the exceptional occurrence which triggered the possibility of human salvation here and now. Actually, a sociologist could have predicted it because "History shows a general growth of rational organization." Since democracy, the total incarnation of Christian principles in this world, was also rational organization, "May we not say . . . that there has always been a democratic tendency." The increased tempo of communication had brought the full expression of what Baldwin called the third and final stage of social evolution, complete individual and social self-consciousness, and what Cooley called rational organization or democracy: "The general or public phase of larger consciousness is what we call Democracy. I mean by this primarily the organized sway of public opinion." [24]

Now the Michigan sociologist hammered forward to establish the thesis of social homogeneity on which Croly based his theory of one-party democracy. Made up of perfectly communicating individuals, society could think and act as one individual. The individual and society were largely creatures of sentiment and emotion; the central fact of human psychology was the urge to act. It was the common man who furnished the moving sentiments, the aspirations for which society must work. The function of leadership was to provide organization for the more or less chaotic impulse of the group. The mass provided the originality in the social process, and the leaders gave it effective and intelligent expression. This did not mean, however, a debasing of leadership. As the highest faculties within an individual controlled his conduct, so "The expression of the group is always superior to the average capacity of its members," and "If a group does not function through its more competent instruments, it is simply because of imperfect organization."

While Cooley believed that sentiment was the basis of human activity, it was not blind sentiment. When the individual and society had reached the stage of total organization of the primary ideals, they would have the environment that would cause them to choose ends which conformed to the highest values of the primary groups. Present American public opinion, Cooley argued, is not "a mere reflection of conditions believed to be inevitable, but seeks principles, finds these principles in human nature, and is determined to conform life to them or know why not." [25]

Cooley was hewing close to the precedent of James Mark Baldwin. He, too, was defining progress as organization and he, too, declared modern man capable of voluntarily following the rules of social organization. Individual conscience was the only necessary social control. A social animal, whose evil or selfish characteristics were present only in an imperfect society, man was now a member of a perfected society and had a perfected conscience. Conscience was rational comprehension of duty. "What are these ethical aims of society?" asked Cooley, are they not "simply rational aims, representing the ideal of efficient total organization?" [26]

Cooley had postulated a rational society understandable through a rational discipline, sociology; he had affirmed that "The ideal aim of intelligence seems to be the rational control of human life"; he had demonstrated the need of such intelligence when he wrote that "There is an evident need of a competent intelligence to watch and supplement the unconscious processes," and that we must "foresee and control the process in which we live. If we can do this we may look for an era of deliberate and assured progress." [27] But this was not creative activity. This was the liberal social philosophy of Lester Frank Ward which Cooley had so violently rejected because it gave man freedom only to conform to rational law even if that law were progressive. This disciple of Emerson was not to be trapped by his own logic, however; he had in mind his earlier statement that there is a "rationality and sequence, not mechanical, consistent with a kind of freedom, which makes possible an organized development of social knowledge." He had begun his synthesis of rational social development and individual freedom by postulating that the world is ideal, not material, and its social laws are spiritual, not mechanical. This would free the creative personality from bondage to Spencer, but not from the determinism of philosophical idealists like Hegel.

Cooley had built on German hypotheses that society was the only meaningful historical environment for man. Like so many of his contemporaries, he accepted the concept of society as a tightly-knit organism with a past and a future. Society had laws of development which demonstrated the past working of a spiritual force and which would also shape the future. Sociology was the study of these laws, the analytical weapon by which the present generation could refute the conservative defense of the *status quo* and prove the inevitability of a better future. But at this point Cooley broke away from those constrictive implications found in the German monistic interpretation that a spiritual force or God was creating progress by flowing through social institutions and that the individual must accept these institutions as the reflection of God's will.

The key to a theory of rationality and freedom he found in a special philosophy of idealism: a dualistic philosophy. He did not identify God with society. God transcended society; God worked through the individual to bring about progress which was the incorporation of resistant brute material within the process of spiritualization.

Regardless of its power and dignity, reason was not man's highest faculty; it must give way to that which guaranteed total human freedom: the creative will and imagination. If man were made by his will and imagination, Cooley the sociologist could make good his earlier poetic assertions that "New right always begins in a revolt against institutions" and "New thoughts are born, not found." He would make sociology functional in a way subordinate to will. He believed that a thorough study of society, a study of its laws of development, would help new thoughts to be born in the present

120

generation. It would help the individual in his efforts to create a future which would be lawful and yet not determined. "Imagination is the prime faculty of a constructive thinker," but imagination could feed on social knowledge. And so he continued,

The only instrument that can in any degree meet the test of prediction, where new problems of higher choice confront the mind, is the instructed imagination . . .

. . . social intelligence is essentially an imaginative grasp of the process going on about us, enabling us to carry this forward into the future and anticipate how it will work.

Intelligent social prediction is contradictory to determinism, because, instead of ignoring the creative will, it accepts it and endeavors by sympathy to enter into it and foresee its working.[28]

For Cooley, then, science, if it was to be creative, had to be related to something like imaginative artistic endeavor. The social scientist could produce objective studies of the past, and to the extent that he could not transcend his studies he was their prisoner, lacking the essentials of freedom, existing on the level of mechanical imitation. If all men acted in this manner, progress would stop, society would atrophy and ultimately die. But if the social scientists used their imaginations, if they gained inspiration from a study of the past, then they could become artists, they could be free to create a new world — free to assist in the unfolding of God's plan for the future. "The artist, in the act of creation, is always free, he is attending to, bringing to clearness and realizing that which is revealed to him alone, unfolding his individuality in the service of the whole . . ."[29]

Like his colleagues and contemporaries, James Mark Baldwin and Herbert Croly, Charles Cooley had developed a philosophy of individual activism drawn from many intellectual currents — from Hegelian idealism, from Darwinian evolution, from American concepts of social science — but most important it was a philosophy of dualism, of transcendentalism; it was a philosophy of evolution that followed the precedent of a great and influential American spokesman — Ralph Waldo Emerson.

Point by point, Cooley had directed all the crosscurrents and contradictions of his writings toward a synthesis implicit in the printed fragments of Emerson's thinking about evolution: Nature was not a mechanism. It was a developing manifestation of an inner spiritual principle that was bringing about self-conscious intelligence and moral maturity in man. Nature was not purely the reflection of the mind of God; it was not completely spiritual. God was not completely immanent in nature but was in part transcendent of a reality that He had evidently not created. Evolution, the spiritualization of matter, the overcoming of inertia, was not automatic. Man was the necessary and active agent of God to bring about the progress which was evolution. Undoubtedly, then, man had free will in that he was the transcendent creator of his world, building its values on those gained from direct inspirational contact with God.

Yes, man was free to overcome this industrial crisis which threatened civilization. But he was free to create that which was preordained, free to fight a battle that had to be won. There was nothing of the William James kind of relativism when Cooley reiterated that "The justification of individualism and self-reliance in art — perhaps everywhere — is that they bring one into some undiscovered or unexplored province of the universal." [30] He had first promised his generation victory over industrialism because of the chance pattern of industrialism itself. He had then promised victory because of the march of sociological law and man's rational ability to understand it. But as the grand culmination of the forces of progress, he promised individual communion with the God who was the motive force of progress.

More than understanding, more than technological knowledge was needed to liberate mankind from its society and from history. Explicitly now a religious prophet, Cooley proclaimed that only a new religion could so free man from his commitments to the past that social evolution could proceed to the utopia which was but a few years ahead. Only a new religion of humanity could discipline the individual into complete harmony with his neighbors. "We need," he affirmed, "the feeling of a larger life without ourselves. . . . It is wholesome to feel oneself part of a great whole, and to expand the individual life into that, to cherish only that part of oneself that contributes to the whole, to estimate oneself and others by capacity to serve the whole." [31]

Charles H. Cooley

For Cooley, the union with the new religion was immediate and intense. "It is God that is working. Life is onward, glorious, transcendent. I am in it; a part of it." He was certain that this feeling was winning the hearts of his countrymen. "Will not the idea of God and the social state tend to merge," he asked rhetorically, "and thus patriotism and religion reinforce each other — a new unity of Church and State?" What was needed then to bring a swift end to the crisis was a religious attitude toward society expressed through "The idealization of the state, the impressing of a unitary life upon the hearts of the people by tradition, poetry, music, architecture, national celebrations and memorials, and by a religion and a philosophy teaching the individual that he is a member of a glorious whole to which he owes devotion . . ." [32]

All this did not deny the creative individual because the unity was not the bonds of historical society but the unity of the true believers who would remake the world in the image of the God of progress. Society and history always must bend before the forces of "Society" and "History." Perhaps it seemed as if his sociological theory postulated that the individual was formed by the society into which he was born and that his standards of judgment were relative to the particular historical moment. He had even written, "The organic view of mind calls for social knowledge as the basis of morality. We live in a system, and to achieve right ends we must learn to understand that system." Nevertheless, he now reaffirmed that the *status quo* could never be equated with right. There was God's "Society," morally superior to society; it was a "Society" that would destroy all societies as it found expression through the "Historical" process of progress. Until the moment of the final establishment of the perfect "Society," right would never coincide with established society, and the individual, caught up in the metaphysical process, was always right in rejecting the *status quo*. "If we accept the idea that life is progress," Cooley wrote, "it is easy to see that no such coincidence is to be expected. If we are moving onward and upward by the formulation of higher ideals and the struggle to obtain them, then our conscience will always be going out from and discrediting the actual forms of power." [33]

123

If that power should strike down one individual and at one spot block progress, the religiously inspired person had the absolute assurance that "the unconscious forces inevitably set to work to correct the wrong. . . . It is a wound against which the moral organism asserts its recuperative energy." [34]

F. H. Johnson and H. D. Lloyd IMMANENT GOD AND CREATIVE MAN

SUPPOSEDLY there pass through the nineteenth century several sharply defined threads of philosophical thought which, by the 1890s, are woven into the substantial pattern of historicism, pragmatism, and scientific naturalism. Delineate the historicism of Hegel, the social science of Comte, the naturalism and evolution of Darwin, blend well and behold — the American generation of 1890 is almost miraculously lifted out of the past, the past of erroneous thinking. The world of eighteenth-century rationalism no longer deludes man into the false security of simplicity in nature. The informing idealism of the Emersons no longer clouds the vision of man so that he thinks he floats through history buoyed by some absolute spiritual force. It is the social scientists, the philosophers of this generation, who are responsible for freeing man to follow his intelligence, and his intelligence alone, in a plastic world that can be understood and manipulated by science.

Surely it was the Baldwins and the Cooleys who provided the Herbert Croly of *Progressive Democracy* and the *New Republic* with the knowledge of reality that allowed him to build a political philosophy free from the restrictions of Hegelian idealism. They had taught him that man is naturally a social animal, a creative, participating part of society. They had taught him that society is free from the determinism of physical law, that it exists within its own history. They had also taught him that society is free from its own history,

125

that it must evolve according to novel problems, not merely by precedent. They had destroyed the mechanical world of the eighteenth century and of Herbert Spencer. They had transcended the spiritual, historical determinism of Hegel. But, most emphatically, they had not hammered out a social philosophy of pure pragmatism or of unalloyed scientific naturalism. With a bland confidence they had taken historicism, relativism, pragmatism, scientific naturalism, and absolute freedom and underwritten them with a guarantee of inevitable progress. They were Darwinians because they believed the scientific method could be used to demonstrate an ultimate spiritual purpose in the universe.

They were not, however, abstract thinkers operating only in the realm of those concepts of technically philosophic and scientific thought which we have been taught to believe exerted an all-powerful influence over the minds of men during the nineteenth and early twentieth century. Evidently, then, they were part of a climate of opinion. They were committed to a set of preconceptions about reality that operated to control their more technical ideas. Those preconceptions molded those ideas into conformity with a certain pattern, whether the ideas could logically blend with that pattern or not. Clearly the important thing for Baldwin, Cooley, and Croly was not one theory of evolution, one theory of social psychology; it was progress. It was progress of a special kind in which the individual had creative free will and yet exercised his freedom to create a world that was lawful and ethical because its laws and ethics were anchored in the reality of an absolute spiritual purpose.

While Croly was dependent on the technical theories of the social psychologists in forging his idea of progress to fit these qualifications, the social psychologists were dependent on the implicit pattern of this idea of progress for the foundation on which to develop their technical theories. Whether Croly absorbed his ideas from Baldwin or Cooley or from one of their like-minded colleagues is not the important thing. The vital point is that he wanted such ideas and could find them. Logically, it should also follow that there were contemporaries thinking and writing the ideas expressed by Baldwin and Cooley in their social psychology.

F. H. Johnson and H. D. Lloyd

Since the metaphysics of Baldwin's and Cooley's fundamental attitude toward evolution seems to parallel so closely that of Emerson, one might well go to the liberal religious tradition of which Emerson had been a part for possible evidence of the continued vitality of this concept of evolution, stretching from the 1840s to the generation of the 1890s. In the decade of the 1880s when the progressive group was finding itself, one of the most energetic voices of the liberal Christian tradition was the Congregational magazine, the *Andover Review*.[1] The new journal was founded in 1880 as a reflection of a liberal change in the faculty of the Andover Seminary, and its opening years were full of drama as American Christianity faced the great issue of evolution. Was there a place for evolution within Christianity or was there a place for Christianity within the philosophy of an evolving natural world? This was the crux of the matter. And it was the meaning of evolution for the Christian tradition that formed the theme for most of the articles in each issue.

One contributor, an Andover clergyman, F. H. Johnson, most consistently dealt with the problem over the years.[2] In a series of articles during the 1880s, which were later published in book form, he argued for Christianity's acceptance of evolution. With great clarity he deliberately fitted evolution into a proof of spiritual purpose and the freedom of man. With almost uncanny precision he outlined a metaphysical proof of this argument which paralleled the one that Baldwin, Cooley, and Croly would use in the next decades.

For his theologically-minded readers, Johnson wrote that Darwin's thesis was in no way a challenge to the agency of God in creation. It was not the doctrine of evolution itself which seemed a challenge to historical Christianity but a philosophy which had come to claim the prestige of Darwin's name. It was the materialism of Herbert Spencer that had attacked Christianity in the years since 1860. Spencer, he declared, claimed that human life was directed along the lines predetermined by physical laws through the mechanism of natural selection. Here was the first major weakness of Spencer, because "Natural selection . . . originates nothing. It is a destructive, not a creative, principle." [3] Rather, contended Johnson,

127

the central part of Darwin's theory of evolution was variation and differentiation. It was by variation and differentiation that evolution and progress took place. Natural selection explained how a species became established once a new form had appeared, but it could not explain the appearance of that form. Evolution had to be considered then as implying a series of sharp breaks from the kind of grinding mechanical law proposed by Spencer. Then the further implication had to be accepted: the life process did not work through restrictive regular natural law but through transcendence over such law. The sudden large changes which brought variations to evolution created new qualities that were unique. " 'Evolution' . . . does not imply that the whole contents of the thing said to be evolved are to be found, or even previously existed, in the antecedents; it affirms, on the contrary, that there not only *may* but *must* be something in the result that did not exist in the antecedents." [4]

Christians should gladly admit that man was part of nature because this in no way endangered his spiritual qualities. Instead, Johnson observed, evolution as unexplained differentiation marked by the emergence of unique qualities clearly demonstrated that the physical world was given meaning only by the spiritual principles which informed it. Mind, the mind of God, was the only causal agency in the world; and man was therefore free from the control of physical law. He had the creative freedom of his intelligence to make moral choices.

Man's transcendence over his physical origins was proven by his history. The first man, as an animal, had no sense of right or wrong; he was governed by instinct. The traditional Christian concept of the fall from pristine grace to the necessity of making individual choices involving the possibility of error was really an upward step in the evolutionary process. The process of evolution through inorganic, organic, sentient, and intelligent physical forms all pointed to its culmination in the self-conscious and self-determining will in man. Up to a certain point in physical evolution, man, as an animal, was forced to conform to his external environment. Then, after a sudden leap in physical evolution, man became part of a social rather than a physical environment. Man was now an autonomous force which, acting through his society, made the external world conform to his desires and will.

Here Johnson anticipated the key point of Baldwin's social psychology that the primitive social man, lifted to autonomy by physical evolution, had the potential of perfection within him. It had been made clear by anthropologists studying primitive man, Johnson continued, that his mind was developed far beyond his immediate needs. This could only mean that at a certain level man acquired the intelligence necessary to carry out his own development. He had the potential not only of goodness but also of mental qualities to work out the society necessary to provide the environment for that goodness. As a theologian then, Johnson had abandoned all thought of sin and evil in a positive sense. Within the evolutionary process, sin and evil were to be thought of as inertia, as undeveloped potential. Salvation after death was not the goal for man, salvation for mankind on earth was his goal. Using his intelligence, man would be able to discover this goal in the normal and natural qualities of himself.[5]

As a member of his society, man developed a conscience that led him to follow its sanctions. But this was only his prescriptive conscience because "Conscience in its highest activity . . . derives its sanctions from principles and moving ideals; it is progressive, transcendental; it follows the prophets."[6] Yet in breaking from his society, the individual is not violating the fact that his conscience is part of lawful process in which he seeks the standard of what is natural and normal. There was no violation because Johnson defined the normal and natural in Aristotelian terms. The natural, he wrote, "has more and more come to stand for that which . . . is normal, and for that which . . . has a tendency to the realization of the highest conditions." And he added, "the perfection of rational mind is the goal toward which all things tend."[7]

But in proving man's ability to save himself, to perfect his social world in conformity to God's plan, and in elevating the rational intelligence of man, had Johnson undermined what he had established to defeat Spencer — the variability of the evolutionary process? Had he not substituted a spiritual determinism for a physical one? Had he reduced man's mind to the unoriginal faculty of reason which merely discovered and imitated the spiritual laws of the universe? Johnson did not think so and he was acutely aware of the problem he faced in proving both the spiritual dominance of God's creativity and the creative freedom of man.

Man was free to create, he affirmed, because there was a physical reality as well as a spiritual force working in the world. Philosophers traditionally failed to realize the practical freedom of man in a world that was both material and spiritual. They denied the experience of the common man in order to work out a position abstractly logical but totally unrealistic. They gave way to the compulsion to trap life within the web of artificial metaphysics. After all, said Johnson, what is the experience of the average man? He knows that he exists and that an external world also exists. He knows that through his will and through his intelligence he can modify himself and the external world. He also knows that he, in turn, is changed by the external world operating on him. The average man then thinks of himself as a representative of a spiritual force and believes there is a spiritual reality.

But this man does not go to the extremes of the philosophical idealists like Hegel who then claim that all reality must be related to the self-conscious knower and ultimately the spiritual reality of which he is a part. The average man does not believe that all the physical world around him is but the representation of mind. On the contrary, he knows that a natural environment exists and is governed by certain laws that man cannot alter. But on the other hand, he does not then agree with the materialists like Spencer that reality is only the brute stuff of material existence beyond the power of mental causation.[8]

The error of the technical philosophers, the idealists and the materialists, was their retreat from the most sensitive perceptions of reality, those gained by the majority of men. They could not accept as a true comprehension of the world the uncoordinated dualism by which most men describe reality. And in this they failed utterly in their responsibility as philosophers. The unavoidable truth, according to Johnson, was that we could never go beyond this confused philosophical analysis. Philosophy must accept this statement that

Since we are unable to penetrate to the essential reality of the world by analyzing its parts, and since, as a whole of vast complexity, it far transcends the range of our comprehension, therefore, it is reasonable to reject any system which professes to deduce all our knowledge from a single scientific principle. . . . it is reasonable to believe that we make our nearest approach to reality when we entertain as real a plurality of principles, as aspects of the world, which we are not able directly to combine into an harmonious whole.[9]

Theologically speaking, this meant that God was immanent in the world and yet transcendent of it. God was spiritualizing the world, and he was represented in it to the extent that his spiritual purpose had become part of the world. But the world was not just the projection of God's mind. It was a reality that existed outside God's spiritual purpose and had to be conquered by spiritual forces, and Johnson pointed out, it was this fact which made human freedom possible. If the world were merely the representation of spirit as in Hegel's philosophy, man would have no choice but to conform to that representation because it would directly express the purpose of spirit. But if the world existed outside spiritual purpose, man, in conforming to that purpose, would be creative in changing his physical environment. He had the further assurance of his creative freedom because he was the indispensable agent by which God's purpose was eventuated here. "It is the *activity* of the subordinate beings that furnishes the opportunity for the Supreme to work." [10]

In a world where God was immanent and transcendent, what finally then was the function of human intelligence, especially in relation to that unavoidable problem of evolution? Rational intelligence through science could discover lawful nature. Because God had expressed himself through evolution, a regular, almost mechanical, pattern had been left behind to be discovered and understood. But as the evolutionary process continued, inevitably there must be changes in science; changes, that is, in the methods and the tentative hypotheses. This did not challenge the fact of scientific truth as the revelation of God's purpose; only the means of knowledge of that purpose changed. The world of science would be marked, therefore, with surface change, as with the development of Darwin's thesis; underneath, however, all would be stable and lawful.

The same situation prevailed in the world of morality. Here, too, men must face the fact that the process of spiritualization meant change. Here, too, "Living experience is continually carrying us to a position in advance of our formulated doctrines and compels their modification." Here, too, men must admit even the relativity of the Bible, that "Every scheme of doctrine assuming to be drawn from the Bible has been dominated by the moral ideal of its age, and more or less consciously adjusted to it." But again men had to understand that change was taking place within a lawful process, that morality had an unshakeable foundation. Johnson's readers should be aware of the bounds of moral relativity; ". . . revelation, as interpreted by reason," he assured them, "though flexible, is not indefinitely so." It was also formative and controlling. ". . . there is," he continued, "a permanent and reliable substratum to our knowledge . . ." [11]

There would be changing expressions of the process but there was a moral certainty to it which could be known and which would hold good for all times. But this rational quality of the grand design of history in no way limited the freedom of man because he did not really discover it except as it existed in the past; the future outline of progress he created himself. He was free not only from a materialistic absolute but also from an idealistic one. The transcendental spiritual quality of evolution was such that it could never be fully understood by science or any kind of reason. To understand evolution man must transcend his environment. Evolution was in fact a living thing in whose constant creation the individual shared by immediate, intuitive contact with God. Science and reason were subordinate ways of thinking and knowing because Johnson postulated ". . . that reason leans upon imagination at every step, that all our organized, connected knowledge of things has been gained through its use; that it is the sole constructive faculty; and that without its activity, conscious or unconscious, we could have nothing but isolated, unintelligible sensations." [12]

The all-embracing power of spiritual forces that contained and controlled the physical laws affirmed by Johnson and by the *Andover*

Review was not the only position of liberal Christian philosophy during the 1880s. Standing in stark contrast to this attempt to place evolution within Christianity is the philosophy of the Free Religious movement which also developed out of a transcendental background. Its chief spokesman, Francis Abbot, has received much attention from modern scholars because it has been assumed he is more representative of the naturalistic, positivistic outlook that is supposed to have become typical of American thinking by the 1890s.[13]

Free Religion has been used as evidence that transcendentalism failed to survive the influx of scientific prestige after the Civil War. Science and its corollary, rationalism, would not tolerate the essential mysticism of the earlier philosophy. There followed the ironic paradox that the thought system of the first Americans who accepted the idea of evolution was undermined and then overridden by subsequent implications of that idea.

Nowhere has this change been more ably described than in Stow Persons' study of Free Religion's divergence from transcendentalism. The relation of parent to offspring, wrote Persons, becomes tenuous for "Actually a major intellectual revolution separated them." Free Religion was a religion of humanity, a rational religion that found transcendentalism too mystical for a scientific age. The new religion accepted naturalistic evolution, and according to its understanding of evolutionary meaning,

. . . intellectual and moral qualities were accumulations of inherited racial experience, in contrast to that of transcendentalism which placed its faith in the original intuitive faculties of the mind. The new philosophy was sometimes called "neo-sensationalism" or "the philosophy of experience," by contemporaries because it explained *a priori* ideas on the basis of hereditary transmission of accumulated experience. Popular or semi-philosophical thought had come full cycle when the sensationalism in its Lockean-Unitarian form, rejected by transcendentalism, returned to constitute the basis of the neo-rationalism which now in turn undermined transcendentalism.[14]

For Abbot, the central meaning of Darwin was that the world of nature and man could be completely known through the rationality of the scientific method. Abbot, then, accepted most of the Spencerian outlook with one crucial difference. Abbot was a liberal who believed in man's ability to perfect his society. He must be able to transcend his immediate society to have standards by which to judge it and reform it. Man's freedom, he contended, consisted in his independence from the arbitrary conditions of his particular society and his obedience to the laws of nature discoverable by reason. Up to the stage of civilization, man had been the prisoner of natural laws as in Spencer's thesis. Then, however, man had become a moral creature capable of understanding and cooperating with natural law. He could escape its more wasteful mechanisms, such as natural selection, and bring it much more quickly along the road of progress toward the final perfect state of human society. But against the intuition and creative imagination that Johnson believed made man superior to natural law, Abbot assumed that the individual found freedom by conforming to the laws of the universe. For this "scientific" theologian, "reform was identical with the science of society." [15]

This very direct parallel to the eighteenth-century method of using natural law as a lever to reform society, which postulated man's freedom from his society to conform to natural law, had an even more important expression in the sociological system of Lester Frank Ward.[16] It is the distinction of Ward that he was the first major systematic sociologist in America to challenge the conservative orthodoxy of Spencer and his major American advocate, William Graham Sumner. Born in the Middle West in 1841, Ward had fought his way up from poverty to the security of a position as a government clerk in Washington, D.C. There, during his evening hours, he diligently pursued knowledge and self-improvement in night-school classes.

Fascinated by the new scientific ideas then entering the climate of opinion, he joined the forces of science in the battle with the religious groups hostile to evolution. Somehow he found the time to edit the proscientific and agnostic journal the *Iconoclast* without halting further studies which became increasingly focused on science. It was a concentration that so prepared him as a specialist that he gained the position of chief paleontologist in the United States Geological Survey. It was also at this time that the energetic Ward began to publish the sociological treatises that eventually brought him to

Brown University as an academic sociologist. Enthusiastically, even vehemently, however, he defined his sociology as the message of social reform. And quite naturally so, because sociology described the social process which, in turn, had to be described as social progress. Man had to understand and participate in the forward movement of which he was a part; it was the responsibility and duty of sociology to enable him to do this intelligently.

While Ward carefully designed his sociological analysis to destroy the conservative individualism, the message of quietism and determinism of Spencer, he was confident that it could be done by using Spencer's own metaphysical outlook. More than this, the fiercely agnostic Ward felt ungrudging admiration for this man, Spencer, who had made the materialistic nature of the world an unassailable doctrine that forever freed man from the ignorance of theology and philosophical idealism. In his initial book, *Dynamic Sociology*, Ward completely identified himself with the basic naturalism of Spencer and with the heritage of Auguste Comte's social science. Ward's theory of knowledge, the only possible theory of knowledge, rested squarely on the positivism of Comte and Spencer. Positivism was the scientific attitude — it was concerned with the real and tangible in nature; it worked with the data of the senses "because only sense knowledge is accessible to us." [17]

Comte, declared Ward, was correct in his theory of the stages of man's intellectual evolution from the theological, through the metaphysical, to the culmination of positivism. Happily, man had now arrived at the positive level and had abandoned the search for final causes which had marked the two stages of human immaturity. But Ward differed from Comte by insisting that man could still make use of the concept of efficient causes. It was on the basis of knowledge of efficient causes that science fulfilled its purpose — prevision. All science, natural and social, was of the same nature although the greater complexity of the material of social science resisted to a greater degree the reduction of its phenomena to exact mathematical formulas. When its knowledge was formalized, however, the social scientist would be able to predict the activities of the social world as the natural scientist predicted the activities of the physical.

135

The phenomena of the social world, like those of the physical, were regular and uniform, conforming to natural law. There was no room for a notion of free will. Explicitly, Ward fought to teach his contemporaries that the whole idea of free will had no place in the world of the 1880s, that it was an immature theory which man had believed during his youthful theological stage of development. Clearly, it could be seen that if social history was the work of the spontaneous activities of its individual members, there could be no science of society. If there was free will, "There could certainly be no science of action, no philosophy of history, no sociology. There would be no social phenomena but only arbitrary actions due to no true cause, and all power of prevision and prediction would be wanting." [18]

This could never be for Ward because his burning purpose was to prove man's ability to create a better world through the use of reason, a better world sanctioned by irrefutable natural law. The great task of Ward, then, was to demonstrate why man, as part of a mechanical naturalistic evolutionary process, did not have to conform to his immediate place in that process as Spencer declared. Quietly Ward began to define evolution in Spencerian terms. Evolution, he outlined, was mechanistic, working through a mechanical distribution of matter and energy. This was a monistic universe of physical force undergoing constant evolution in the direction of progress. That change was solely the product of matter in motion. "An initial motion inhering in the primary form of matter is . . . the sole source of all causation and the true first cause." And yet Ward, in order to support his liberal beliefs, had to demonstrate that the human mind had the power of controlling to an extent these mechanical forces of which it was theoretically but a passive reflection.

His answer involved a tortuous use of logic that is reminiscent of that used by Croly in *The Promise of American Life*. Where Croly was demonstrating the possibility of human freedom when man must adhere to historical tradition, Ward had to demonstrate freedom within the bonds of physical law. Mind was the product of natural law, declared Ward, but that did not constrain it to be pas-

136

sive. Evolution had to be understood as a creative process driven forward into new synthetic advances by the constant conflict which characterized the universe. In this upward process matter brought forth life, and life brought forth mind. Carefully, he pointed out that this did not contradict his materialistic monism. Mind was still part of the physical world, a physical force. "The view that matter and spirit are one is true monism and I believe it is true science, but it means only that the material world contains all the elements of intelligence and will and these are in fact as rigidly determined as are the winds or the electric current." [19]

Nevertheless, Ward was broadening his definition of mind. Intelligence and will were parts of mind. Where could he fit in the concept of will which he had read out of the positivistic final stage of intellectual evolution? Gradually, he was creating a tension between a blanket affirmation that nothing involved with his definition of will contradicted absolute law and the necessity of using will as the motive force of human evolution. Desire, or will, he wrote, was the source of all human striving. Reason was but the tool of the will, used by it in determining the best methods of serving itself. Yet these desires, this will, were rigidly determined and capable of precise description. "Psychology is the physics of the mind and its phenomena are as uniform — and its law exact as are those of the physics of the inorganic world." It was possible to know in advance all of man's actions if all the involved factors were known.

From the inclusion of desires, the central fact of will, within monistic mechanical evolution, it was possible for Ward to look forward to a science of morality. Standing in the British utilitarian tradition, he insisted that ethics must be conceived as the "minimization of pain and the maximization of pleasure." Morality was the greatest maximum pleasure for mankind. On the other hand, however, he described morality as an altruism rooted in the instinctive gregarious nature of man. It would be difficult for Ward to overcome what he considered the conservative doctrine of individual selfishness by a straightforward moral theory of pleasure and pain in which each individual acted in his own behalf. So it was that Ward fell back on a theory of instinctive altruism that marked the social solidarity of mankind when it emerged from the domination of the laws of biological evolution.

Even when Ward had thus transcended the atomic individualism of Spencer, his philosophy of reform was still entangled in the materialistic monism of the British writer. There was no real justification for a belief that the individual could transcend his immediate environment in order to criticize it constructively. In his own way Ward had reached the same impasse as Croly.

It was not in Ward's direction, then, but to the kind of thinking done by Johnson that many young reformers turned in the 1880s. The confusions that Ward had struggled with were cut through by the journalist son of a Dutch Reformed minister of New York City. Born in 1847, Henry Demarest Lloyd was a contemporary of the self-trained sociologist and came to full intellectual maturity at the same time. Lloyd's ideas of the 1880s forecast those of the generation of 1890 to 1914.[20] Like Johnson, Lloyd vigorously rejected Spencer, and he shared the Andover theologian's metaphysics of idealistic dualism. And with poetic clarity and enthusiasm he connected those abstract principles with a dynamic theory of practical reform. It is Lloyd who is perhaps the first true spokesman for the American religion of progress. His writings have within them every major sociological and psychological point utilized by Baldwin and Cooley to build the science of social psychology. His analysis of the American economic scene and of economic theory parallels and anticipates that of Ely, Patten, and Veblen. His political and educational concepts seem almost the text from which Croly copied the material for *Progressive Democracy*. His religious views could have been the direct inspiration for Walter Rauschenbusch.

The formative intellectual experience of this remarkable man is part of what is becoming a familiar pattern; he broke loose from the Calvinistic restrictive pessimism of his youth to express the absolute freedom of man: absolute freedom, however, that involved a full acceptance by each individual of moral responsibility for the world in which he lived; absolute freedom to battle endlessly evil and sin and corruption; absolute freedom to make the world ethical in conformance to the word of Almighty God. It is a pattern, not of the total rejection of Calvinism, but of the affirmation of real creative individualism within tradition. If this is a contradiction of true Calvinism, it is nevertheless a spiritual movement that owes much to precepts of the founding fathers of puritanical Protestantism.

Intensely ambitious and yet self-searchingly concerned with his conscience, in much the same manner as Cooley, Lloyd came into contact with the waves of outside intellectual unrest during his years as an undergraduate at Columbia University and as a law student. Here he was awakened to an interest in the social sciences by Francis Lieber, became involved in the good government movement of the 1870s and the American Free Trade League, and developed his lasting passion for having a hand in public affairs. This desire to have a voice in the molding of public opinion led him to abandon law for journalism. It took him from New York to Chicago and a post on the *Tribune*. While working for the *Tribune* and observing the life of the booming young metropolis, he began to move beyond the conservative, respectable liberalism of his New York days. Gradually he came to sense that there was a real crisis in America, a crisis so severe that peripheral reform could not save the country. As editorial writer for his newspaper, he began his analysis of the crisis and those who were most responsible for it. Increasingly his editorials focused an attack on the industrial leaders of the day and moved so far beyond orthodoxy that his views forced his retirement from the *Tribune*. He then went on to express his ideas in magazine and book form — ideas that outlined and expressed the nature of America's critical problem and a solution for it.

For the *Tribune*'s readers Lloyd had become a radical preaching the necessity of a basic reorganization of society — this attitude, he felt, reflected the worst aspects of America's crisis, the blindness of its citizens. For Lloyd was not radical; he was conservative. He did not wish to preach revolution, to advocate the overthrow of established institutions. The truth of the situation was that established society had broken down — that was the crisis. The conservatives, in the name of stability, were defending anarchy; they were the ones who would destroy civilization by refusing to save it. Lloyd was the true conservative because he recognized that society had already radically changed. Hitting hard at the literary defenders of the *status quo* who argued that any discussion of existing class relationships might lead to revolution, Lloyd answered:

The revolution has already occurred. That took place when the mighty wheels of the new industry whirled the peasant and his children away from his little homestead, the artisan away from his cottage loom and the village shop and non-competitive brotherhood. . . . The new industry has broken up the brotherhoods of the old industry. . . . That is the revolution. And the gospel of the revolution is the doctrine that you can do anything with your fellow man provided you do it in the market.[21]

In the course of the breakup of the old economic system, the social relations on which values rested were destroyed with the result that, in Lloyd's estimation, his generation was wandering, confused and bewildered, without guidance from any standard of ethics. This situation, if allowed to continue, would be completely disastrous for the very existence of civilization because it implied a moral anarchy in which each individual fought every other individual. This was the law of tooth and claw when men disguised chaos under the name of competition and ceased to treat men as human beings, but rather as material commodities. If this disintegration of man's sense of a common humanity were not checked, civilization would perish because conscience represented the social heritage of man, that which raised him above the animal level. Without organized society, the social heritage could not be preserved and the isolated individual would revert to a brute level of existence.

The average American, Lloyd continued, could not understand the extremity of the crisis because he had been nurtured in a tradition that had taught him the erroneous doctrine that man was a self-sufficient individual and his society was merely an artificial form created for his convenience. He was not aware of what it would mean if society were to disappear; nor did he have the intellectual concepts to reformulate the basic doctrines of democracy from extreme individualism to cooperative social solidarity.

But Americans must be informed of the danger. They must learn the principles that could save them. They must grasp that what they believed were infallible natural principles of individualism were merely mistaken concepts produced by the immediate environment of the American frontier. Spreading seemingly inexhaustible resources before the European immigrant, the West had seduced him into believing that the individual was self-sufficient and self-determining. And always as the pressure of social problems had encroached on the settler, he could move farther west — preserving his illusion of self-contained autonomy. Now the frontier was gone; now Americans had to face reality: "Our young men can no longer go West; they must go up or down. Not new land, but new virtue must be the outlet for the future. . . . We cannot, hereafter, as in the past, recover freedom by going to the prairies; we must find it in the society of the good." [22]

The material forms of the new economy must somehow be infused with the truly democratic spirit of cooperation. This would be a desperate task, a race against time. As long as democratic institutions existed, there was a chance for an aroused and re-educated electorate to save itself through the use of those institutions. Now with ever-increasing class cleavage, the basis of democracy, a homogeneous people able to decide together on important issues, was being destroyed. Anarchy was making democracy impossible and democracy was the only means of ending the anarchy. Would the American people act in time? Could they rise to the occasion and swiftly shake themselves loose from those erroneous attitudes which placed them at the philosophical mercy of the so-called conservatives who defended the chaotic *status quo*? Was it possible for them to learn and to act before it was too late? This note of urgency surged through Lloyd's prose as he, a lone individual, did his part to arouse his readers so that they, in turn, might alert their neighbors.

With determination, Lloyd analyzed the steel chain of ideas held by the conservatives and most clearly expressed by the academic political economists of the day. They justified the current anarchy with a set of principles postulating the artificial and mechanical nature of society divided into isolated individual members; they postulated that labor must be treated as a commodity controlled by iron laws of competition. There could be no human feelings in this kind of society and its economic relations because, in the final analysis, this social and economic system was rooted in physical science. For these men, man and society were caught in a deterministic process governed by immutable natural laws, the most important of which was natural selection. The shadow of Spencerian philosophy clouded Lloyd's aspirations for the salvation of American life. While attacking the evils of unregulated capitalism, he had to rout the metaphysics used in their defense.

Lloyd struck directly at Spencer's fallacious position which postulated that man was controlled by physical law, that man was a self-contained atom, and that society was an artificial and mechanical aggregation of these atoms. Sufficient proof now existed, declared Lloyd, to prove instead that "Man is the creator and redeemer of himself and society." Man was free from the control of physical law because he was not born with a given set of psychological traits that connected him to the world of nature. Instead he was born with a character marked by its plasticity, its capacity to learn and to grow. This potential person was then turned into a human being by his society. And society was in no way to be correlated with the world of nature. Society moved through history, a shifting social environment. This was the first lesson for Americans, the existence of a real society, that "there is a people, and it is as different from a mere juxtaposition of persons as a globe of glass from the handful of sand out of which it was melted." [23]

If the social nature of man were established, it followed that there were no permanent principles of society or of human nature. With each changing environment, society altered its precepts and values in order to adjust to new problems. With the reformulation of these precepts and values the character of the individual members of society also was reoriented. Here was a vast world of fluid relativity, of possibility and potential. When all this had been comprehended by his generation, Lloyd was certain that they would realize that the

same revolution must take place in Political Economy as has been made in law by Sir Henry Maine. No such universal law as Ricardo claimed; no such perfected structure as Lowe's; no body of revealed truth — infallible guide of conduct on one hand, and prophesying on the other the future.

Man must be free to make his own future, and to be free he must know that

There is no truth, it is to be made. There is no absolute truth, final, and never will be. There will be whatever truth is created, as music is created, more truth beyond to be not discovered but manufactured.[24]

Lloyd was breaking sharply with his contemporary and fellow liberal Ward in repudiating the applicability of the positivistic tradition of science to society. The attempt to equate social life with the rigid concepts of physics and mathematics was ridiculous and in its conservative use contemptible. He wrote scathingly,

"Scientific" is the word conceitedly arrogated to themselves by the dull people who assume that they know the laws of currency, trade, and other departments of social economy, and quote these laws against every proposal of reform.

But he affirmed,

There is no surer test of the title of scholars to be called cultivated, than whether they have mastered the fact that in social science the "laws" that rule men are the laws that men make. . . . No man is scientific who does not grasp the truth that the "laws" of currency, employment, wealth change as the ideas and ideals of men change. . . . The only true science is that which listens even in political economy to the whispers of the poet and the reformer, and classifies that which IS only as a bridge between that which was and that which is to be.[25]

But just how free was the individual who was part of society and how free was the society which was part of history? If the individual was a social product, was he not just as unfree as if he were completely the puppet of biologically determined psychological traits? His values, his standards of judgment, could only represent what his society had taught. He would have social ethics, he would escape the anarchy that would destroy civilization, but his ethics would be those of social conformity. He could never rise above the level of his society at any given historical period. He could not criticize it; he could not change it. Progress would be impossible.

Even more serious, the whole concept of progress would be meaningless if history were defined as a series of equally valid societies.

Each generation would be different; each would be free from physical determinism; each could adjust to the new situations it faced; and always the values expressed in this adjustment would be as ethically valid as the adjustments of every other generation. Every society was ethical and was not to be criticized for falling away from any moral standards because morality could only be defined as the existing society. Had Lloyd lifted man from physical evolution only to conform to a society drifting through meaningless history?

Most serious of all perhaps were the implications of the immediate crisis. If man was humanized by his society, if his character and personality were created by society, what hope was there for a world in which society was disintegrating under the impact of industrialism? Were not the viciously competitive individuals of the business world the inevitable product of this situation? How could men reform themselves and build a new society, when their whole experience was in a sense antisocial? Was this not the final ironic paradox that Lloyd faced — that just because they were socially determined, his generation was hopelessly antisocial?

It was not as a sociologist, however, that Lloyd came to save his contemporaries. His was not the task of social reorganization but social salvation. He was the prophet of a new religion come to inspire and uplift. "Ultimately," he exhorted, "everyone is the people — but no such millennial social entity exists now." "The people is . . . the name of an ideal. . . . A multitude becomes a people as it becomes united in faith and works." [26]

Man was not the prisoner of his society. The society of the moment with its faulty traditions and institutions was an entangling web of evil from which the individual must extricate himself to find salvation in the true "Society" through the sublimation of self in the service of the whole. In turn, the transitions, the changes of history, were not the essence of true "History," which was the unfolding of the progressive laws of the absolute, cutting through the irrelevancies, the accidental occurrences of mundane history. Man and society changed within the historical process but in accordance with a fixed plan and toward the complete fruition of the perfect society of total cooperation and brotherhood. "History" and "Humanity" were capable of change but only within the set limits of a pre-established scheme of progress.

Here was the philosophical basis of Lloyd's religion. With approval he cited Mazzini that "The basis of the new religion will be the recognition of the law of progress." This law was based on the fact that an ideal "History" was carrying man and society upward to culmination in an ideal "Human Nature" in an ideal "Society." Here was the guarantee that progress was meaningful, that man had ethical standards by which to judge himself and his society. Here was the guarantee that man had real freedom in working to attain this goal. There was tension between the ideal "History" and history, between human nature and "Human Nature," between society and "Society." This was no simple idealistic philosophy in which spirit directly and immanently informed the world and history, and made man and society reflections of its presence. Once again, therefore, Lloyd was assuming a dualism between a real world that had to be conquered and an ideal that had to conquer. Once again he found freedom for man in the creative mediation between the ideal and the real. The individual was free from his society in order to transcend it, to learn through inspiration what society should become, and then return to reform it according to this pattern of prevision.

In expressing this philosophy of idealistic dualism, Lloyd, like Cooley, was saved from the tortuous delving of Baldwin by a direct knowledge of Emerson. His notebooks and correspondence, like the journals of Cooley, are packed with references to Emerson. It was Emerson who filled Lloyd with admiration as the greatest thinker of the nineteenth century; it was Emerson above all others who understood man and nature. Smoothly, then, Lloyd's metaphysics flowed in simple poetic terms understandable to the nontechnical reader. He stated the fundamental precept of Emerson, the conquest of material form by spirit, the constant process of striving and creation in which man shared. "Pushing upward and outward through all the forms of nature is life, urging on all the variations of matter from the mollusc to man in perpetual aspiration to express itself better and better." [27]

Then Lloyd expressed with almost intuitive ease what Baldwin

had called on the entire history of philosophy to elaborate: the qualified, even limited nature of God. God, Lloyd affirmed, neither knew
nor completely controlled the future. The essential definition of God
was creative power. And it was man's unique responsibility to be
the creative agent of God as the creator of himself and society. For
man, "Authority is not a pre-existing standard, outside of humanity,
which it receives as legislation from a superior power; but *is* created
by mankind, piece by piece. It is not fixed, but changing. It is not
absolute but relative." All of the concrete and tangible institutions
which made up society, even all the established relations between
men which were so much of the definition of society, had no existence except as the creative expression of man's mind and will; they
were but "outward expressions of inner conceptions of the individual." [28]

As men followed their natural inclination and the sense of deity
within the creative process that was the striving after perfection, all
their immediate institutions and relations were to be viewed as
temporary way stations in man's infinite forward journey. Man was
in constant rebellion against what he had created because once
established it became a limitation on further freedom of growth. It
must follow then, declared Lloyd, quoting Emerson, that "The
highest virtue is always against the law . . . To consecrate oneself
to the right is always to move on a little in advance. The same spirit
of progress which creates an institution hastens . . . to displace it
by something better." [29]

The prophet of this transcendent religion, Lloyd gave his adherents the assurance that all this creative effort was justified; that the
individual truly had superior standards in view when he rejected
established society; and that the statements insisting that man was
"the God of society," that "he is its creator," that "he is not under the
law," that "he creates the law" did not lead to a corroding and
immoral relativism. All statements that seemed to imply the complete autonomy of man lost their element of relativity when they
were read within the proper context. While man could be defined as
the god of himself and society, in the final analysis, "Humanity is
not God but the priesthood of God. There could be no more suicidal

phrase than 'worship of Humanity.'" Expounding clearly the dualism of Emerson, Lloyd pointed out that on the level of the real world "The highest virtue is against the law." But this was only a partial description of virtue and law. There was a higher law above human law; here man's highest ethical duty was reversed; here "Liberty is not escape from law, but the use of law. . . . the more law the more liberty." [30]

With the inconsistent logic of Emerson, Lloyd described how the individual could rise above the law of his society to cooperate with the law of the ideal absolute. For Emerson, man came into contact with spiritual reality by living fully in the world of nature because while nature was not spirit, it contained spiritual principles. In the philosophical manner of Cooley, Lloyd substituted society for Emerson's nature. It was society that man should live in and know because it was his natural environment — live in and know it because while he would ultimately transcend it, still the ideal "is here at least in some measure." It was by immersing oneself in society that one gained the inspiration to grasp the fuller extent of the ideal which was not yet expressed in mundane forms. Men could come to know the ideal as it was expressed in their institutions and social relations. Such knowledge or sensitivity was in a way the prerequisite for obtaining that view of total reality which allowed man to become cognizant of the future. Full participation in immediate society released man from its bonds to become the creative agent of God, which was his highest calling. All men, who were truly men in the sense that they were creative, started with objective knowledge but then moved to transcendent imagination as the highest capacity of man's intelligence. All creative men were in this sense poets: "The poet is the creator, maker, because he sees the ideal which is the reality toward which we move, and by holding up the picture fires men to pursue. What is called imagination is but the clearest vision." [31]

This was the beauty of Lloyd's religion of progress. The faithful knew they were free from natural law; they knew they were free from history; they knew they were free from immediate society; they knew they were free from a monistic spiritual force. And yet they knew their creative efforts would be ethically progressive; they knew they were cooperating with a God who would conquer the resisting material world. Joyfully, Lloyd could promise that

The secret of reform is not to attempt to force human nature from its inevitable channels . . . but to detect and assist the unfolding of the new forms which grow out of the old. . . . The progress of humanity . . . is proceeding according to an intelligent plan, that line of march is irresistible, and the reformer's work is to remove one by one the obstructions in its way, strip off from growing man the outworn, outgrown forms at the instant of transition from one period to another. . . . Mankind's progress is towards absolute truth.[32]

And now it becomes clear why beneath Lloyd's grim sense of crisis there bubbled up an ebullient optimism. His deep-lying attitude in this period of social anarchy was a full-throated optimism. Running along with his emphasis that evolution was progress, generated by a spiritual force of which man was a freely creative partner, Lloyd now outlined a theory of evolution distinctly Aristotelian in nature. What was it that he had written? The reformer had only to remove obstructions from the movement of progress; he had only to detect and assist the unfolding of new forms. On the mundane level, on the level of the real world, evolution was the maturing of a social potentiality whose character man could understand. Knowing the final state òf progress, a perfect cooperative commonwealth, the reformer could be efficient in his efforts to change his society. It was true enough that he needed to experiment in the area of means, but illuminated always by the goal, the experimental road would cut relatively straight ahead.

This meant that the reformer was a free agent but he could be scientific also. Lloyd was demonstrating how his generation could have all the advantages of Ward's science of society in its fight to rebuild its social environment without any of the troublesome vestiges of physical determinism or individualistic ethics.

With each step back to the eighteenth century, through the science of society and Aristotelian evolution, Lloyd's optimism heightened and its accompanying enthusiasm seemed to complete the circle by drawing Lloyd still farther back to an even more pristine exposition of the philosophy of the Enlightenment. The central thesis of the eighteenth-century belief in progress was the simplicity of the progressive process. A few key principles available to all men would serve to guide society toward perfection. Indeed progress was a paradoxical term for the *philosophes* to use, for the standard of progress was the character of the natural man. Progress was the return to man's original state in history, cut off from all the irrelevancies, the entangling and corrupting complexities of society so firmly embedded in historical tradition. Against this outlook of abstraction, reduction, and universalism the philosophical idealism of the nineteenth century rebelled and instead set out to prove that progress was a process of increasing complexity, impossible of abstraction or reduction to universal easily comprehensible principles. Lloyd, like his fellow Americans who adhered to philosophical idealism, agreed that the pattern of progress was one of increasing complexity, of constant expansion of personality, and of development of novelty. He agreed that progress could never be fully defined or attained.

Then, however, Lloyd had postulated that spiritual evolution as it found expression in this world had the character of Aristotelian evolution; it was the gradual unfolding of a potential toward the final culmination of perfection. He had argued that reformers could grasp the end of this process and so understand its working out and indeed facilitate and speed its full fruition. The assurance of this kind of evolution made possible a science of society. Society could be studied, analyzed; the sociologist would come to know where his immediate society stood in the path of development and what its next form should be. But Lloyd went further in contradicting his idealistic definition of progress. He brought in a full-fledged primitivism as the final capstone of his use of the eighteenth-century reform theory in late nineteenth-century America. The individual and society were evolving to find the expression of their full potentiality. Why was Lloyd so certain what that would be? Why was he so certain that fellow reformers could so easily follow a set of standards in reshaping society? We knew what the full potentiality of society would be, Lloyd affirmed with full confidence, because its final characteristics would be those of the natural man, the primitive man.

Evolution or progress was toward a society that would provide expression for the full potentiality of the original human being, the man who existed at the beginning of history.

The *philosophes* had made the mistake of assuming that the natural man was a self-sufficient individual, perfect unto himself without the benefit of society. Swiftly the sophisticated, historical-minded conservatives of the nineteenth century had taken advantage of this untenable postulate. Why had the original man fallen from his pristine purity? Why was he part of society? Why had the perfect individual been the cause for an imperfect society? Why was progress defined as the escape from the civilization which held man above the animal level? Obviously the concept of the natural man was ridiculous. Man was a member of society; he had always been a member of society.

Of course, man was social in nature. Lloyd had argued this point to destroy the individualism of Spencer. But merely stating that man was social, as the historical-minded conservatives had, did not begin to define the meaning of social. They had stated that it meant man was the product of his immediate social environment. In this they erred totally, admonished Lloyd. The truth, which anthropologists and sociologists were now making clear, was that primitive man was social. There was no such thing as isolated individuals in history. The original man had lived in family groups. Lloyd knew what Baldwin and Cooley would prove a decade later, that men had always been members of a community, gaining their personality and very being from this social relationship. Within the family group man had lived a life of love; the family was a perfect social institution.

And now reformers could explain why, if man was good, history had been marked by evil and error. Men in face-to-face contacts must love each other. In close proximity, in a really integrated society, men would produce a cooperative commonwealth. History recounted a series of societies marked by competition and not cooperation only because men had not been able to communicate effectively with each other beyond their families and other comparable small groups. Between men there had been ignorance and therefore mistrust, mistrust and therefore hatred, hatred and therefore no love.

F. H. Johnson and H. D. Lloyd

If the love of the family group could spread to all of society then the world would become the Heavenly City of God on Earth. This was why Lloyd wrote, "The whole theory of true reform is to set free the 'inward perfecting principle within the individual and society,' to use Aristotle's words, which when released from interceptions and oppressions can be easily guided to move to its proper ends." [33]

This was why Lloyd actually gloried in the crisis that industrialism had brought. The overwhelming changes in economic life had brought anarchy and endangered civilization by destroying the partial control of love over history through its operation in various small close-knit groups. All the world was being broken into its smallest component parts — separate individuals — mistrust, fear, and hatred were coming to mark all human relations. But at the same time as industrialism was whirling the individual away from the incomplete cooperative groups which had struggled to sustain civilization, it was hammering out, through its factories and steel mills, the environment that might spell the total salvation of mankind. "Already through modern industry," he proclaimed, "the physical contact of all peoples is an almost accomplished fact," and he continued triumphantly, "We are on the eve of another of the great expansions — or extensions — which have made up the civilization, evangelization of the world." [34]

Industrialism, urbanism, the technological revolution in communications and transportation were reassembling the fragmented individuals into one great tight-knit worldwide community which would have the qualities of the original family group. This was the social environment of the total cooperative commonwealth that would bring out man's full capacity to love his neighbor. This would be social perfection.

Impatiently, the fervent Lloyd began to execute an exact sociological study of American society to demonstrate how close his generation was to triumph over the forces of anarchy. He was waiting for a Baldwin or a Cooley to "write a book on 'Social Selection' showing how the institutional variations of society have been produced, and giving a scientific sanction to the processes of reform, and a scientific place to the idealizing faculty." And he reiterated,

151

What we need today is the historian of humanity, the philosopher of the true society, who will discover to men how great is the extent to which they are living love. . . . Ours is the era of the new Newton who will work out the attraction of men for each other as the gravitating force which explains the position, motion and relations of the social atoms and the social masses.[35]

Until the younger generation produced such scholars, Lloyd would accept the responsibility of beginning to outline the growing social power of love. His was the task of putting sociology to work as social reform. Who was it, Lloyd asked, who was most influenced by the new social discipline of the industrial system? Who had been uprooted from the tradition of history, the traditions of fear and hatred and selfishness, and left free to be influenced by the socializing forces of the day and to express his fundamental goodness? Clearly, it was the working man who fitted this pattern. Labor was the actual force which would usher in the cooperative commonwealth.

The reformer, that aristocrat among men, should associate himself with the struggles of labor to escape the oppression of the heartless capitalism of the day. In forging an alliance with labor, the reformer was gaining the economic, political, and social strength necessary to carry through the reorganization of society along the lines of the coming perfectly integrated community. The reformer was not calling in labor as a class but as the group that most nearly represented the natural normal man, as the group that would respond most quickly therefore to the battle against anarchy for the salvation of mankind. With the brute strength of labor delivering the majority of votes, the reformer would lead a peaceful revolution. It was not even a revolution because the impersonal forces of industrialism were stripping men of their erroneous historical tradition and allowing their natural altruism to flower. Speaking for those who had to remake society, the radical yet conservative Lloyd wrote, "Our work is not to create but to continue one or two simple principles of sympathy. . . . We no more need a destruction of existing institutions and the creation of new ones than we need a new body of social principles." [36]

F. H. Johnson and H. D. Lloyd

The reform movement could be called a labor movement only insofar as labor was closest to the state of natural altruism. But paradoxically, Lloyd defined this natural altruism, this normal state of man, in middle-class terms. Vehemently, he wrote that he was class conscious only in the sense that he was "opposed to all classes." He was certain that in working with the labor movement Americans were ending classes and bringing about an essentially classless society; he was certain that "the proletariat is being continually destroyed, burnt out. It will be the middle class that will survive and will furnish the human material of the new order." [37]

Progress was coming because it was the spiritual purpose of evolution; progress was coming because the positive laws of society pointed toward it; progress was coming because industry was providing the proper environment for it; progress was coming because labor would vote it in. Yet progress was not coming swiftly enough for the mercurial Lloyd. Progress, after all, was more than the mechanics of the perfectly organized community; progress was its spirit. Progress was a sense of fraternity; progress was a spiritual attitude. Progress was love. Progress was a religion, the religion of humanity. Was it not possible, therefore, that near the climax of evolution, man would be caught up in the religious attitude which marked the climax? Was it not possible that this religious feeling would be evangelical in the sense that it would lift men over the last hurdles of an impeding history with its inertia and ignorance and falsely inculcated attitudes of fear and selfishness? Was it not possible that within the next decades the world would be miraculously and completely delivered from sin to salvation?

There was every reason to expect such a revival. The upward evolution of man's intellectual outlook had brought him to the point where he was able to see that he had to become a participant in a religion celebrating progress and the unity of humanity. During the first part of evolution, man had been under the guidance of physical laws. Progress had been painful, the slow result of man's blind efforts to strive upward, prompted by his instinct. Then, biological development had finally given man self-conscious intelligence, the expanding ability to understand and control his future. Understanding the social process meant a comprehension of the central role of love, it meant that "Men are at last becoming conscious of love — till now a blind force. They are seeing that the socializations they have accomplished in their homes, their brotherhoods, their States, have been motivated by the greatest of all forces. Love has been one of the arts; it is now passing into the domain of conscious science." [38]

From the acceptance of the fact of love underlying human life, they had learned also what would be verified later by the social psychologists: "That a community can think together and act together, can feel; that public opinion, scientifically is an entity, not a fortuitous collision of individual thoughts." Lloyd made this empirical fact and its recognition the basis for his religion. "Then will the basis be laid," he exclaimed, "in the demonstration of this great and new fact, for a new religion . . . a new belief in the common origin, aim and destiny of mankind." The sociology of solidarity, of altruism, of love was the basis of the religion of group love. In turn, religion, however, lifted its sociological foundation out of its heritage of mechanical causation and made it plastic, fluid, and expansive in the creative hands of man's self — conscious intelligence and will. Swiftly and magnificently, Lloyd's generation was proceeding to cut off all ties with the past and make a new history, the history of the first truly religious age. All the aspects of the era of perfect social cooperation would be blended together by man's spirituality. It was within the framework of spiritual unity that the various concrete phases of reform should be carried out.[39]

Spiritual unity, however, found symbolic and real representation in the political state. Of all man's institutions, the state most nearly was the focus for the association of all the community; since all men were citizens, the state had infinite potentiality as a cohesive force. Gathering together the energies of the community, directing them efficiently to the problem to be solved, the government was the only available agency for the reconstruction of the economy to conform to man's freshly freed altruism. Competition must be strictly limited and regulated; cooperation must be established and encouraged. The state would act temporarily, therefore, as the counselor and if necessary as the policeman, to see that the economic side of the community lost the last vestiges of cut-throat selfishness, which had marked the period of social chaos and anarchy. It would encourage what was coming inevitably: the kind of competition that is found within the well-adjusted family; competition motivated by friendship and directed toward group well-being. Without a hierarchy, without forced discipline or coercion, the organism of the family worked together and all of society was to share this economic outlook.

The family organism in its economic activity was, of course, the model for the cooperative commonwealth; nowhere was this more true than in the character of the state itself. Anticipating Croly, Lloyd described the politics of social solidarity — politics that would naturally do without that central and traditional American political institution, the two-party system. Let Americans ask themselves, What was the historical basis of the two parties? Was it not in the reaction of the seventeenth- and eighteenth-century liberals against monarchical absolutism? Filled with fear of the unchecked will of despotic kings, unable to rise above their experience, the people had been willing to shackle their own will and work with a limited government of indirect representation which led inevitably to parties. Then this period of political revolution had merged with economic revolution and there no longer was any will of the people. Society was broken into fragments and these fragments continued bloodless war among themselves: it was a competition that found representation in the two-party system.

Now that a real society was emerging from this chaos, a unified and self-willed community, democratic in organization and purpose, there was no need for the people to fear an absolute will and suffer limited government; the only will was their own. There was no need for two parties to represent competing interests; there was only the single interest of the cooperative commonwealth. What we need in politics, continued Lloyd, is peace and cooperation rather than to "put the discharge of duties of vital importance into the hands of passion, prejudice, whim and trimming."

The type of government to be evolved, he wrote, was anticipated by the American political boss. Regular government, working under the handicap of constitutional limitations and divided legislatures, was not capable of action. The boss, in terms of political science, was a separation of administrative and executive power from the competition and irrationalism of general elections. This was the direction the political forms of the cooperative commonwealth would take. A permanent executive and administrative group would be built up, based on "election by education, which Emerson prophesied," of men who "represent the deliberate and intelligent will of the people." These guardians of the community's welfare would consult the will of the people through types of direct representation. Together, the community and its leaders would move ahead creating a living fundamental law as it was needed instead of attempting to conform to dead abstractions which must destroy all spontaneity, all life.[40]

Richard T. Ely THE ECONOMIST
AS CHRISTIAN AND PROPHET

With brilliant clarity and emotional force, Henry Demarest Lloyd had forged a philosophy of reform for Americans. It was radical in intent yet persuasively conservative in its method and immediate goals; it was fraternally minded but it depended on the initiative of the individual; it guaranteed success while asserting creative free will; it denied the economic nature of man and yet it affirmed that a changing economic environment was inexorably guiding mankind toward the cooperative commonwealth. It was idealistic, inspirational, and religious in quality; nevertheless, it created a razor-sharp weapon of attack against current institutions and their ideological defense. Surely and with a deft hand, Lloyd had demonstrated how to outflank the conservative defense. The steel chain of ideas, which protected the *status quo* and its supposed universal archtypical principles from change, was to be dissolved in the acid relativism of history. The concept of a swiftly running current of history with its endless novelty was to be firmly anchored in the authority of Darwin and in the implication that evolution must mean change. But, at the same time, the reformer was to make it clear that biological evolution had nothing to do with history.

Then let the circle of logic begin to tighten around the Spencers, the William Graham Sumners, and all other apologists of the inevitability of individualistic competition. History was the record of an endlessly changing succession of social environments. In each one, man, the product of his environment, rebuilt his institutions and ideas to facilitate adjustment. Institutions and ideas were relative to a limited historical situation and were then outdated as history passed them by. Men's ideas were always shaped by their institutions and their institutions were always shaped by their environment, of which the most basic factor was the economic. The defenders of individualistic competition in late nineteenth-century America were upholding institutions that no longer existed; they were using ideas that in the historical sense were dead, that had lost their meaning when the historical environment had moved away from them.

This was the magnificently destructive dialectical weapon forged by Henry Demarest Lloyd. This American, standing at the threshold of the twentieth century, however, could hardly claim author's copyrights for it. Nor could he even more proudly seek recognition for the reformer's path of retreat from this monster of debilitating relativism. Carl Becker, in his essay on the eighteenth century, suggested the pragmatic utility of believing, at one and the same time, that man was the product of his environment and that he had universal qualities. The reformers of that century had to demonstrate that man was capable of regeneration, that he was not bound by original sin, and that a better environment would provide a better man. Having destroyed, to their satisfaction, the conservative defense of the *status quo*, based on an insistence of innately evil qualities of man, they must, as moral men, substitute a code of values for those which they had destroyed. And so they proclaimed that man, in civilization, had been led astray from the essential goodness of the universal natural order. If he could strip off the errors of his artificial institutional life, if he could conform to the pattern of nature, then all would be well. Paradoxically, they returned to history to confirm the natural qualities of man. They worked, therefore, with two histories, the history of change and error and the history of permanence and good.

This, too, was Lloyd's method of escape from relativity, from meaningless existence without moral values. There were two histories, the real which must be transcended and the ideal which must be materialized on earth. But he defined the ideal in the earthy terms of the primitive man and forecast its triumph through an Aristotelian type of evolution, which would come full cycle in the universalization of the altruism of the prehistorical family group.

Lloyd had pointed the way to the perfect kind of economic reform. All that was established in economics, institutions, and principles was outmoded. The industrial revolution, however, was a novel historical force. The reformer need not concern himself with manufacturing the values, the social mores that would adjust man to his new economic environment. In a way, industrialism was absolutely destructive and absolutely creative. Working within history as tradition, as day by day occurrences, as chance and error, industrialism was freeing man from history as past experience. If evolution were Aristotelian, the straight-line movement of a potential force, pushing aside the superfluous, the unnecessary, the inert aspects of the world, until it reached full fruition, then the reformer could look at industrialism as the culminating push of evolution to that perfect state. Truly, in burning out tradition, in obliterating the excess baggage of the social heritage, industrialism was allowing, for the first time during the history of civilization, the natural qualities of man, his altruistic social character, to be completely expressed.

It was with the greatest possible *élan* that Lloyd had pushed his economic criticism. While he was waiting for the social psychologists to confirm his analysis of human nature, he was joined by a group of academic economists in this attack on the citadel of American conservative thought, the principles of orthodox political economy.[1]

One of the most important leaders of the young rebels among the economists was Richard T. Ely.[2] He was a member of a whole generation of youthful scholars who had made a pilgrimage to Germany to escape the platitudes of economic classicism so firmly entrenched in American colleges during the 1870s and 1880s. It was in cooperation with these fellow rebels returning to America in the 1880s that Ely helped organize the American Economic Association in 1885. This was a group dedicated to the overthrow of accepted academic economic theory and to its replacement with an economics that would be both more scientific and more liberal.

With roots deep in puritan New England, the Ely family had

gradually edged westward until, in 1854, Richard T. Ely was born in Fredonia, New York. His mid-nineteenth-century branch of the family still clung stubbornly to the strictest tenets of Calvinism, urged by a rigidly pious Presbyterian father. But young Ely reacted violently against the bleak doctrine of predestination, which doomed the vast majority of men to eternal damnation, and as he weakened family ties by the long trip to New York City, he rapidly sought a more optimistic, more mellow interpretation of Christianity.

Rapidly, too, the young pilgrim from rural New York began to grasp the richness of civilization. Reaching out for the cosmopolitanism offered by Lloyd's Columbia, avidly pushing his way through knowledge, the enthusiastic Ely earned a traveling fellowship to Germany to follow up what had seemed a real interest in philosophy. Once at the University of Halle, however, he soon discovered that he did not want to be indoctrinated in the fine points of abstract and unworldly logic. Philosophy meant an understanding of the world, this world; it meant a grasp of immediate developments, not speculation about nonexistent absolutes. Impatient with irrelevant metaphysics, he followed the advice of friends and transferred to the University of Heidelberg; here he came to understand philosophy as knowledge of man's environment through the tutelage of economists like Karl Knies and Bluntschli. Ely was now convinced that the key to understanding was a grasp of the economic process.

Process was the magic word that Ely learned so well in Germany. Admiringly, he listened to his almost belligerent German mentors blast the foundations of English classical economics, and incidentally, therefore, American academic political economy; these teachers presented the young American with a critical history of economic thought. English economics, even in the guise of Spencerian evolution, was rooted in the materialism, the rationalism, and the individualism of the eighteenth century. The English school used such terms as private property, self-interest, and competition as if they were principles which should operate perfectly in every society, at every historical period. Knies, however, calling in the authority of colleagues like Wilhelm Roscher and Bruno Hildebrand, termed this kind of thinking fantasy. To the carefully listening Ely, it was pointed out that man was part of history, that all his concepts were products of historical development and were valid only within particular cultures and at particular times. Little intelligence was needed, therefore, to see that the precepts of the classical economists could not be applied to the economies of all countries, or to all periods of history. As a matter of fact it was doubtful whether they still applied to the England whose economic environment had produced them because, inexorably, history would move on, changing the English environment so that new ideas would be needed there.

Beyond historical relativism, which undermined the possible universality of the technical classical doctrines, Ely also was taught by his German professors that the ethics of the English economists had always been in error, because they postulated a self-sustaining individual who voluntarily entered into social relations with his fellows. It was the essence of social truth, the Germans insisted, that man was absolutely dependent on his society, that the individual was created by society. Ethics must take into account, then, this fact of the reality of society and the dependence of man upon it for his personality. There could be no abstract economic man nor economic values that were distinguishable from the totality of society. Ethics must be social not individual, social and not economic.

Filled with enthusiasm for these principles which freed him from the tenets of classical political economy that reminded him so much of the dark despair of orthodox Calvinism, Ely came back to a teaching post at Johns Hopkins ready to do battle against the determinism of economic theory which coldly and impersonally insisted on the necessary economic damnation of the vast majority of men in this world. Boldly, the young knight-errant hurled down a challenge almost immediately to his elders in his *The Past and Present of Political Economy*.[3] It was only a few years earlier, Ely recounted, that the profession of economics had celebrated the centennial of *The Wealth of Nations* which symbolized the birth of a specialized science of economic life. In this century, English thinkers had continued the dominance begun by Adam Smith. When one spoke of economic thinking, one naturally had in mind the English classical tradition. Now, however, Ely announced it was his sad duty as a historian to lower the curtain on a past that had been so full of glory. English thought was the past of political economy; it was not the present. Somewhere between 1776 and 1884, younger economists had forgotten Smith's emphasis on history and statistics. They had not followed science — the path that would have given the profession vitality. They had lost contact with reality, and reality had passed them by.

When the English past was compared with the present, the German present in political economy, all the faults and inadequacies of the English position became glaringly apparent. The central method of the English school had been deductive and in a sense idealistic. The men of this tradition had assumed certain premises, based only on their own minds, and had evolved an economic system without recourse to the knowledge of the external world. All this was obviously then outdated, he continued, because we, of the new generation, realized that science cannot be based on idealistic and deductive philosophy; it was realistic and inductive, that was why we had come to base our thinking on German precedent that accepted the outer world as a source of principles and studied it empirically, inductively. The unscientific basis of all previous economic thinking in this country must, therefore, necessarily call into question its major tenets: that universal self-interest was the basic cause of all economic phenomena; that all men loved ease and were averse to exertion; that there was no friction in economic life; and that "The beneficent powers of nature . . . arrange things so that the best good of all is attained by the unrestrained action of self-interest." [4]

This whole system had been given the dignity of natural law; its postulates were called the reflection of universal attributes of man and nature. Now, with the knowledge drawn from the German economists, Ely declared, we could scientifically affirm that there were no natural economic laws, that there was only the growth and development of new concepts of economics, which differed with the particular context of the time and place in which they found expression, that "In every stage of its progress, the theory of political economy is the generalization of truths recognized up to a certain point of time, and this theory cannot be declared complete, either as respects its form or substance." [5]

All of this was by way of preparing for the grand assault on that major bulwark of conservative economics Herbert Spencer. Spencer had claimed the title of evolutionist and yet he had embedded the static principles of classical economy in his theory of evolution. For practical purposes, he had used the authority of Darwin to support eighteenth-century concepts of natural law. Here, certainly, was no true statement of Darwin's theory of evolution, which chained man to a set of simple mechanical principles that operated outside the softening process of time.

In the first place, wrote Ely, the meaning of Darwin was change, growth, and novelty. There could not be one set of principles operating in evolution. Second, it was clear that man was no longer even part of a complex stream of physical evolution. Slowly, man had developed along the lines of capacity for learning and of ability to act according to acquired knowledge rather than by biological instinct. Finally, this plasticity of human nature had reached an absolute point of differentiation, separating man radically from other animals. Now his traditional life was all important; he was a social animal, not a biological one. Now history and not nature was his meaningful environment.

The necessary corollary of this process of growth out of a life of instinct into a life of social training was the fact of man's truly social nature. Individualism and competition were meaningful concepts within biological evolution guided by survival of the fittest. When man's environment became his society and its historical tradition, his nature was not given him at birth through biology; he gained his character and his personality from society. He had then the capacity for learning and the equal quality of cooperating within his new social environment. The entire notion of man as a separate, atomic individual was left behind in man's animal past. Men were integral parts of their societies and could only be defined in terms of that society.

Now to confront Spencer with this armory of weapons brought

home from Germany: Who was this Herbert Spencer? An Englishman of the second half of the nineteenth century. What were his ideas? That man was an atomic individual whose highest ethical behavior was complete self-sufficiency and competitive zest. How were the man and his ideas to be explained? As part of English history. Where could one find the environmental conditions in English history that would encourage men to think in terms of individual self-sufficiency and competition? Not in the second half of the nineteenth century but in the first half.

At the end of the eighteenth century, the industrial revolution had begun, and it had destroyed whatever unity existed among men; they were disengaged from any close relationships to one another; they came together in cities, and when they met, they met as strangers. And they, therefore, met as enemies. All was social chaos. The philosophy of individualism with its idea of negative, prescriptive rights was the direct result of such a situation. Each man treated other men harshly, wanting only to protect his own position. Inevitably, there had appeared a philosophy which justified this existence, the *laissez-faire* doctrines of Adam Smith.

There grew up the elaboration of this rationalization of a situation that men could not avoid. Seeing men cut off from meaningful social relations, social philosophers wrote that the normal state of man was isolated individualism, and this was a value that should be encouraged. Finding men engaged in a cutthroat struggle for existence, they wrote that competition was the normal kind of social relationship that should be encouraged. Knowing man only in this competitive struggle for material existence, they assumed that the definition of man was the economic man in which the individual followed a simple calculus of pleasure and pain. They praised the virtue, therefore, of pursuing pleasure and avoiding pain. Bewildered and demoralized by the overwhelming forces of industrialism, they accepted man's inability to control his environment, and they came to praise passive acceptance as the very highest virtue, the only means to happiness. To give man dignity, they endowed industrialism with a certain grandeur by describing it as an expression of inexorable natural law. They had made the philosophical mistake that

164

had plagued all of mankind until the present generation had discovered historical relativism. They had ascribed universality to the experience of one group of people, sharply circumscribed by barriers of space and time.

But they had built such an imposing logical edifice that it had continued to seduce subsequent generations to such an extent that the younger men were blinded to historical change and continued to offer devotion to the outmoded precepts; and in a way, the worst offender was Herbert Spencer. Cognizant as he was of the doctrines of modern science and evolution, he should have followed the inductive method of study of his society; he should have realized that evolution meant constantly changing environments and, therefore, constantly changing ideas, principles, and values. Instead, he clung stubbornly to the outlook of the English generation which had first undergone industrialism. He continued to defend the dated principles and values of that generation. He refused to admit that a new era needed new ideas and new values. He could only reiterate blindly the sterile doctrine of the age of social disintegration: that liberty was mainly negative and political.[6]

Within English thinking, however, there were sensitive men who did take the growth of a new economic order into consideration. There were Englishmen who were moving in the direction suggested by the German economists. The key transitional figure here was John Stuart Mill. Steeped in the statics of the old utilitarianism, he had risen above it to express the fact of man's social responsibility in a world of new economic factors. Equal in stature to any of Ely's German heroes, however, was Thomas Hill Green who carried on the change started by Mill. It was Green who had written that liberty was to be defined in positive terms, related to the expansion of the powers and potentialities of the individual through a reciprocal relationship to society that included duties as well as rights. Consigning Spencer to an outmoded age, Ely then rejoiced: "As Adam Smith's philosophy of liberty is an expression of the eighteenth century, Thomas Hill Green's view may be looked upon as an expression of the philosophy of liberty with which the twentieth century opens."[7]

Ely had made it clear that because he was a scientist he could not believe in any creeds; because he was aware of history, he knew that there was no final definition of truth in any historical period. Did this mean, then, that he believed Green's ethical philosophy was as transient and insubstantial as Spencer's? Did this mean that moving on into the twentieth century, new economic forms would require new theories about human nature and society and values? Was he prepared to declare the complete ethical neutrality of science and history, qualified by an ethics of adjustment to an immediate, if passing, environment?

With simple and innocent clarity, Ely answered these questions in this manner. "Science is not religious revelation but a progressive unfolding of truth." Here, summed up in brief, is the key to the unconscious and all-important presumptions of Ely's climate of opinion. Proudly, he cut the connection of science from anything like a direct religious control of the facts man knew. Just as proudly, he brought religion back into the scientific world, a religion controlled and upheld by the concrete and unarguable facts of science; it was a religion of a progressive unfolding of truth. Science dealt with facts and the facts of the world spelled a pattern of progressive growth. Bluntly and self-confidently, Ely had expounded this version of science as the basis of the American Economic Association. The members of this young group of liberals, he wrote, who had banded together to make academic economics more scientific, were determined to direct the economic and social growth of mankind. They were prepared to "ascertain the laws of progress, and to show men how to make use of them." [8]

But how could there be laws of progress in a world of historical relativism in which each generation was neither better nor worse than any other? Historical relativism, Ely affirmed, was a term which applied to history as man had known it in the past. It was a history of endless and fruitless struggles, of error and evil. Science, however, revealed another "history," a progressive "History." His readers, Ely continued, could understand this dualism between everyday history and "History" if they thought back to the key concepts of Aristotle. Historical relativism postulated that every state of man was natural. The eighteenth-century rationalists had stated that the original condition of man was the natural one. Accepting Aristotle, however, the natural state of man, on which ethics could be rooted, was the final, perfected stage. If the evolution of man were the inevitable development of his potential perfectibility, the work of the economic scientist and the reformer was to strip away the obstacles that stood in the way of this perfecting principle: "The ethical aim of reformers is to render general that excellence which at the time is isolated. . . . The germs of a better future always exist in the present . . ." The social scientist could cut through the irrelevancies and lawlessness of history to discover the meaningful laws of "History." [9]

Furthermore, and most wonderful of all, Ely was in position to tell his contemporaries that the economic scientists had discovered the laws of progress; they had come into possession of the trend of Aristotelian evolution toward perfection. They knew what the final social life of man would be. Indeed, men were rapidly approaching this era. The social philosophy of Thomas Hill Green was an exposition of the ethical life of that society. Green's thinking was the product of "History," whereas Spencer's had merely reflected the pressures of history. And how could the economists, the social scientists, the sensitive thinker like Green be certain that their analysis of human nature and society was final, above the corroding influence of historical relativism? How could they be sure that their statements were not the reflection of a passing, historical environment? Liberals could be sure, Ely confidently proclaimed, because they had ascertained that the values of the culminating society were the values of the natural, original man. They had discovered that there were two human natures: the one, the imperfect, created by historical situations; the other, the perfect one, established in the first human beings. The reformer was in a position to say, therefore, that if man could escape from history, the final fruition of social evolution would take place in the universalization of the character of the natural man and "History" would at last stand free from history. This did not mean, wrote Ely, that the modern liberal denied the social nature of man. That would be a contradiction of his very insistence that values must be social, that man's highest ethical achievement was cooperation. No, it meant that, finally, social scientists had realized the primitive man was a social man. The original men did not live as isolated creatures, they lived in tight-knit, family groups based on man's love for his brother.[10]

The laws of progress, the process of Aristotelian evolution, "History" — all found concrete expression in history, and Ely had an explanation of their working in the everyday world. The character of the original family group of man had not been capable of more than limited extension to larger social groupings. As men gathered together in ever-greater social groups, the intimacy of the family broke down. Love ceased to be the fundamental principle of human life; it was replaced by mistrust, suspicion, fear, and hatred. History, until roughly the beginning of the nineteenth century, had been marked by tension between truly socialized groups, competing within an encompassing impersonal social environment. Civilization had been created on the basis of the groups who were capable of love in spite of constant, surrounding warfare. The economic structure of family agriculture and small industrial units had ensured the survival of the fundamental altruistic social unit. Then, industrialism had come, the unity of the small groups was shattered, and all men were on the way to becoming, for the first time, isolated and, therefore, distrustful individuals. The entire heritage of civilization was endangered as life became almost totally competitive. This was the crisis. This was the crisis to which the young Ely had returned from his student days in Germany. This was the crisis which had made it morally imperative to destroy the constrictive principles of Herbert Spencer, principles which had encouraged apathy in the face of disaster.[11]

But the crisis was also opportunity. In the midst of upheaval, there was the opportunity to remake society along the lines of social solidarity. Industrialism making men into individuals was tearing them loose from their acquired personal characteristics, associated with mutually distrustful classes. Industrialism was obliterating the history which had given men personalities alien to their innate capacity for love. Industrialism was making all men equal and, therefore, brothers. This fearful negative force that had made the world plastic, that provided the opportunity for the reformer to attack successfully the outmoded institutions of competition, however, was also a tremendous positive force making inevitable the cooperative commonwealth. It had made all men equal for the first time in the history of civilization, equal in their escape from history. Now it was making them equal brothers in the creative, fruitful sense of restoring their original capacity for loving those with whom they were in intimate contact. Industrialism meant the establishment of a worldwide social web in which humanity was like one great family. The factory, the city, the railroad, the telegraph, and the inexpensive newspaper had conquered the problems of space and time which had kept men apart.[12]

In terms of history, this was crisis, danger, and opportunity. And Ely's generation must struggle mightily to see that opportunity triumphed over danger; otherwise civilization would perish. But they fought with the assurance that "History" was on their side. If history revealed no steady progression toward the perfection of social solidarity, which could issue out of the crisis, a reading of "History" did. The economic scientist, continued Ely, saw the progression of economic forms tending toward this culmination. Economic forms followed the parallel of the development of human nature from infancy to youth to maturity. The infancy of mankind was marked by the economic forms of hunting and fishing and later pastoral pursuits. As humanity reached its youthful period, agriculture and then handicrafts had been pursued. Finally, as men reached social maturity, they entered the industrial stage of economic life. Here, at first, was the crisis, identified by competition. This was but the initial phase of industrialism, however, and it was giving way now to economic concentration. This phase, too, would give way until the last phase of this last stage of man's economic life would be defined as integration or cooperation.[13]

This was the inexorable course of economic evolution. Those who fought on the side of the future were not destined to lose. Yet Ely warned that it rested with his generation to see whether the forces of social union would triumph over the forces of social disintegration. The dignity of man rested on the fact that he, personally, was responsible for the fruition of this process of evolution. Science revealed the outlines of progress, but everything depended on whether man willed and created a world that would fulfill this destiny. It was to the honor of man, Ely wrote, that the will of man "is a main factor in all politico-economic phenomena, and this will must be regarded by students of society as itself a creative energy, introducing new forces." [14]

Struggling with history to fulfill their "History," Ely advised his generation that a great source of energy to achieve victory over the momentary anarchy could be found through cooperation with the growing labor movement. Labor was the group, at the end of the nineteenth century, most influenced by industrialism. The workers in the factories, taken out of the small shops and off the farms, had been stripped of their past injurious habits. The same workers were those who were most integrated into the new face-to-face communities of the urban environment. It was because labor had been disciplined to achieve the characteristics of the culminating social utopia that it was in the vanguard of what so-called conservatives called social unrest. Sensing instinctively how far the actual conditions of the competitive world were from the ideal, labor was demanding that present society abandon its attempt to retain institutions and values which were self-destructive. [15]

Ely wrote, echoing Lloyd, that the labor movement was truly conservative; the liberals who guided its potential power were conservative. This was not a doctrine of class warfare nor a philosophy of leveling. Ely, too, believed that leadership should and would come from exceptional individuals. Ely, too, believed that this revolution would take place without the forceful overthrow of any of the institutional framework of the present. He, too, advanced the paradox that while competition, associated with the middle class, must be sharply circumscribed, still the classless society of the future would find its values, its leaderships, its character in the middle class. [16]

To prove the conservative nature of his adherence to the labor movement, Ely opened a biting attack on a tradition he believed foreign to America, the socialism of the great European thinkers like

Richard T. Ely

Karl Marx. As a broad philosophical position, this brand of socialism had reached the proper conclusions about the nature of progress.
It called for an end to the present chaos of individualism and selfishness. It recognized altruism as the fundamental principle of social
life. But it erred in its specific program of reform. Its basic economic
principles of the common ownership of the means of production,
the common management of production, and the distribution of
income by common authority would defeat its own aim of seeking
the complete development of individual potentiality. Such an economic program would bring into being a centralized, monolithic type
of government and society, grinding out a kind of mechanical
equality for all individuals. This would crush out all creative individualism and spontaneity.[17]

European socialism had developed this erroneous attitude of
mechanical individualism because historical European Christianity,
in attacking socialism, had driven its leaders to atheism. And from
atheism, they had come to believe that social causation was determined by material forces; they had postulated that progress would
automatically eventuate from the working of inexorable economic
laws. Socialist leaders, then, had fallen into the same false philosophy
of the economic man as had the opponents of social progress, the
Herbert Spencer type of conservative. But Ely was ready to lift his
economic determinism into the realm of human freedom. In his
earlier years, he had come to dislike the mental maneuverings of
technical philosophy. Always impatient with detail, he never attempted the tortuous rationalizations of Croly or Baldwin or even
the instinctive philosophizing of Cooley or Lloyd. Without great
effort, he stated the central tenets of their technical idealism in terms
of what seemed to him traditional Christian theology. He would
prove that spiritual force controlled material forms.

European socialism had followed the wrong road in rejecting
Christianity, a road with a dead end. But the values, the goals, which
socialism represented, were the living ones of the future, because
they were spiritual. European Christianity had suffered more than
socialism in this clash, because it had set itself against a movement
that had to find expression if God was to triumph. American Christi-

171

anity was in the same danger of identifying itself with those who defended the chaotic *status quo*. If it did, Ely warned, the labor movement would go on without the leadership of the church. This would be a great tragedy, because labor was actually Christian in its make-up and aims. "Christianity," he declared, "is primarily concerned with the world, and it is the mission of Christianity to bring to pass here a kingdom of righteousness and to rescue from the evil one and redeem all our social relations." [18] Labor, then, was fulfilling this mission but it needed the church to inform it of the proper dignity and place of the individual in this mission and the final leadership of Christ.

The world was God's creation, and it was He who had endowed the individual with his innate capacity of love. Christ told us, he continued, that there were only two commandments which must be followed: the first is to love God, the second to love your neighbor. Under the fatherhood of God, all men were brothers, and if they were to be Christians, they must treat each other in the spirit of fraternity. Now Ely, exhorting his fellow Americans, qualified his social determinism as he declared that Christianity was a unique spiritual influence. Although man had a social nature, a perfected society could not be reached without the influence of Christianity. It was Christianity alone which insisted on the absolute spiritual equality of all men and which insisted that its communicants treat each other as brothers. It was Christianity alone which defined individual salvation in terms of a perfect unity, transcending the individual. Its sacraments of baptism and communion brought individual regeneration by making the individual conscious of his place in God's society. The rite of baptism reinforced the feeling of fraternity by providing a tangible symbol of the unity of those baptized under the fatherhood of God. Communion was the recurring symbol of the fatherhood of God which once again reminded man of the universal brotherhood of mankind.[19]

Solemnly, Ely pointed out to the leaders of the church that they would fail to fulfill man's responsibility to God if they neglected this opportunity to connect the church with the labor movement. God had placed man in the world to save it, Ely wrote. All His earliest

172

revelations to the Hebrew prophets emphasized that religion must be socially regenerative. With the coming of Christ, God had made it possible for man to go beyond social reform to social perfection. The coming of Christ had eliminated evil as an instinctive part of human nature. From this point on in history, man had free will to choose to follow God and to save his soul by saving the world. From this point on, sin was a conscious choice to be selfish and unsocial. Unfortunately, the early church fathers had so concentrated on the first commandment to love God that they had forgotten the second, to love your neighbor. Centering all attention on God, without realizing that He was also in His children, they had forgotten that God had placed man in the world to save it. The church had become subservient to conservative, antiprogressive, and anti-Christian vested interests. Happily, the economic crisis had given the church a chance to redeem itself and to become the leader in bringing about the Kingdom of God on Earth.[20]

Implicitly, without conscious effort, Ely, then, had stated the dualistic idealism of his fellow liberals. God, the great spiritual force, was supreme power. His will would triumph. The material world was His creation. But, for practical purposes, the material world had an independent existence. God was not completely immanent. He stood, transcendent, outside His creation. There was a material world to conquer, to spiritualize. And man was God's necessary agent in this progressive task. Reason and science would reveal the sociological laws of progress, operating through man's past, and they could provide assurance that inexorable forces were bringing about a social utopia, the Kingdom of God on Earth. But, finally, man must exercise his freedom, his creative will to construct those laws in the future. He must transcend his present to gain spiritual insight into the future and to gain the inspiration necessary to materialize this vision.

Simon Patten THE ECONOMIST
AS BIOLOGIST AND PROPHET

Rooted in the history of American economic thought, there stands the stubbornly honest and curiously twisted figure of Simon Patten. While Ely escaped easily from his family to the capital of eastern cosmopolitanism, Patten struggled almost hopelessly against the inherited Calvinism that controlled his old New England family on the Illinois prairie. When Ely easily dismissed the technicalities of German philosophy to follow his instinctive optimism, Patten forced himself to reject all authority and to formulate an elaborate metaphysics for himself. As the friendly, outgoing Ely returned from abroad to easy academic triumph, the shy, maladroit Illinois farm boy was an isolated, unemployed Ph.D., back from Germany, all but rejected by his hardworking, farming parents. And yet, somehow out of the psychological despair that brought Patten to blindness, he fought back to publish a far more original criticism of the American academic profession of economics. Tenaciously, and with tremendous courage, Patten carved out a successful career in economic theory.[1]

Without friends, without a family, and without poise or grace, he forced every social scientist of his generation to take his labored writings into account or face the devastating criticism of one of the most informed and most subtle minds of the day. Perhaps it was an almost mystical kind of inspiration, which Patten drew from his overwhelming love of nature, that drove him on to lonely fame. He had to be famous to make men understand what had been revealed to him on the lush Illinois prairie — the beauty and the bounty of nature that was the most magnificent fact of man's life. It was a fact that somehow the majority of men had missed. Somehow they had been blinded by religious leaders who had deformed God and nature by writing of Him as a God of wrath who had created his children in sin and evil from which there was no escape. This was a heresy, which now had secular support in the doctrines of conservative political economy. What a terrible picture of nature the professors offered mankind, composed as it was of inevitable pain and cruelty, competition by tooth and claw, jealousy and selfishness. Knowing overwhelmingly the truth, the beauty and goodness of life defined pantheistically as God, man, and physical nature, Patten conquered his own weaknesses in order to bring his generation to the same satisfying vision.

To rescue God and man and nature, the most critical blow Patten could strike would be against that very stronghold of heresy which held all thinking Americans spellbound, the English classical economic tradition. It was this labor of love, published as *The Premises of Political Economy*, in 1885, which lifted Patten out of himself and which gave him the academic chair at Pennsylvania that guaranteed his future influence.[2]

Patten recognized Spencer as the enemy of the day, but unlike Ely, he felt competent to criticize in technical terms the economic tradition of which Spencer was a part. The major thinker of that tradition was Ricardo. And thus Patten directed at Ricardo those concepts of historical relativism that he, too, had learned in Germany. The core of Ricardo's position, wrote Patten, was an attempt to explain human economic behavior and institutions in terms of a physical nature of declining resources. It was clear, Patten pointed out, that the fertility of land did not directly control rent and prices. If one looked beyond England and beyond the provincial attitude that this local environment was universal, then one saw many countries with varying fertility of land, all of whose rents and prices varied greatly. Here was certain proof that economic life depended more on the attitudes of societies than on physical nature. It was the social environment, not the physical, which explained man's history.[3]

Bluntly, directly, Patten told his readers what this single fact meant for *laissez-faire* conservatism. If the doctrines of Ricardo and the other classical economists were not universally true, then a different civilization was possible. The door was opened for the reform of the *status quo*. If human nature were the creation of immediate social environments, then change in that environment must be reflected immediately in the characteristics and attitudes of men. What the classical economists and Spencer had not realized was that the concepts of the natural man and evolution, motivated by the survival of the fittest, did not apply to civilization. Primitive man had been controlled by his biological instincts; he was the slave of his passions; he reacted directly to changes in the physical environment; the strongest men survived.

But, wrote Patten, evolution did not really proceed through the mechanism of survival of the fittest. Certain physical types did develop by such struggle. They had only a limited potential, however, and soon reached a limit of growth that was not progressive. They adjusted too well to one specific environment and lost their capacity for a change in structure. The weaker organisms were driven out of the favorable environment and forced into a harsher, more complex situation, which demanded the development of generalized rather than specialized capacities. Such had been the case with man, Patten continued. As a weak animal, prey to the more successfully specialized predators, man developed his abilities to adjust to many kinds of conditions; intelligence and cooperative traits were forced to grow by man's very failures. Increasingly, the biological organism which was man outgrew the faculty for adjustment to one environmental situation; increasingly, he learned to use his intelligence in cooperation with his fellows to make the best of any environment; and soon he was making his own environment. He had transcended his primitive, natural forebears and was no longer controlled by a group of simple instincts like the pleasure-pain calculus of the British utilitarians.

Man was part of his own history, a social tradition passed down through time. His values and desires depended on this heritage. There was an intimate relation, however, between this social environment and the physical world. Society always was influenced by the brute facts of nature. Changes in nature and changing adjustments of society to it blended together to give meaning to the real world in which man lived. This was the economic world. Fundamental to all society was its economic basis, compounded in each generation of the adjustment of history and nature. Ideas and values helped to create the new synthesis but once it was made, it, in turn, forced the inherited cultural tradition to conform to it.[4]

On this acutely logical beginning, Patten began to build a much more complete criticism of his American and English masters in a series of biting articles. His generation was conscious that it was going through an age of transition; it questioned the ideas and values that it had inherited. More and more, too, it was accused by its elders of endangering civilization by this irreverence. If one reasoned, however, from the facts of social life, this attitude was clearly mistaken and only reflected the environmental conditioning of the older people. Patten's contemporaries, who had come of age in the 1880s, had also inherited laws, habits, and prejudices suited to the limited and artificial surroundings of their ancestors. Under the pressure of a new economic environment, they knew they must reject this heritage from the past and work out their own adjustment of ideas, values, and economic facts.

Furthermore, they had a new intellectual attitude, built on a knowledge of history and evolution, that enabled a clear-cut criticism of the past. In a very exciting way, this knowledge made possible, for the first time in history, a rationally conscious synthesis of values and brute experience. The last great synthesis of ideas and experience, that at the end of the eighteenth century, had been molded by the science of that century, Newtonian physics, which had forced men to think in terms of natural laws, of a static world of fixed and simple principles. This, necessarily, had been the model of economic thought. Theorists had to speculate about the natural, economic man who did not change through history. There had to be a Ricardo. This was the economics of primitivism as it tried to force history to agree with the presupposition that a perfectly lawful and finished creation had been accomplished at the beginning of time; indeed, that time had no meaning.[5]

Patten and his fellow economists were aware, however, that all economy was progressive, not primitive; that society was an organic unity, no longer dependent on nature; that it changed through time; that there was time and not perfection. Here was the ironic humor of Herbert Spencer's position, Patten wryly added. Spencer wrote in terms of evolution and the sense of the reality of time and yet he always returned to static perfection. Here, Patten diagnosed, was a man who had adjusted to the intellectual currents of the modern age, but who had failed to lift his values out of the past.[6]

Why couldn't the Spencers realize that the understanding of evolution and history as real movement through time necessitated a comparable revolution in values? Once perceive that society was an organism moving through time, and the individualistic ethics, based on the mechanism of eighteenth-century physics, was impossible. The concepts of the selfish pursuit of pleasure and avoidance of pain and of a self-adjusting economy, making possible *laissez faire*, could be held when men thought of themselves as comparable to physical atoms, held in precise regularity by physical law. If, however, human life was cooperative social life, constantly working out group adjustments to changing environments, the values of men must be social and cooperative. The health and coordination of the social unit was the highest aim of its members.[7]

Then, suddenly, Patten found himself off this easy ideological road. Stubbornly, he was ready to follow the full implications of his historical relativism. It was most unfortunate and irritating for this honest puritan to realize the primitivism of his contemporary, liberal social scientists. Like himself, they were arguing that man was created by his immediate social environment. Similarly, they used this point to destroy the absolutist rationalism of the *laissez-faire* conservatives. But what did they do then? They committed themselves to the same fallacy that they had attacked so vigorously in Spencer. They announced that the reformers' work ended in this negative task of destroying erroneous doctrine; they assumed that men, freed from error and injurious institutions, would move directly toward perfection. They believed that the new cities automatically were expressions of a perfect society, rooted in an innately social man. They made the social definition of man instinctive. They postulated the same kind of static human nature as had the utilitarians, even though they labeled its characteristics social rather than individual. They, too, had no sense of the meaning of time, based on true appreciation of evolution.[8]

This meant, continued Patten, that sociological thinking in America, in spite of protestations to the contrary, was still under the dominance of biological thinking. Even in the 1890s, the younger sociologists had not escaped the influence of Ward, who taught them to use direct parallels between biology and sociology. Like the older man, they denied that this link existed and affirmed that society had a history above the influence of physical law. But they were just as inconsistent as Ward was in *The Psychic Factors of Civilization*. Here, Ward argued that progress was the result of psychological forces, not physiological. And yet he defined this major psychological factor, desire, in such a way that it became a mere expression of physiological impulses. Until the younger sociologists stopped defining man's social nature in instinctive terms, they, too, would never really express the true dependence of the individual on his social environment. They, too, would never be able to outline the positive steps necessary to create an environment that would make man a better individual.[9]

Almost stridently, Patten relegated his contemporaries to the eighteenth century. They had firmly rooted themselves in the tradition of science. They had gladly accepted evolution and historicism, but they still defined science and evolution and historicism in the terms of the Enlightenment. Proudly, they had accepted Comte's theory of the three stages of human thinking and placed themselves at the culminating summit of scientific thinking. What they did not realize was that there was no real difference between the theological and metaphysical stages and their conception of science. Everything, for them, fitted a hierarchical pattern; everything had to have an explanation; everything could be simplified to a few key prin-

179

ciples. This kind of science did not incorporate a sense of time, of open endedness. There must be, declared Patten, a higher kind of thinking than this level of science. A few economists, like himself, had reached it; they understood that history was the record of changing economic syntheses which could only be studied by inductive methods. There could be no comparison between these syntheses, no parallels drawn, no deductions applied. Objective knowledge about the specific environment was possible, but this knowledge did not form into hierarchical areas of law; it was distinct and unique for each generation.[10]

With poignant nostalgia, Patten consciously surrendered the eighteenth-century natural man. He outlined for his fellow liberals the tremendous appeal that this past outlook held for them. What better way was there to smash through an aristocracy of inherited rights than to affirm the freedom and equality of all men? What easier justification of equality than to ascribe all differences in men to the crushing weight of social injustice? The reformers of the 1890s, however, must do their work without a fixed yardstick of human nature to measure their success and guide their efforts.

With the fervor, dignity, and assurance of an ancient Hebrew prophet, Patten shouldered the responsibility of providing a substitute guide and guarantee of progress to replace the natural man. It was a difficult job, however. The reformers and Patten had elaborated the meaning of history and evolution, which had to mean change. The negative freeing of man from absolute principles was solidly established. All agreed that changing environments necessitated changing ideas, values, and institutions, indeed no one could escape the need to adjust constantly to fresh situations. But was such adjustment reform if it did not have the dignity of a substantial moral position behind it? Was this definition of reform anything more than Burke's definition of conservatism? Was not man essentially passive, finding his values in inescapable brute factors? Had Patten given man any more freedom in anticipating and conforming to the fresh economic situation than Ward had in declaring that man must anticipate physical evolution and bring himself into harmony with it?

Stubbornly, Patten believed that his thesis of man in history did embody these values. And, in a way, it rested on the psychological inheritance of man. Progress, he declared, was not adjustment; it was the expression of the creative capacity always to move beyond the immediate environment and to be working to build a new and better world. Of course, there were always unchangeable physical characteristics of the situation that man could not alter, but the synthesis of social tradition with brute factors always gave scope to man's capacity to create the essentials of a society which was spiritual and physical. Individual psychology, then, was composed of motor and sensory feeling. Through the senses, man gained knowledge of the objective environment; through his motor reactions, he expressed his values and desires. The individual did not adjust or conform to the external world presented to him by the senses as the lower animals did. Instead, he merely used such information to make his motor reactions more intelligently effective as he sought to blend unchangeable factors into the social situation he wished to construct.[11]

If these were the universal attributes of human nature, however, if the individual always acted this way, why was America in a crisis, brought on by a continued loyalty to past environments? Why were not the individuals of the present exercising their motor reactions to create, instead of being content to imitate? Patten who had written this analysis of sensory and motor qualities in *The Theory of Social Forces*, published in 1896, was aware of the contradiction. Toward the end of this essay, he had declared that mankind was not operating normally, and he added, "To put itself into a normal condition, the race must construct an artificial channel from the point where it left the normal line of progress to the point where it now is." [12]

A strange and tortuous magnum opus, *The Development of English Thought*, appeared three years later, in 1899. It explained why, if men were normally creative and, therefore, progressive, they had somehow lost this faculty. It also explained how normal progress was to be attained. The opening statement was a strategic retreat from the optimism of his first analysis of human psychology.[13] Determinism, rather than creativity, was the keynote of the universal sensory and motor activities. It was true that men reacted through motor responses, so that their adjustment to an environment, known through the senses, was not purely mechanical. But while the senses were passive, their influence over motor reactions was still formative. As sense experience increased, it was interrelated and associated, growing into complex patterns. Ultimately, one sense fact could call forth in the individual mind a rich picture of the environment. This, in turn, resulted in a complex motor response which also followed a pattern. Patten was now arguing that man's choices were intimately connected to his objective situation in life; so much so that creativity was almost conformity.[14]

Indeed, the struggling Patten now would not even argue that progress came from transcendence over the restricting, surrounding, concrete world. Rather, he declared, the repetition of certain motor responses, ensuring the type of survival dictated by the environment, made them part of man's heredity; they became difficult to change or to eliminate. The stage was set for a disharmony between individuals and the environment because the environment began to move away from these hardened motor patterns. History became a series of conflicts between new environments and old motor reactions. This strife was the necessary condition of man's progress. Innocently, Patten postulated that if men could totally adjust to the environment, conditions would become static and progress would cease. Men would have no sense of living in a social world as well as in contact with nature; they would never realize that there was an area of free choice in bringing society into better adjustment with the evolving physical environment.

This was individual psychology but men did not live as individuals, they lived in groups. Social life paralleled directly the responses of its individual members. Blended together in tight-knit communities, men pooled their sense experience and shared common motor responses to the environment. Collectively, this knowledge and reaction became the character of historical nations. Each nation had lived in different environments; each had developed different patterns of responses, which had become stamped on the nervous patterns of its citizens. These peculiar traditions defined the natures of the various peoples of the world. There was no universal human nature.[15]

Patten was backtracking. He had to deny the universality of human nature and the normality of reform in order to explain the troubles of his generation. Yet somehow he had to condemn the present as a deviation from a definable moral standard. He had now nicely accomplished his first task. But, seemingly, he was even more bogged down in the quagmire of his dialectic as he sought for an objective moral standard to use as a lever to condemn the *status quo* and to use as a transcendent goal to inspire his contemporaries to pursue progress. Even more decisively, he had proved the futility of searching for a universal definition of progress. More completely than ever, he had entangled man in historical relativism and denied him a real free will.

With apparent ease, however, Patten began to save himself by inserting a series of absolutes at strategic places in his theories. The first of these was the division of human history into just two great economic eras. Until the seventeenth century, humanity had labored in a deficit or pain economy; since that time, men had moved toward a surplus or pleasure economy. This was a crucial absolute because it interacted with four universal character traits that Patten also suddenly discovered. Irrespective of time or place, men always divided into four personality groups: clingers, sensualists, stalwarts, and mugwumps. The over-reaching pain economy of the past, how-ever, encouraged men to be either sensualists or clingers. In a harsh world of deficit, most men reacted as clingers; they were timid and conservative; they saw nature as evil and overwhelming; they were incapable of cooperation beyond the local group. They were the prey of the sensualists who appeared when there was a slight increase in material wealth. It was still a deficit economy, but a minority of cunning, ruthlessly selfish men could exploit the clingers to build a narrowly secure and rich existence for themselves. Feudal life of serf and noble exemplified perfectly this historical pattern.[16]

Then the commercial revolution began and a new class appeared. On the borderline, between the pain and pleasure economies, a middle class appeared in seventeenth-century England. These were the stalwarts, men who rejected the debasing passions of the sensualists in order to follow the discipline of difficult creeds and ideals; these were radicals, democrats, and utopianists. Freed from the fear of a deficit economy, their fundamental attitude was independence and self-determination. These were the puritans, the followers of Calvin.[17]

Unfortunately, increasing wealth began to corrupt the middle class and to produce the mugwumps, a leisure class so free from fear that they desired freedom from work. They ceased to take part in an ongoing world; their motor responses decayed and they lived by sense knowledge. They developed their analytic power and consciously subverted will and desire. Sterile and critical, they deserted the Calvinism of the middle class to drift in an emotionless agnosticism.

Unconsciously, Patten, who had rejected Spencer for generalizing from English experience, used English history as the clearest expression of the inevitable course of social evolution for all humanity. It was easy to describe moral standards and progress when they could be associated with a specific historical situation. It was not difficult to relate the situation in America to an English background. Stalwarts, sensualists, and mugwumps could be delineated in the American middle-class situation. The moral standards for men to follow were the virtues of the stalwarts; progress was the destruction of the sensualists and the mugwumps, and the triumph of the stalwarts.

The crisis, the struggle of America in the 1890s, revolved around the interactions of these classes. Industrialism was really still in its infancy. A surplus economy had not yet overcome the patterns of response from the ages of deficit. Many men were still clingers who could not resist the exploitation of the sensualists. Actually the large capitalists of the present were anachronisms in the new society. They were still sensualists with a narrow, antisocial outlook. The real middle class, the stalwarts, had not been able to defeat them because of the influence of the mugwumps. As the sensualists and the stalwarts, the natural actors, had been locked in mortal combat, the mugwumps held the balance of power. Although they were not in basic sympathy with the sensualists, their philosophy protected this vicious group. The mugwumps, in describing the world in the analytic terms of a self-regulating machine, justified the *laissez-faire* individualism behind which the sensualists had hidden. They had influenced young intellectuals not to follow the activism and moralism of the stalwarts by deriding driving religious enthusiasm.[18]

But, Patten assured his fellow Calvinists, reformers, and stalwarts that they must triumph because social evolution supported them. They had to triumph because they represented the final stage of social evolution, the religious. And it was the religious man who had the critical advantage of all other men. It was only the religious who were not prisoners of the economic environment.

Patten had moved from economics to religion to prove the inevitability of progress. The rich new economic environment would make possible a bountiful life for all men; the goal of progress was the lifting of all men to a cooperative commonwealth, marked by the development of the full potentialities of all men. It would be a Christian community in the true sense of the fraternal love which would mark all social relations. It was economic wealth which allowed men to rise above the fear and the selfishness of past history to act with complete altruism.

On the other hand, the passive new economy could not create the cooperative society. This had to be accomplished by men actively destroying the obstacles to its establishment. Only the stalwarts could do this by their ability to transcend any particular economic environment. All the other personality types reflected localized conditions; their characters were held within the national traditions, based on solidified motor responses. But the stalwarts had gone through so many different economic environments that their original motor responses could no longer be called into action by any particular material situation. They were free to follow the emphasis of religious thinking to transcend the *status quo*. Proudly, Patten declared, "As a race we no longer see the world as it is, but as we make it. We are not satisfied with a bare reality, but struggle for some Utopia created by our fancies." [19]

But Patten was not yet able to be proud of this philosophy of progress. In many ways, logic had driven this book away from his deeper feelings. In searching for a dynamic quality or group to shatter the complacency of the present, he had returned to the Calvinism of his heritage, a surging force, but a cruel one. His poetic feeling for complete beauty and goodness, his spiritual yearning for a Christlike Christianity of fraternal love, conflicted at every step with his stalwarts. If the cooperative commonwealth were cooperative and loving, an escape from competition, a democracy of true equality, then there was something awkward about the group and the means to bring about his historical victory.

The stalwarts, he had proclaimed, in the heat of the moment, would win through the most bitter kind of competition. One of their strongest traits was an intolerance of other attitudes; another was their sense of superiority; still another was their conviction that the unrighteous should be forcibly eliminated. As Patten grimly warned, "A race that has gone through Calvinism cannot become truly democratic." The clingers, the sensualists, and the mugwumps, the majority of mankind, were not suitable human material for the coming altruistic society; they therefore would be physically destroyed.[20]

Patten's love of a gentle and generous nature and Christianity built up an intolerable tension with this technical outline of progress, and the Pennsylvania economist continued a search for a theory of progress that would square with his economic emphasis, his historical relativism, but would incorporate methods of Christian cooperation that would better express the basic friendliness of the world.

With dramatic thoroughness, the now mature Patten decided to go back to first principles to cut through his problems. He had incorporated psychology with his economics and historicism. In many respects, however, he never got beyond Lockean sensationalism in his theorizing. Sensationalism continued to introduce more determinism into his beliefs than he really desired. It was time for a new approach to psychology. *Heredity and Social Progress*, published in 1903, was substantial testimony of years of intense thinking since *The Development of English Thought*.[21]

Immediately, Patten attacked his own favorite environmentalism.

In blunt terms, he announced that the physical environment was not rich enough to ensure progress. There was in nature a law of diminishing returns. In no way could the reformers argue that external environmental conditions would automatically produce progress. Progress must come from within man. There must be the possibility of free will within human psychology. Darwin replaced Locke as the formative influence on psychological theory. Sensationalism meant passivity; a reading of Darwin, however, proved the active and truly creative nature of man. Evolution, when studied, implied not adjustment to specific situations but the creation of novel physical and psychological attributes which allowed the organism freedom from the restrictive aspects of its environment. Patten was going to prove, on the authority of Darwin, that evolution moved forward through successive novelties.

In human evolution, therefore, progress depended on the reservoir of individual plasticity and potentiality. Parents, who adjusted successfully to an environment and created a surplus for the family, developed acquired characters which, in turn, allowed for an even richer and more successful life. They then passed these acquired characteristics down to their children — not in the Lamarckian sense of direct hereditary transmission, but in the sense that the richer social environment allowed the children to develop new personality traits which did become part of their heredity.[22]

Progress, in terms of increasing human potentiality, was, therefore, largely a humanly inspired process. The successful adjustment of the parents to an environment was not mechanical but intelligent, imposing a social pattern on the physical surroundings. The offspring, whose physical heredity benefited from this richer social heritage, immediately transcended their material surroundings to build a still richer society, which controlled nature to an even greater degree. It was a psychological process that increasingly gave man power over the physical world.

Once more Patten was back to his assertion, made before *The Development of English Thought*, that all humans were progressive; he did not need an exclusive class of reformers like the stalwarts. Precisely and strongly, he pointed to the important connection of this

fact with his definition of progress as universally democratic, altruistic, and Christian. The development of human potentiality, he
insisted, was a process of differentiation, and human progress was
a process of differentiation. The more men became differentiated
from each other, the more potentialities could flower out. If men
tried to further progress through competition, intolerance, and elimination, they would limit the possibilities of progress. With this statement, Patten had destroyed his once beloved stalwarts. It was only
through the attempt to incorporate all of mankind into the progress
of civilization, he continued, that differentiation within mankind
would be assured. "Progress," he wrote, "is not the making of the
strong but that protection of the weak by which differentiation becomes possible." [23]

So now, through a clever use of Darwin, Patten had given his
philosophy of progress the altruistic, Christian means he longed for.
By rejecting sensationalism and environmentalism, he could postulate more human freedom than ever before. His new, biological
emphasis seemed to incorporate a completely tolerant, radical
pluralism. But radical pluralism, as Baldwin had argued, hardly
guaranteed progress towards a specific historic cooperative commonwealth. Many amazing things, however, could be done with Patten's
statement that "The original germ cell has a capacity for consciousness" as he was soon to demonstrate. After twenty years of intense
speculation, of wandering through vast storehouses of social and
physical knowledge, Patten, at last, had a feeling of certainty. All
the contradictions, the false starts of the past, were overcome. The
inspiration of Darwinian biology had given Patten insight into human
evolution as cooperative and creative, as altruistic and Christian.
It had given him final proof that it was leading to a culminating,
social utopia. Radical pluralism broke men loose from the present
to choose their destinies as individuals, but innate qualities would
reassemble them as integral parts of a unified community.

Patten was swiftly returning Darwinian evolution to a subordinate
relation to that most fundamental theory of evolution which was
Aristotle's. Novelty, as he finally defined it, was not novelty at all.
The development of potentialities in succeeding generations was not

real transcendence over their forebears. It now turned out that Patten believed that the germ cells of the original man contained dormant within themselves all possible novelties and potentialities. There was an unchanging human nature, but there was novelty and potentiality and development because all aspects of this nature had not had the time or the opportunity to find expression. The achievement of a parental generation, in making a creatively successful adjustment to an environment, lay in the fact that the richer environmental situation they built would permit their children to unfold more aspects of their permanent nature.

In Patten's words:

Natural characters are made active only by surplus energy. A deficit renders them dormant and causes conduct to be determined by the acquired characters of the present environment. Persons and classes living under a perpetual deficit have no opportunity to reveal their natural character. They must be controlled by tradition and imitation until a surplus destroys the dominance of acquired characters.[24]

Patten was home, back to the Enlightenment; his intellectual wanderings were over; he had stubbornly thought through the relation of reform to the knowledge of the day; and if he returned to the position of the reformers of the 1890s whom he had criticized, he had done so on his own terms. Historical relativism was still central in his mind. Man had a personality which was the product of the immediate environment. The economic basis of society was still a fundamental concept. The economic structure determined whether acquired personality or man's natural one would triumph. Evolution was the key to his whole position as he insisted on novelty, differentiation, chance, and creativity. Indeed, no one took Darwin more seriously than Patten because it was through the authority of Darwin that the culminating development of Aristotelian evolution could be proved.

This was the climax of Patten's essay into biological theory. He had concluded with a demonstration of what social progress was and how it could be achieved. He had arrived at that magic concept which made reform infallible: a world with two histories, peopled with men who had two personalities. He had suggested how this concept should be used. Now with his dialectical position secure, Patten was to proceed in subsequent books to drive home the practicality of his views for immediate reform.

Straightforward and uncomplex, a textbook for liberals and by far his easiest to read, Patten's next book, *The New Basis of Civilization*, concentrated on an elaboration of the two histories.[25] The overwhelming aspect of the young century, he wrote, was the ongoing, economic revolution. The overwhelming difficulty, which flowed in its wake, was the inability of men to adjust their thinking to the new environment. The challenge for liberals was to bring man's attitudes, values, and institutions into harmony with the material surroundings. While this might appear a difficult task, it was only so if one refused to see the precedents, the standards that could guide men through the revolutionary situation. These guides centered around a permanent human nature. The biological inheritance of primitive man was rooted in the family group, characterized by altruism. This was the normal human evolutionary unit. Its values were the ones that man should use to organize the industrial world.

History had not been the history of the control of society by family values because until the present there had been no methods of organizing and coordinating society to follow these values. Disorganized society, the civilized life that men had known, had been marked by selfishness and exploitation. But selfishness was not really part of man's nature; it was something imposed on him by the artificial environment of civilization. Indeed, this perversion of human nature had not even been the history of the majority of mankind. Most men, those who had been exploited, had remained true to their innate natures. It had only been the exploiters who had been corrupted.

There have flowed then, side by side, two streams of life, one bearing the working poor, who perpetuate themselves through the qualities generated by the stress and mutual dependence of the primitive world, and the other bearing the aristocracies, who dominate by means of the laws and traditions giving them control of the social surplus.[26]

190

Simon Patten

With awesome majesty, the new environment of industrialism was grinding the aristocracies into the dust of memory and freeing the Christian goodness of the common man to beautify the world. Inexorably, mankind was rising to its full potential because "Economic life will make them more social by reviving the impulses of the primitive world," and "The growth and influence of cities are renewing and intensifying in all classes the motives to cooperation." [27] What a magnificent message for the reformers! Theirs was but the negative job of destroying the vestiges of history which had become part of man's personality through the influence of a series of inadequate social environments. Positive values would flourish automatically when the destructive task was finished because this economic environment of industrialism was absolutely novel and different in restoring the plenty of primitive society. Instead of forcing an acquired, historical character on man, it was the environment which would encourage the natural man to express himself fully. The "History," which had been locked in the germ cells of the universal man, could, at last, free itself from the history of tradition and custom and hardened institutions.

This was the benign theme of *The New Basis of Civilization*; it was not Patten's final statement. He had not exhausted his calling as religious prophet to his generation. There were many things he had to say and write. The simple thesis of this last book would be misunderstood as his total contribution. And it was not enough in this hour of crisis. Even with total victory at hand, Patten was frightened. There was chaos in this interregnum between two generations.

If men relaxed and waited for the workings of the fresh environment to educate society, to lift it out of the crisis, it might be too late. Civilization might be so shattered, men so hopelessly isolated, that the powerful cohesive forces of industry would be in vain. Men must act. They must throw all their energies into the glorious effort to save their civilization. They must sense the spiritual exaltation of their mission and be inspired by its religious nature. He had to tell them that their fate was in their own hands; theirs was the responsibility and the duty. Evolution depended on the creative freedom of mankind.

Patten had returned to the tremendous task of supplying primitivism and rationalism with a spiritual and idealistic basis which lifted man above simple adjustment to the environment. This time, however, he was ready; he had thirty years of philosophical delvings behind him; his vision was clear. In 1911 he produced his great synthesis, *The Social Basis of Religion*.[28] It was a book that pulled economic determinism and cosmic destiny together in a poetic clearness which transcended the muddy prose and complicated reasoning of his earlier writing.

Drawing upon his full dignity as one of the important philosophers of the American Enlightenment, Patten sharply called upon his fellow liberals to abandon the contented materialism of inevitable progress. Behold, he called out, the terrible danger that befronts us. Our new surplus economy, our new pleasure economy, far from automatically saving us, has brought the nation to the point of corruption. As it has developed, men have lost their moral fiber and relaxed. They have done so, however, before they escaped the psychic heritage from the pain economy. Unconsciously, they are still the prisoners of the fear which has been ground into their personalities by the series of deficit environments through which humanity has passed. The relations of society are still, then, governed by fear from which men cannot escape because the partial pleasure economy has robbed them of their will to act. Mankind can drift indefinitely in this halfway state between the pain and pleasure economies unless they receive inspiration from Christianity. Uplifted by religious fervor and the love which is Christ's message, they can rise above their injurious traditions and become free to remake society along the lines of the full potentiality of the coming pleasure economy.[29]

Repeating the innocent contradiction of his comrade Ely, Patten assured his generation that this revival of Christianity, which would allow transcendence over material conditions, was occurring "because favorable environing conditions have replaced race antagonisms with a spirit of social cooperation." Made possible by economic changes, the religious upsurge would carry man over this period of transition into the immediate and total expression of his normal self. The religious man was, by definition, the normal man. And Patten insisted, as he returned to the everyday world in another way, that the normal man, freed from his past traditions by religion, was only now reaching the social truth that man's intelligence was free from the control of both tradition and physical law.

The preface of *The Social Basis of Religion* vividly sets the stage for the presentation of this irreconcilable confusion in ideas. The only possible philosophy for an era that had known Darwin was pragmatism. It was pragmatism that recognized a constantly changing world, spurred on by sudden novelties. It was pragmatism that stated directly the creative freedom of man's intelligence. Linking pragmatism with the future and characterizing himself as one of its champions, Patten, however, relegated even William James to the outmoded past. They were both, he admitted, the intellectual heirs of John Stuart Mill, but James took his inspiration from Mill's earlier writing. His pragmatism, therefore, was of a primitive type, a radical empiricism whose test was personal satisfaction. But the later Mill was Patten's guide, and under this inspiration, he began to define a pragmatism that appeared, at first glance, close to that toward which Dewey was working. His own pragmatism, Patten affirmed, was social and its tests "are objective and are measured by the social results of action." It was a pragmatism that had four criteria, seemingly very modern, and very far from Aristotle and the *philosophes*.

First, the tests of truth are objective and social. . . . The only valid personal test is whether or not individual action conforms to social standards. . . .

Second, there are no universal laws. . . . The test of truth is action. . . .

Third, Skepticism affords no test of truth. . . .

Fourth, the psychic test of truth as a relation between an idea and its object is defective. . . . Truth is a relation between thought and act, and not between feeling and its external cause. . . .[30]

Here, in these criteria, was the highwater mark of Patten's commitment to a mode of thought that was not absolute. They were significantly not part of the regular flow of his mind; rather they were principles that were not to furnish the positive support for the main constructive argument of the book, but were to be used solely for negation and destruction. Firmly rooted in the preface, in dramatic contradiction to these pragmatic points, was the central and positive theme of this work.

Continuing the analysis of his intellectual debt to Mill, Patten began to use a different vocabulary and to think in different terms. Mill, he wrote, had passed beyond the stage of empiricism which had so influenced James. Mill had been converted by Auguste Comte to the use of universal historical proofs to establish social laws. True enough, continued the American economist, Comte and Mill were wrong but only in detail. Their general philosophy of universal historical stages was correct! This self-styled pragmatist, who had advanced as the central criterion of his philosophy the proposition that there were no universal laws, now openly insisted that human thought had three necessary stages of development, but that Comte's description of them was defective. The first stage was the theological as Comte had stated; the second stage, however, included both Comte's metaphysical and positive stages; and the final stage was the pragmatic.[31]

With almost breath-taking agility, with a sleight of hand that was both marvelous and tragic, because it fooled no one so much as it did Patten himself, he had maneuvered the central ideas of his time — evolution, pragmatism, historicism — into a pattern directly parallel to that used by the *philosophes* to destroy their conservative opponents.

These eighteenth-century liberals wrote that the things conservatives defended, historical tradition and social custom, were ephemeral and unsubstantial. They were not relevant to the real nature of man and the world; through the use of reason and through the discovery of natural law they would, therefore, be destroyed. Then nineteenth-century philosophy shattered the *philosophes'* ideal of static perfection, the ideal of autonomous reason. Man was replaced in the flow of history or in the course of evolution; he had to accept the present for what it was and nothing more.

This was the beauty of Patten's theory of evolution. The ideas of the nineteenth century, the ideas of a Hegel and a Spencer, men who

194

denied free will, were wrong, absolutely wrong, because they were outdated, because they belonged to the second stage of mental evolution. Men were now to be free because they had no choice but to be free. They were part of the final stage of mental evolution, the pragmatic. Nor did Patten need to be concerned with the merits of pragmatism as a theory and whether it fitted the facts of evolution; there was no option connected with society's acceptance of pragmatism as its way of thinking.

If there is a paradox for us in the idea of forcing men to be free, there was none for this American social philosopher. Exactly as the *philosophes* had done, he equated freedom with the ability of man to conform to absolute standards not found in current society. Pragmatism and historicism were weapons to use against enemies. They were tools to prepare for the future, not real philosophies to live with, but to be discarded upon the final approach to utopia.

Nothing shows this more clearly than Patten's discussion of psychology and religion, the heart of his final philosophy. Wielding the knife of modernism, he criticized the conservatives for holding to a pre-evolutionary conception of thought, for believing that thought was "a definite, pre-determined product of some mechanism, material or otherwise, molded by pre-determined conditions." Instead we must accept the genetic theory of thought that there was no mechanism for producing ideas, that we must judge the mind "by its products instead of by its structure or antecedents," that we gained ideas from the society of which we were a part.[32]

This, in turn, was his tool to clear the ground for his perfected society because he must show that the present character of man could be changed, that such weaknesses as selfishness were not innate as the conservatives claimed. Human psychology, he insisted, was not the product of natural law, but of tradition. Unfortunately, the controlling concepts of Western civilization had been molded in the Near East when that region was undergoing unfavorable climatic changes with the tragic result that our culture had centered around the ideas of conflict and despair. The plastic part of human nature had been shaped by this philosophy into its present imperfect pattern, a pattern conservatives called inherent.

Patten, however, made it clear that the plastic was but part of human nature because, with the conservative position outflanked, he was ready to drop the evolutionary approach; it had served its negative purpose. His final purpose was to arrive at perfection, a goal that might be embarrassed by a thoroughgoing philosophy of evolution. Because man had reached the pragmatic stage, because he was, therefore, able to transcend his immediate environment, mankind was on the verge of perfection — a perfection made possible by the innate, universal side of human nature, by man's instinct for social cooperation that was beyond the control of the environment. This inner, irreducible part of man was his religious nature. Throughout history, it had fought against an adverse environment and the acquired psychological traits. As Patten wrote, "The conflict of religion is between social habit and social feeling. The spiritual is the inner self in contrast to the social self. It is suppressed heredity battling with the routine and habit of the external world." [33]

Now, he drove home to his readers, in the final pragmatic phase of evolution, man was free to alter the *status quo* so that his inner self could at last flower out and reach perfection. Historicism and pragmatism helped to consign conservative doctrines to the shifting sands of history, helped to manipulate and change present institutions, but they would be left behind when Patten led society into the sheltering arms of a rational, static utopia.

If there is any doubt of Patten's fundamental debt to the Enlightenment, it is stilled by his elaboration of methods of social study. Warming to his task as guide to the promised land, he offered the foolproof technique to clarify the innate elements of human psychology on which the new world would be constructed. It was an economic method of approach, which, he emphasized, was not similar to that of the physical sciences. That method, he wrote, included observation, experiment, and verification which depended for effectiveness upon the isolation of the object to be studied. Incapable of isolation, however, society must be compared with itself as it passed through distinct epochs which were economic in origin. The results of such study would disclose the common or universal qualities of man and nature and strip away the acquired, the debilitating traits foisted on man by injurious social environments. In Patten's own words,

> We regard many characters as natural that are acquired, because they appear so regularly in current events, while the underlying natural traits, seen only in distorted forms, are misjudged and underestimated. In this way, sympathy is displaced by selfishness, religion sinks into superstition, democracy yields to imperialism, cooperation is displaced by class struggle. Competition gives way to monopoly, and liberty to absolute power. . . . Economic interpretation gives the only method that will unravel the tangled skein of social events and permit us to reach the ultimate through whose dominance alone the goal of civilization may be reached.[34]

Patten's optimistic message to reformers then read something like this: All that was good was the result of general laws that were enduring and which would furnish the plan of progress. All that was evil was the result of specific economic conditions that could be isolated and overcome. The economic interpretation would clarify these general laws and the abnormal conditions that kept them from working. Moreover, the reformers could rest assured that the economic interpretation would be utilized by a growing number of people in the future — utilized because, as Patten had written earlier, the thought of mankind went though the three stages of the theological, the metaphysical, and the pragmatic. The economic interpretation, he affirmed, was merely one way of thinking pragmatically. It was pragmatic because it was genetic, it was concerned with the growth and development of normal characteristics. But let Patten himself describe his conception of the pragmatic, the genetic type of thinking:

> Cut off all the acquired factors and disregard the psychic abnormalities of depressed conditions, and simple reality stands revealed that may be tested by the method of agreement and verified by the normal as seen in the present. This is the genetic as contrasted with the structural view of thought, and is a legitimate consequence of the displacement of the mechanical view of the universe by the evolutionary. . . . The genetic . . . is synthetic and its reality is revealed in the normal, which expresses for the moment that which extends into the past and will continue into the future. . . . The normal is the permanent, the abiding and the good.[35]

Having demonstrated his method by which the principles of the perfect society could become known, Patten now expressed his theory of what the future would be like. Because men were reaching the pragmatic stage of thought, because they could use the economic interpretation of history, because there was now a favorable economic environment, men were consciously discarding their false historical traditions and beginning to use their natural instincts, they were beginning to be truly religious. Then, becoming religious, they became normal, following their instinct to act in a completely brotherly and social manner. A perfect cooperative commonwealth, therefore, was to be anticipated in the near future. Patten, jettisoning completely his historicism and pragmatism, now offered a poetic vision that denied history and free will as completely as had Plato's utopia.

. . . a socialized world can no more have a dozen religions than it can have a dozen sciences in one field. . . . So also there can be but one morality, and this will be made effective by the motives that prompt men to lead normal lives. . . . A truly social morality will be more authoritative than any traditional code could be. . . . As society progresses and as the men who compose it become more normal, the same concept will be held by all at maturity. Everyone in his development will go through all the epochs of thought development of which this higher concept has arisen.[36]

Patten had blended together the belief in man's freedom as a creator and the belief in man's participation in a lawful world process through the same technique used by his liberal contemporaries. He, too, could postulate a material world that man could transcend and control; he, too, could postulate a spiritual force that was working to conquer the material world and to bring it under the design of spiritual law. He could declare that God needed man's assistance in this process of spiritualization. In a dualistic philosophy, which distinguished sharply between matter and spirit, he could proclaim both the freedom and responsibility of man. Finally, he could describe the reconciliation of spirit and matter through religious mysticism: "The person, lost in the onward flow, gets his joy in a service that helps the super-pulse to grow."

Thorstein Veblen THE ECONOMIST AS SCIENTIST AND PROPHET

WHAT relation existed between science and progress? Each passing year after 1890 increased the depth and ramifications of this question, and was the answer of Ely and Patten sufficient? They had written that science underwrote a philosophy of possible progress. They had pointed to the relativism implicit in Darwinism, which must affirm that man was bound to no established institutions or traditions, but that he must create a new social structure and new ideals in an evolving world. With determined vigor, therefore, the two pioneering economists argued that their generation should make progress its conscious goal. If the world were not predetermined, but a world of unforeseen possibilities, then, certainly, man should attempt to formulate those possibilities. Was this, then, the relation of science to a theory of progress?

Quietly, and with a grim humor, a younger colleague of these two economists, one who already dated them as part of a dead tradition, began to lay open to critical analysis the assumptions of the vocal progressives. Thorstein Veblen made himself known to the world of academic economics at the beginning of the 1890s.[1] A strange convert to economics with a Ph.D. in philosophy, obtained completely in American universities, Veblen perhaps was won to economics by the pressure of economic circumstances. If anything, his biography has a theme of isolation and loneliness more extreme than that which plagued Simon Patten. Veblen had not only the problem of the scholar's maladjustment in a rural home but also the burden of an immigrant's son outside the centuries of continuity on which Patten could lean. Like Patten, he compounded his misfortunes with a personality both withdrawn and belligerent. If there was no opportunity for a Thorstein Veblen in the prim and proper academic world of 1885, his stubbornness would make one, if not in philosophy, then in economics. In the end, it must be economics, because, by 1890, Veblen could define philosophy only in economic terms. This was not retreat but victory, final and total.

Thorstein Veblen, then, was pure intelligence. He had cut his ties with an unsympathetic family and Midwestern rural community; he had no feeling for the old-world traditions of that family or community; nor could he spontaneously accept the myths of the present America, which scorned him for his lack of personality and background. Such a declaration of war from his contemporaries surely precluded any acceptance of America's historical traditions. If the necessary environment for critical thinking is a certain sense of having no commitments to the past or present or future, then no man was more adequately prepared for his function of critic than Veblen.

Decisively, this outcast, this free-floating brain made apparent the advantages of his social problems for philosophical analysis. What was the relation between science and progress? It certainly was not what Patten and Ely had written. Science and progress could not be discussed together. One had to choose to follow science and objective, tangible knowledge or to follow progress and the whole vague and meaningless realm of value. In a brilliant preview of what Becker was to attempt a generation later in his *Heavenly City*, Veblen analyzed the historical connection of science and philosophy since the first serious formulation of scientific theory in those marvelously fruitful centuries after the collapse of the medieval age. From the first, rational man grasped that science was the one means of knowing whose results could be guaranteed as true. From the first, then, men had used science to learn facts about the world they lived in, and they had modified their beliefs to conform to this information. But more than they modified beliefs to the facts, men still forced facts to conform to their beliefs. Until the very present time, men had championed science only to twist its findings and even its philosophy to their inherited prejudices. Until now, in 1890, the Western world had claimed to be scientific without really abandoning the prescientific bases of culture.

But why had this happened? Because, wrote Veblen, anticipating Becker, man was not rational. He did not live by the use of his free intelligence, operating through the fact finding tool of science. Man was a creature of history. His personality, his character, was shaped by the traditions he had received from the past and through the behavior pattern he developed to fit the institutional structure of his time, a structure which was itself formed by tradition. Man's basic outlook on the world, then, was the result of habit, not of intelligence. Man's habitual views about his surrounding environments were in no sense scientific, created as they were in past eras, controlled by beliefs in magic and mysterious forces. This belief in spiritual powers, which shaped history, had become embodied in Western civilization as the tradition of progress. Somehow, the European world was certain that history was ascending toward a triumphant climax. This was the central theme of Western civilization — this belief in inevitable progress.

This myth was antithetical to an understanding of true science, the science of a Charles Darwin. Here, explicitly, the philosophy of true science was set down. There was change, constant change, but it was impersonal. Man was part of the physical world whose movement could not be defined in terms of good or bad; it could only be explained in tangible facts that could not be associated with moral values. Veblen was the first thoroughgoing American prophet of what Becker was to call the twentieth-century climate of opinion, that age which realized the meaningless quality of existence and which chose to live by the one certainty left: the scientific fact.

Veblen first assaulted the entire basis of economic theory in 1898 with his article, "Why is Economics not an Evolutionary Science?" [2] The previous generation, he pointed out, had believed it was scientific because it demanded a realistic examination of the facts of economic life. Accuracy and observation, objectivity and induction, were its watchwords. And, surely, these were scientific words. Nor could that generation be called unscientific because it did not correlate these facts into a close-knit body of theory, even a concept of process. Nevertheless, Veblen affirmed, economics was not an evolutionary science and there could be no science which was not firmly rooted in an understanding of evolution. What separated Veblen and true science from the past was not technical views but the all-important difference in spiritual attitude which later scholars would call the climate of opinion.

Veblen, calling on the authority of Darwin, wrote that the economic scientist focused his attention on causal relationships, but he never went beyond the immediate factors for his answers. The post-Darwinian asked only about the conservation of energy or the persistence of quantity. The superiority of the modern scientists, he continued, was "their refusal to go back of the colorless sequence of phenomena and seek higher ground for their ultimate syntheses, and . . . in their having shown how this colorless impersonal sequence of cause and effect can be made use of for theory proper, by virtue of its cumulative character." [3]

This outlook was in sharp contrast to pre-Darwinian science, which was the framework for all earlier economic writers. Without exception, their detailed knowledge was put into irrelevant form, because the end they always served was the establishment of an absolute spiritual truth. As part of the unbroken line of intellectual history of man from primitivism to Darwin, the classical economists shared the assumption that nature operated in the human characteristics of propensity and will power. The first great weaknesses of past economics, then, was the belief that some force was pushing the world along the path of progress. The second fundamental error was the conception of human nature as hedonistic, passive, inert, immutably given.

Standing with the progressive generation, momentarily at least, Veblen could agree that a true comprehension of evolution resulted in a theory of history as relativism and not as fixed process; therefore, human nature must also be relative, not fixed. Postulating that man was carried along by impersonal forces toward some specific goal, the older economists could have no appreciation of the fact that man was active, that his desires changed and created change, that human "activity is itself the substantial part of the process." Previous economists could not entertain such a theory of human nature, because the element of chance would upset calculations about mechanical progress. Replace progress with the evolutionary fact of historical relativism, and theories of human nature would inevitably change too.

What evidence did Veblen have that economic theory was almost all pre-Darwinian? How could he back up the assertions of his article? In rapid succession, he published three articles on "The Preconceptions of Economic Science," intended to provide the historical proof of his thesis.[4]

Economics, as a formal theory, he wrote, might be said to have begun in the eighteenth century, and in the very citadel of the *philosophes*, France. By common consent, the physiocrats made the first conscious attempt to formulate the laws of economic science. Just as clearly, however, those enlightened ones had not escaped the animism of their savage forebears. Progress, inevitable and absolute, was their central thesis, and they connected progress to the laws of nature. It was an abstract nature to be sure, and yet it was very real — so much so that the physiocrats' central economic thesis was the productivity of those who helped nature. It was the farmer who, above all, created an increment in the vital forces through which progress worked.

When one crossed the channel to England and to the writings of Adam Smith, one met a more sophisticated and more scientific approach to economic reality. Smith was blessed with an environmental background that enabled him, as an Englishman, to surpass his French contemporaries. Isolated from the wars of the continent, endowed with an unbroken continuity of history, seizing leadership in commerce because of geography and this history of peace, the English, in general, could think in less animistic, less personal and willful terms than the French. It was possible for them to think in mechanical terms; the expanding economy, which was now in the process of industrialization, pushed concrete, matter-of-fact knowledge into a position of prestige where it could effectively compete with the irrationalities of spiritual tradition. But, while Smith's writings were marked by a realistic grasp of the economic processes of his day, he still fitted them into a framework that was the design of God and that progressed according to God's teleological plan.

The movement away from animism that marked Smith's writings, however, was accelerated by those English writers who succeeded him as the purveyors of economic tradition. The utilitarians talked less and less of God's beneficent hand ordering the relations of things and wrote instead of the mathematical laws that defined capital, labor, land, and supply and demand, and which were integrated in a frictionless and beneficent competitive system. But the utilitarians, then, had not really escaped the animistic trait of belief in a meliorative trend.

Soon their attenuated animism was reduced still more by men like John Stuart Mill who attacked the continued tradition of hedonism. Once such an attack was made in the name of a more flexible and active human nature, one of the major attitudes of the economic theory of the physiocrats, Smith, and the utilitarians had to weaken. This was the doctrine of natural rights, which had found support in a world of regular economic law based on regular psychological interests. But if the individual were "something more than the field of intersection of natural forces that work out in human conduct," how could natural right be defined?

And then the truly classical economists, Marshall and Cairnes, denied the whole concept of economics as the expression of a meliorative trend. Science, these Englishmen concluded, had no room for such nonscientific concepts of progress. Now, this English trend to reduce animism and reach objectivity neared a climax as Cairnes and Marshall refused to admit anything but mathematical laws as capable of expressing the impersonal economic world.

Nevertheless, Veblen warned, this trend toward mathematical objectivity had not brought economics to the level of a true science. Cairnes and Marshall, perhaps, had rid economics of the besetting sin of animism, but they had not escaped the institutional framework evolved for the expression of that animism.They rejected laws of

progress, but they could not think beyond normal laws. They elaborated scientific laws which they considered adequate descriptions of
economics and then tested the scientific reality of those laws by
logically forcing experience to coincide with their hypothetical laws.
They had done everything to make economics into a science except
to relate it to reality in the form of matter-of-fact events. As a result,
they were just as much prisoners of their climate of opinion as were
their less emancipated, less scientific predecessors. The mathematical laws of the classicists were just as much an expression of the
values and traditions of the moment as were the natural rights and
goals of progress held by the Enlightenment. What was needed to
make economics a science was to carry this trend away from animism
to its logical conclusion, to place economics in the sweep of history,
considered absolutely as meaningless change, so that there were no
normal laws either for institutions or for men.

Surprisingly, the cynical, amoral Veblen was waxing enthusiastic
and eloquent about the certain, immediate, final transformation of
his economic profession to true, objective, scientific endeavor. He,
who did not believe in progress, had just recounted the progress of
economic thought to a point of culmination. He, who did not believe
in the predictability of man, was prepared to predict man's future.
He could predict man's actions, because he was loyal to the psychology of the Enlightenment which he had attacked; he knew how man
would react in a given environmental situation, because man had a
fixed nature.

One of the ironic masterpieces of Veblen's prose is his description
of the hedonistic definition of human nature:

The hedonistic conception of man is that of a lightning calculator
of pleasures and pains, who oscillates like a homogeneous globule
of desire of happiness under the impulse of stimuli that shift him
about the area, but leave him intact. He has neither antecedent nor
consequent. He is an isolated, definitive human datum, in stable
equilibrium except for the buffets of the impinging forces that displace him in one direction or another. Self-imposed in elemental
space, he spins symmetrically about his own spiritual axis until the
parallelogram of forces bears down upon him, whereupon he follows
the line of the resultant. When the force of the impact is spent, he

comes to rest, a self-contained globule of desire as before. Spiritually, the hedonistic man is not a prime mover. He is not the seat of a process of living, except in the sense that he is subject to a series of permutations enforced upon him by circumstances external and alien to him.[5]

The exponent of evolution as complete indeterminism, Veblen had criticized this hedonism and insisted that man was a prime mover, a seat of the process of living. Strangely, however, as he outlined his criticism of the tradition of scientific economics, this theme had become increasingly inconsequential. He had stated as his initial premise the two great errors of past economics, a belief in progress and an unchangeable human nature. But the emphasis of his critical analysis had more and more centered on animism as the basic weakness of the idea of progress. There could be no science if men believed that nature had such human qualities as will and propensity. He had admired the classic writers like Marshall and Cairnes who had translated economic behavior into colorless statements. He had never praised the German historical economists and their emphasis on man's will.

With each of these articles at the turn of the century, Veblen committed himself more and more to the thesis that concrete, material forces determined what men think and do, and that economic science, indeed, was only interested in charting the impact of economic institutions on man. Did this mean, then, that Veblen had returned to the classical definition that "Spiritually . . . man is not a prime mover . . . that he is subject to a series of permutations enforced upon him by circumstances external and alien to him . . . that he spins symmetrically about his own spiritual axis until the parallelogram of forces bears down upon him"? Was he not saying that there could be no science if men believed that men have such human qualities as will?

One might now write irreverently in Veblen's manner that, at this point, Veblen began to revolve around his own theoretical axis, which was progress. In perhaps his most famous essay, "The Place of Science in Modern Civilization," [6] Veblen elaborated the method by which one could believe in a more active personality than that of

Thorstein Veblen

hedonism and yet keep this individual personality from upsetting the regularity of economic phenomena. Modern Western civilization, Veblen began, had proved itself superior to all other civilizations before the highest of all courts — that of the survival of the fittest in the struggle for existence. Why had this happened? It was because of the matter-of-fact quality of our life, because modern man had given his allegiance to science, because it was the scientist alone who passed on the value and truth of all things.

The question Veblen was most interested in answering, however, was why science had become the controlling element of culture. He began this answer in the most peculiar form of a malicious attack on pragmatism as a psychological theory of individual activity. "The teleological bent of intelligence," Veblen wrote, "is an hereditary trait settled upon the race by the selective action of forces that look to no end. The foundations of pragmatic intelligence are not pragmatic, nor even personal or sensible." [7] But he was not content to stop here; this was not even pragmatism, this hereditary trait of looking to the future with no end in mind; this was curiosity. Pragmatism, the attempt to use intelligence to solve particular problems within particular contexts, was neither a hereditary trait nor a creative outlook.

Primitive man, more controlled by instinct than culture, was motivated to gain knowledge by an instinct of idle curiosity, which had no interest in expedient action. This constant seeking for an objective understanding of the world led to an ever-richer tradition of factual knowledge, which coincided with concrete reality. But as culture developed, this trait was overcome by that of pragmatism, which had been and was a body of maxims of expedient conduct, which did nothing to increase man's constructive knowledge of the world. Unfortunately, civilization through history had really been barbaric in the sense that its basis was force and fraud, both of which naturally accentuated pragmatism as the guide of expedient conduct in a society of mastery and subservience. As Veblen put it, "A shrewd adaptation to this system of graded dignity and servitude becomes a matter of life and death, and men learn to think in these terms as ultimate and definitive." [8]

Now, Veblen declared, salvation has begun for the Western world. Industry became a part of the economy, and workmanship replaced exploitation as the leading cultural trait. "This, of course, amounts to saying . . . that the law of cause and effect was given the first place, as contrasted with dialectical consistency and authentic tradition." The scientist, therefore, had become the leader of our society, and Veblen asked, "How far is the scientific quest of matter-of-fact knowledge consonant with the inherited intellectual aptitudes and propensities of the normal man? And, What foothold has science in the modern culture?"[9]

Happily, Veblen continued, there was a real logical consistency between modern science and savage human nature which guaranteed a permanent place for science in man's future. The ages of barbarian civilization had not been long enough to alter man's primitive characteristics. Furthermore, the cultural habits, such as pragmatism, had been followed only by the aristocrats while the mass of men had lived the vulgar life and so had retained their virgin purity. The idle curiosity of the savage, then, was the direct ancestor of the scientific spirit of civilization. "It is like science in that it has no ulterior motive beyond the idle craving for a systematic correlation of data," but he added, "it is unlike science in that its standardization and correlation of data run in terms of the free play of imputed personal initiative rather than in terms of the constraint of objective cause and effect."[10] There was a certain tension in Veblen's estimation, therefore, between the ways of civilization and savagery on this intellectual level. In many ways, the machine process had removed certain artificial historical additions to human nature which characterized barbarian civilization and allowed the original savage human traits to find expression once more. But the machine process had the added task not only of stripping off barbarian historical traits but also of suppressing the animistic element of man's savage nature.

Such a qualification seems to have saved Veblen from following Ely and Patten the whole way through the paradox of primitivism, progress, and industrialism. Slowly, but surely, Veblen's intellectual analysis of the science of economics was taking shape as that most perfect of radical philosophies. He had placed previous economists and, therefore, the conservatives who leaned on them in the untenable position of holding to pre-Darwinian concepts, which did not grasp that the world, society, and man must all change. Having demonstrated that all existing institutions and traditions were outdated in a new world, he managed to turn his theoretical position of moral neutralism into a prophetic platform. He affirmed that moral neutralism was morally right because it returned men to their primitive qualities. Holding to a theory of cultural stages, from savagery to barbarism to civilization, he began to define civilization, at its highest intellectual level of science, as a return to savagery; he began that paradoxical procession which concluded that industrialism was the basis of civilization because the complexity it created returned men to their natural simplicity. But finally Veblen, unlike Richard T. Ely and Simon Patten, declared that there was a certain fundamental discord between savagery and industrial, scientific matter-of-factness.

Gradually, however, as Veblen continued to write, he brought his history of man to a logical summary in *The Instinct of Workmanship*, which made it apparent that this discord was the logical necessity for making this paradox rational.[11] How else could Veblen, the precise philosopher, explain why savagery was overwhelmed by barbarism if there were not one clearly definable fault in primitive man? In a way, this theory of discord may be the proudly intellectual Veblen's manner of proving to himself that there was a crucial place for reason in a world that was overwhelmingly the product of emotion and brute force.

Man had always been the prisoner of his immediate environment which meant that the majority of men were the prisoners of a few who exploited them. Now Veblen was going to demonstrate that man could escape from his bondage to tradition and to the exploiters. Economic theory was basically a theory of reform; the method of science was a method of reason, and the purpose of reason was to distinguish between the true and the false and to help men to live by truth. For the first time in history, the economic environment allowed man's rational element free play to overcome his more emotional other self. No, this was not a neutral philosophy Veblen was constructing block by block, but a philosophy of reform filled with all the dynamite of enthusiasm and interest.

From the very beginning of his economic writing, then, there had been the tremendous motivation to destroy conservative thought, not because it was unscientific, but because it blocked reform. From the very beginning, he had published in the cause of progress. In 1892 he had begun his attack with an article on Herbert Spencer which demonstrated Veblen's criterion of progress: the cooperative commonwealth that would emerge from the cultural crisis caused by industrialism. Spencer had published an essay, "From Freedom to Bondage," lamenting the rise of socialism.[12] He had used two criticisms: first, that there was no real grievance by which one could excuse the presence of socialism; statistics proved the steady rise in the standard of living; second, and more important, socialism would destroy human liberty. To these accusations, Veblen answered by agreeing that the masses were better off in terms of absolute standards; the socialist agitation was led by men who were relatively well off. The secret of the growth of socialism, Veblen believed, at this point, was the very success of the capitalistic system of private property, which encouraged men to think of prestige in terms of material wealth. The majority of men naturally competed to be able to display more property. Envy was driving the less well-to-do classes to think in terms of socialism, which would guarantee them a more equitable share of the nation's wealth.

But like Spencer, Veblen agreed that the relevant question was socialism and liberty, and it was here that he prepared a full answer. If private property and the urge to emulate one's neighbors in material ways could be circumscribed, Veblen theorized that a far healthier and wealthier nation would emerge. It was not true, as Spencer insisted, that governmental control of the economy would end human liberty. Spencer held up as the only two possible types of human society that of status and that of contract. Ancient man, for Spencer, had lived in a world of status, ruled by a military hierarchy and bureaucracy which choked all initiative. Gradually, men had won their freedom from these institutions to a free society based on contract that was anchored on the institutions of private property and competition.

A more perceptive reading of history, according to Veblen, however, revealed the development of a society neither of status nor contract among the English-speaking peoples. This was the society of constitutional government, operating through impersonal law and impersonal institutions. As against a society of status, where men were subject to personal authority, enshrined in prescription and privilege, the English tradition was a system of subjection to the will of the social organism that was expressed in an impersonal law.

This, clearly, was a tradition very foreign to the idea that society was run by contract and based on private property. Man was free from unjust and arbitrary actions by the government; he was protected by law; but he was responsible to his society and his life was regulated by its laws. There was no logical reason, then, continued Veblen, why the government could not regulate industry within the constitutional tradition without returning society to the bondage of status.[13]

Suddenly, in reading Veblen's glowing description of constitutional government, one is made aware that he had begun to equate this historical position with socialism. Suddenly and without logical transition, Veblen had ceased to equate socialism with the selfishness engendered by capitalism and had associated it with what he considered the best of all social philosophies.

Veblen was finding something in socialism that its great prophet, Karl Marx, had not expressed. Ruthlessly, Veblen had destroyed Marx as a precise thinker. With great care, he had placed Marx in perspective for his readers as a self-contained and highly original theoretician. "Except as a whole and except in the light of its postulates and aims, the Marxian system is not only not tenable, but it is not even intelligible. . . . There is no system of economic theory more logical than that of Marx." [14] Marx, Veblen contended, stood or fell with his system as a whole; he could not be criticized in detail. But what of this logical masterpiece, and what of its postulates? It was a house of cards constructed of pure irrelevancies, Veblen declared; it rested on two metaphysical traditions, the natural-rights liberal school of economists and Hegelian romanticism.

From Hegel, Marx borrowed the idea of progress, necessary progress, culminating in the classless society. From the English, he took his concept of the exploitation of labor by capital and the laborer's claim to the whole product of his labor. He merged the Hegelian notion of a mysterious, upward movement through conflict, expressed by a necessary triadic scheme of thesis, antithesis, and synthesis, with an English-utilitarian view of psychology. There was nothing really materialistic about Marx's theory of the class struggle, Veblen declared; this class struggle was motivated by conscious self-interest. "It is in fact a piece of hedonism and is related to Bentham rather than to Hegel."

When these criticisms were in, what was left in Marx that was of value? Nothing, Veblen declared, but socialism.

From minor points like the labor theory of value, through the major idea of the increasing proletarianization of society, to the necessity of the class struggle, there was nothing that needed to be read in Marx. He was a metaphysician, pure and simple, who never took account of the facts of the surrounding environment, nor was he sensitive enough to begin to question the bases of his metaphysics as the doctrines of Darwin came to liberate men from metaphysics. If Marx had been truly materialistic in accepting the facts of the environment as determining and if he had understood what Darwin was trying to express, he would have developed "a concept of a process of cumulative change in social structure and function; but this process, being essentially a cumulative sequence of causation, opaque and unteleological, could not, without an infusion of pious fancy by the speculator, be asserted to involve progress as distinct from retrogression or to tend to a realization or self-realization of the human spirit or of anything else. Neither could it conceivably be asserted to lead up to a final term, a goal to which all lines of the process should converge and beyond which the process would not go, such as the assumed goal of the Marxian process of class struggle, which is conceived to cease in the classless economic structure of the socialistic final term." [15]

Thorstein Veblen

Yet, Veblen wrote approvingly of the followers of Marx, the younger socialists who had abandoned Marx's false premises to link socialism with Darwin rather than with Hegel. But what was there left in socialism worth continuing? There was evidently Veblen's definition of socialism as constitutional government or rule by impersonal and equal law. There was the increasing affirmation of Veblen that the so-called contract society of the day had not obliterated rule by status. There was the growing enthusiasm of Veblen that the really material processes of life, the factual environment of industrialism, were working to bring society to create true freedom for all men within the rationality of the machine process. The worth of Marx and socialism was not found in their logic but in their struggle to free man from his bondage to socially wasteful institutions; it was the goal of the cooperative commonwealth, based on an appreciation of man's basic worthwhile instincts, that freed socialism from the imperfections of theory and made it a cause to be championed.

Gradually, and one might say inevitably, Veblen had to fuse his science and his socialism. The tremendous surge of emotion that welled up in his writing and dissented from capitalism guaranteed that science should become the weapon of social value. Veblen could not become the first modern economist as he had become the first thoroughgoing critic of past economics. He would not describe American conditions with complete objectivity, without praise or censure, as was fitting in a world without values. At this point, one is reminded of the description of Hume, in Becker's *Heavenly City*, who, in his *Dialogues Concerning Natural Religion*, came to the conclusion that reason could not establish the existence or the goodness of God and, for that matter, the foundation for any system of values. Hume then locked the manuscript away in his desk and turned to the study of history, where one could establish a system of values based on the permanent characteristics of man, because, in Hume's own words, "mankind are so much the same, in all times and places, that history informs us of nothing new or strange in this particular. Its chief use is only to discover the constant and universal principles of human nature."

Veblen had not locked his manuscript away; he had asserted and reasserted that reason, the scientific method of the post-Darwinian epoch, could not establish values. He had even denied the ability of history to perform such deeds because man changed constantly throughout history. But, when Veblen began to write his descriptions of American social and economic science, when he began to discuss subjects other than the theory of science, his philosophy of history and of human psychology shifted radically. Ely and Patten, too, had used evolution and historical relativism to undermine the theories of their opponents, but they had based their positive values on a set of absolute principles, the principles of the natural man who stood above history and who was more than a complex of shifting habits and desires. They were careful to replace what they destroyed. And so it was with Veblen, who denied his role as reformer, who delighted in the destruction of conservative absolutes, but who presented for the edification of his liberal readers a set of values, the altruistic ethics of the natural man, in the tradition of his fellow reformers, Ely and Patten.

Even in his scientific essays, so coldly and calculatingly critical and objective, the idea of the natural man had become a prominent theme. In his important essay, "The Place of Science in Modern Civilization," while he was discussing the fact that modern civilization was now under the influence of science and was "peculiarly matter-of-fact," Veblen asked the question, "how far is the scientific quest of matter-of-fact knowledge consonant with the inherited intellectual aptitudes and propensities of the normal man?" He answered it by writing, "It may seem a curious paradox that the latest and most perfect flowering of the western civilization is more nearly akin to the spiritual life of the serfs and villeins than it is to that of the grange or the abbey";[16] this meant, in the context of the essay, that modern science coincided very closely with the qualities of the normal man who in the era of savagery was motivated by the instinct of idle curiosity, which was also the foundation for modern science. It meant that the savage traits like idle curiosity had been carried largely uncorrupted in the lower classes through history. It meant that these traits were overpowered superficially in the next stage of history, the barbaric, by the characteristics of the aristocrats, the barbaric aristocrats who dwelt in grange and abbey. It meant that Veblen believed modern conditions were making possible the revival of the savage spiritual life.

These were the very terms used by Patten when he divided men into aristocrats, who were creatures of history, creatures of cumulative habit; and into members of the lower classes, who retained the qualities of their original savage state, who were submerged but not obliterated by history, and who were now re-emerging to stamp the new epoch with their permanent and good characteristics. This theme of contrasting a lost Garden of Eden with the evils of the present and forecasting the return of this primitive purity under the discipline of industrial conditions, this "outmoded" philosophy which was used so enthusiastically by Ely and Patten, became the biting edge of Veblen's criticism of his America and his solution to its problems.

Concurrently with his scholarly articles, Veblen published a series of books on which his popular fame was based. Certainly the first of these, the description of the economic manners of the American upper class, the celebrated *Theory of the Leisure Class*, would have been meaningless if Veblen had remained faithful to his statement that he was not making value judgments.[17] The whole theory of history and anthropology of the book was designed to give the reader standards by which to criticize the foibles of America's middle class. Here was no presentation of facts within an evolutionary process without a beginning, without direction, and without a culmination. This was destructive humor with a purpose — to educate an audience that would never read the esoteric, academic articles. This was social satire to destroy loyalty to an established order that had no rational excuse for existence. This was the critical irony of contrast between the pretentiousness of a decadent present and the virile strength of man's vulgar, but beautiful, savage past. This was the qualified promise that the ridiculous antics of the leisured were a step upward from barbarism to the final achievement of civilization.

The ironic humor of the *Theory of the Leisure Class* rests always on the social behavior termed conspicuous waste and conspicuous consumption. Here were the leaders of American capitalistic society, striving desperately to demonstrate their ability to avoid constructive work while, at the same time, they must also demonstrate their economic security by lavishly purchasing those symbolic goods and services that must also have no connection with rational, purposive, creative economic behavior. Was this then the climax of civilization, that cultured women must wear unbearable clothes which proved so plainly that the wearers could not and need not work; or that the male leaders of society should assiduously pursue meaningless games? This, of course, was the tremendous, rollicking joke that Veblen shared with his readers. The poor stuffed shirts, adding further starch to their shirts as evidence of civilization, were really revealing the barbaric cultural level to which they belonged. With the vehemence of the prophet who would laugh the unfaithful from the temple of culture, Veblen never allowed the reader from one page to another to forget that every action of the so-called cultured unfrocked the emptiness of their claim to civilization.

The Victorians who abhorred barbarism were barbaric; this priggish generation who shied away from life was barbaric; the spotless upholders of propriety were barbaric. Surely, Veblen was vengeance, and vengeance was Veblen, as he suddenly introduced barbarism like some horrid, unclean nightmare into the midst of the sterile parlor of the *fin de siècle*. It was funny, it was uproarious, to consider one's pristine maiden aunt, surrounded by unread books and overworked maids, as the glaring representative of barbarism.[18]

But even if the young irreverent college student wanted to believe that his elders, who considered him as a basic threat to civilization, were themselves the true enemies of culture, was the will to believe enough? Clearly, inexorably, Veblen could prove, even to the college student, that all this so-called culture was barbarism in disguise. Yes, Veblen would prove the essential connection.

What was conspicuous waste and consumption, if it were not evidence of ability to live without working? What was the ability to live without working, if it were not evidence of power to exploit? What was the power to exploit but the basic definition of the barbarian age?

Man's long infancy, the age of innocence named savagery, had not known exploitation of man by man. Primitive humanity had lived in simple harmony without the invidious distinction of superior class from inferior class, evidenced by the economic symbols of conspicuous waste and consumption. Gradually, however, the transition was made from homogeneous, peaceful savagery to conflicting, competing, warlike barbarism. The barbarians were the conquerors, those who called themselves nobles, those who lived like parasites on the labor of other men. The full expression of the barbaric stage of social evolution, Veblen continued, was reached in medieval Europe and feudal Japan. It was here that the nonproductive work of the aristocrats was most extensively channeled into warlike activity and the obtruse mysticism of a class of priests.[19]

Even though it somewhat lessened the joke on the present leisure class, Veblen now had to confess that they were not as barbaric as their spiritual ancestors. Although they still lived by exploitation and practiced nonproductive consumption of time, they were not obviously predatory, as were these past historical epochs. Repeating a constant theme, Veblen admitted that capitalism was on the way to civilization as it lifted the leisured class into a quasi-peaceable era which formally observed peace and order. The modern business man was not his pirate forebear. The conditions of his economic system demanded an obedience to law.

Beyond this improvement of the present over the past, so that all that was left of warlike endeavor for the business man was the pursuit of sports, Veblen had to admit still one more basic modern improvement from the height or depth of barbarism. The present was marked by a definite blurring of class lines. The aristocracy and the masses were blending to an unprecedented extent. Veblen was not certain that this was really progress. In one very real sense he felt that the lower class was being corrupted by its ability to imitate the ways, the nonproductive wasteful ways, of the leisure class.

As the common man was freed from strict class discipline, he almost naturally tried to emulate those whom he mistakenly considered his betters. In this way, he was denying the fundamental instinct of workmanship which defined him as a real man, a savage man, and perhaps also a civilized man.[20] Perhaps it was now time for Veblen to make clear just who and what this normal man was, to point out his connection to savagery, and to show how he could be corrupted by the upper classes.

Effortlessly, Veblen explained the relation of savagery to barbarism, history, and evolution. Man, he wrote, was a social animal; society was the immediate human environment. Like the life of other animals, man's social life had always been shaped by the struggle for existence and reflected the process of selective adaptation. Over the sweep of the long unwritten history of humanity, the adaptive process selected certain stable types of temperament and character, which would operate best in man's cooperative effort to survive against a hostile environment. By the time that written history began, evolution had produced the cooperative, altruistic man of savagery. Yet, Veblen continued, there was another aspect of the adaptive process beyond the evolution of deep-rooted personality traits. Men's habits of thought adapted much more quickly to changing environmental circumstances than did these personality traits. It was out of these habits of thought that men developed institutions which were designed to fit the surface changes of history, and man developed secondary superficial personality traits to fit this institutional environment.

This, declared Veblen, was the explanation of barbarism in human history. Under the impact of new situations, men submerged their basic savage nature under barbarian attitudes, which were embodied in barbarian institutions. But the essence of institutions was their relation to the times of which they were a part, in contrast to the timelessness of savagery. The surface environment of man was always changing; this change always forced a new adjustment by institutions to the new environment; the environment had always moved on by the time the institutions were adjusted; institutions, then, were always out of joint with present circumstances.

This was the promise and despair of the present, wrote Veblen, carefully guiding his followers toward the desired conclusion. The new conditions of the modern world were breaking the spell of the barbarian historical environment, and they were allowing the normal savage character of man a chance to stand forth, unsuppressed by acquired attitudes. The development of large-scale business enterprise had been diluting the hold of barbaric qualities on the aristocratic class that had become, in turn, a capitalistic class. Although he retained the exploitive instinct of the barbaric aristocrat, the capitalist was disciplined by his own economic creation to act in such a peaceful and tolerant manner that an even more revolutionary class could appear: the worker. Industrialism was now producing, among the factory workers, the irreverent attitude toward the values of capitalism which was rapidly carrying the workers into a new historical era. This was the hope of the present.

Briefly, it was true, Veblen argued, that the present institutional unsettlement contained an element of despair. The masses had always remained outside of history in the sense that they had not been directly conditioned to barbaric attitudes; passively, they had always remained true to their historical savage background, although they were not in a position to influence society positively. Here, at the moment of the breaking of historical class divisions, there was not only the possibility that the leisure class would partake of the values of savagery but also that the masses would accept the values of the leisured. Indeed, this corruption was evidenced at every side as the workers followed the curse of economic envy — the very cause Veblen had used earlier to explain the rise of socialism.

But, while Veblen might momentarily inject this sober note of caution into his analysis of the disintegration of modern society, the logic of his argument must inevitably lift the reader toward an effervescent optimism. The values of the leisure class were historical values, created by a limited historical situation and necessarily ephemeral; they had no vital power that would ensure their preservation once the conditions that created them were gone. On the other hand, the masses, who were now briefly tempted by these values, were committed by nature to the values of savagery, which were not historical fashions, but inherent character traits that would not be outdated. Furthermore, the conditions of the new historical environment, industrialism, were actually encouraging the resurgence of these primitive qualities. Inexorably, inevitably, the leisure class must disappear, ground as it was between the historical conditions of industrialism and the permanent human personality that was descended from prehistory. The logical setting for Veblen's next book was, therefore, also inevitably established. He had to expound on this process by which the current economic structure was destroying the business civilization and giving rise to the reappearance of savage man. And so he had to write *The Theory of Business Enterprise*.[21]

Modern society was living in two worlds: an old world of history and convention and a new world of industrial environment. This was the opening premise of *The Theory of Business Enterprise*, and the conflicts of the two worlds were the dramatic theme of the book. One understood the basic structure of the present, Veblen recounted, if one grasped that its controlling element was the machine, and if one further understood the ramifications of the hegemony of the machine. In brief, the machine meant standardization of the economy and, ultimately, the whole of life. It was the logic of the machine to destroy human whim and to replace it with rational discipline and order. It was the logic of the machine to produce goods as economically as possible and to distribute them as efficiently and equally as possible. All men were equal before the machine, and all must work efficiently, with certainty and expedition, to keep the machine process working with the regularity of clockwork. This was the final definition of the influence of the machine on human life — that it forced all men to keep pace with the machine's ability to produce and distribute with the regularity of a clock. The machine demanded that men become as rational as the machine.[22]

Over the past centuries, the machine had succeeded in creating an economy, standardized in production and services. There had come to "prevail a degree of standardization and precise mechanical adjustment of the details of every day life, which presumes a facile and unbroken working of all those processes that minister to these standardized human wants." [23] This was the brute fact of existence at the moment — man's well-being was carried along by an economic system of clocklike regularity and clocklike balance. Rationally accepting the machine-delineated world in which they lived, men must train themselves to keep the economy in perfect balance so that full production and distribution of standardized products and services could continue.

Modern society was not rationally adjusted to its economic environment, however, because its leaders were blinded to the facts of the present by their commitment to past conventional values and attitudes. Modern society was controlled by businessmen who acted on assumptions that were historically valid in the seventeenth and eighteenth centuries. This was the conflict between history and the current environment, engendered by the failure of the businessman to comprehend the needs of the day.

The economic beliefs of the businessman, Veblen continued, could be summed up as the belief in private property and the freedom of contract. These sprang from the period in English history when traditional agricultural life became commercial activity. At this moment of confusion, individuals, sensing their freedom from the past and their power to create, postulated that they were naturally the productive unit of the economy and that they naturally had full freedom to dispose of the property they so creatively owned.[24]

To prevent anarchy and to protect their property, these Englishmen of an era of handicraft and petty trade, developed representative and constitutional government. They established an impersonal law, upheld by their own representation in parliament, to protect their absolute rights in the individual ownership and disposal of property. In a very real way, they began to cut their bonds with the barbaric past. The barbaric attitude toward the state had been dynastic with the life of the community directed toward the attainment of honorific gains in meaningless warfare. Now the English businessman had put the state under the control of business for the rational motive of economic expansion and under the direction of the rational authority of a constitution, which guaranteed rule by objective law rather than personal whim. Under the peaceful protection of law and order, business had logically given birth to the machine as the indispensable instrument for greater economic expansion. Business originated the machine and became dependent on it, but the needs of the child soon outgrew the capacity of the parent.[25]

While it was true, therefore, that business was much more rational

221

than the barbarian culture out of which it developed, it, nevertheless, was now introducing an irrational element into an economy more perfectly geared to the tempo of the machine. The modern business-man, thinking like his ancestor of an age of anarchy, assumed that his property was absolute when it was so patently interconnected in a seamless economic structure. Acting like his ancestor, who strove for private gain and who helped the economic process to expand, the modern businessman still thought it was permissible to seek private gain in an economy almost completely socialized. The businessman believed that personal pecuniary profit was still permissible in an impersonally rational system. Therefore, the businessman tended to upset the balanced machine process and to protect himself from criticism behind the courts which continued to uphold the legality of the eighteenth-century concepts.

But while the businessmen, their lawyers and judges, tried to interpret "new facts in terms of accredited precedents, rather than a revision of the knowledge drawn from past experience in the matter-of-fact light of new phenomena," the machine had lifted the masses from bondage to this tradition, and the legal structure of absolute property rights was being questioned by the juries who "speak for the untrained sympathies of the vulgar."

The masses no longer took their values from precedent, but from the machine, and "The discipline of the machine process enforces a standardization of conduct and of knowledge in terms of quantitative precision, and inculcates a habit of apprehending and explaining facts in terms of material cause and effect. It involves a valuation of facts, things, relations, and even personal capacity, in terms of force. Its metaphysics is materialism and its point of view is that of causal sequence." [26]

The majority of men involved in the productive work of the factories were leading the way to a fresh adjustment of society to its economic basis. There was no way that business could stop this trend, because the business world had been built around the machine. There could be no retention of the *status quo* by the businessmen. Their choice was suicide if they attempted to bring back barbarism, which would destroy the continuity of impersonal law so indispensable for the business world. On the other hand, if they accepted the machine they must also accept the end of business, because the machine was destroying the institution of private property. "Broadly, the machine discipline acts to disintegrate the institutional heritage of all degrees of antiquity and authenticity. . . . It thereby cuts away that ground of law and order on which business enterprise is founded." [27]

In this strange new world of sterile objectivity, all of mankind would be on the road to salvation; it would be escaping from a history in which men were always torn between outmoded institutional values and new institutional situations. The machine would guarantee that there would be no more ephemeral historical values. ". . . the mechanically trained classes, trained to matter-of-fact habits of thought, show a notable lack of spontaneity in the construction of new myths or conventions as well as in the reconstruction of the old." [28]

With tongue in cheek, Veblen could write that "The machine is a leveler, a vulgarizer, whose end seems to be the extirpation of all that was respectable, noble, and dignified in human intercourse and ideals." [29] What he really meant was that all such historically valid ideals were to be destroyed; barbarism was to be destroyed; and history was to be destroyed, because history was the barbaric age between the purity of savagery, when men lived by truly noble instinct, and civilization, when these instincts could be retained.

The Instinct of Workmanship completed Veblen's grand scheme of outlining the essentials of human life from past to present. At last, he was drawing together all the threads of his discussion of social development through the stages of savagery, barbarism, and the forecast of the civilization that was to be. He was ready to explain fully how civilization was a return to savagery and yet not a simple imitation of the primitive past. Clearly, he would demonstrate that there was no paradox in the blending of the environment of industrial complexity and the spiritual qualities of the prehistoric man.

From an understanding of what human psychology was now like, Veblen reconstructed in detail the conditions that must have made men what they were. "This savage mode of life, which was, and . . .

is native to man, would be characterized by a considerable group solidarity within a relatively small group, living very near the soil, and unremittingly dependent for their daily life on the workmanlike efficiency of all the members of the group. The prime requisite for survival under these conditions would be a propensity unselfishly and impersonally to make the most of all the material means at hand and a penchant for turning all resources of knowledge and materials to account to sustain the life of the group." [30]

This was, of course, Cooley's primary group, and it was the basis for a theory of natural rights. Veblen did not mean that civilization was to be without values. Not at all. Modern man had no need for new values, for new conventions; he had them built in, ready made, from his savage inheritance. Stripped of all that was false and pernicious, man could, at last, go back to the native proclivities that "alone make anything worthwhile." These are the instincts of workmanship that lead men to high social and material productivity and pride in their jobs — the instinct of parental bent which is broader than a family feeling and leads men to a broad humanitarianism and concern for the welfare of the whole community, and the instinct of idle curiosity which is the basis of all progressive knowledge.[31]

As these instincts were expressed through habit and as habits became conventionalized in institutions, a complex pattern of life emerged in which the instincts contaminated each other and led to the regressive stage of barbarism where men came under the habits of predation and self-aggrandizement. This weakness in man was unavoidable. "It appears, then, that so long as the parental solicitude and the sense of workmanship do not lead men to take thought and correct the otherwise unguarded drift of things, the growth of institutions . . . will commonly run at cross purposes with serviceability and the sense of workmanship." [32]

As modern capitalism developed, Veblen saw the progressive freeing of the instinct of workmanship from the bonds of barbarian habits; the machine process made possible the flowering of the instinct of idle curiosity; and the destruction of class divisions and distinctions in the industrial order would further the community spirit of the parental bent.

Above all, the machine process was causing men to think in terms of impersonal sequence. This meant that the instinctive savage attitude of animism, which had served to corrupt the instinct of idle curiosity, was held in check. And it was idle curiosity which served to balance and orient the more basic instincts of workmanship and parental bent. Once freed, therefore, from the debilitating cross-currents of animism, it could efficiently serve its purpose of keeping the two fundamental instincts operating in the most fruitful manner.

The machine had then freed man from history; it had made his truly rational element, idle curiosity, superior to his emotional outlook of animism; and it had been animism which had kept him trapped in history defined as the curse of unending cumulations of habits without value and meaning. Veblen had followed Ely and Patten to state the paradox that man gained creative freedom through the working of an impersonal economic and social force like industrialism.

Indeed, Veblen, as he was about to enter his openly reformist years of World War I and after, began to sound even more suspiciously like the Christian philosopher Ely and the quasi-Christian thinker Patten. Both had agreed that the historical traditions of man, with the exception of Christianity, had worked at cross purposes to his primitive nature. Both had seen in Christianity a spiritual tradition that had kept alive the ideals of primitive goodness; and both had looked to Christianity as a source of cultural stability that would ease the transition of society from its competitive basis to the era of cooperation. Veblen, writing in 1910, followed the pattern of thinking of Ely and Patten almost to the letter. Western civilization, he wrote, is based at the moment on two major traditions, that of competitive business and that of Christianity. It was important, Veblen believed, to discover if they "further and fortify one another? Do they work together without mutual help or hindrance? Or do they mutually inhibit and defeat each other?" [33] These questions were important to Veblen, because he had a still more basic question in mind: Could Western civilization survive if one or the other of these traditions disappeared?

The answers to all of the questions were only to be found through

225

the establishment of their historical background. Christianity, Veblen explained, was based on two principles: humility and brotherly love. It appeared as a force in Western civilization during the collapse of the Roman Empire for two reasons which explain the two principles that were its foundation. In the first instance, that of humility, the discipline of daily life for most of the people was the experience of defeat and the necessity of submission. This was the cultural source of humility in the habits of the day. Brotherly love, however, came not from habit but rather from its destruction. During the period of disaster, "The pride of caste and all the principles of differential dignity and honor fell away, and left mankind naked and unashamed and free to follow the promptings of hereditary savage human nature which make for fellowship and Christian charity." [34] This, to Veblen, explained the lasting power of Christianity through the ages; it was based on a permanent human nature which "springs eternal" when the pressure of conventionality is removed.

As against the bedrock on which Christianity was grounded, Veblen stated that the competitive principle of business went back no farther than the eighteenth century and reflected the cultural values of this limited historical period. Anchored only on ephemeral habits of mind and the institutions that rested on those habits, the competitive principle was disappearing from a world in which the machine process was inculcating new habits of thought.

Veblen was now in a position to answer his questions concerning the relations of Christianity and the competitive system. They did not further each other, they did not help each other, nor did they mutually defeat each other. One was dying, and one was growing stronger. One represented a phase of Western civilization, and one represented the essence of it. Western civilization would survive, therefore, the disappearance of the competitive principle. The machine process with its impetus to the savage instincts of workmanship, idle curiosity, and parental bent would further the development of the Christian tradition. Expressing as much enthusiasm as was possible in his scientific and objective prose, Veblen wrote:

"There is little in the current situation to keep the natural right of pecuniary discretion in touch with the impulsive bias of brotherly love, and there is in the spiritual discipline of the situation much that makes for an effective discrepancy between the two. Except for a possible reversion to a cultural situation strongly characterized by ideals of emulation and status, the ancient racial bias embodied in the Christian principle of brotherhood should logically continue to gain ground at the expense of the pecuniary morals of competitive business." [35]

Veblen's faith in inexorable progress is much less apparent than that of Ely and Patten; [36] but it is also inescapably evident that he shared their paradoxical concept of progress defined as a return to primitive human qualities, set free by industrialism — a concept shared by other thinkers of their generation.

Walter Rauschenbusch PROPHET

T HERE is a great deal of Veblenian humor in the fact that Veblen began his academic career as a philosopher. Veblen must have enjoyed the irony of his ruthless criticism of the irrelevant logic-choppers who had ignored his genius. There is a still finer irony, however, in the relation of Veblen's scientific economic postulates to the first important writing he published in his youthful philosophic years. Interpreting and analyzing Kant's critique of judgment, he outlined the essentials of the problem of reconciling practical reason and pure reason.[1] According to Kant, he wrote, man had the faculty of practical reason, which guaranteed freedom to the individual as men used this reason to exert causality on their environment. Men grasped their world through understanding and chose modes of acting that stamped them as creative individuals. But if each individual acted freely according to his unique experience, what then was morality? What were the common standards against which his choices could be measured? Somehow, continued the Veblen of 1880, Kant believed that this practical, creative reason, or understanding, was sublimated to and contained within a world of pure reason which controlled men's actions. Arguing closely, in orthodox metaphysical language, Veblen pointed to the necessary conclusion of a final strict determinism, an idealistic determinism in which "The idea of what the world was to be precedes and conditions the world as it actually comes into existence."[2] There was a final cause.

But, in practical terms, Veblen concluded, men could ignore the intimate presence of the final cause because, while it was an ideal all-embracing force, it found expression in the immediate, material aspects of life and men could only discover final meaning, piece by piece, through induction, through the scientific method. ". . . by induction alone can we get such knowledge as will enable us to forecast the future; and knowledge which shall help us to forecast the future — to tell what will take place under given circumstances and as the result of given actions — is the only knowledge which can serve as a guide in practical life, whether moral or otherwise." [3]

Veblen had cut the traditional Gordian knot of philosophy posed by Kant: how to reconcile human free will and divine moral determinism. Self-confidently, he had affirmed that induction could take the place of philosophical discussion, that the persistent use of human intelligence could discover, in the unfolding of history, what abstract logic could not attain. And Veblen's own writings, as an economist, were to serve as the triumphant proof of his philosophical position. He had rejected metaphysics, he had even rejected the idea of final cause, he had placed his faith entirely in induction and science; and then, by abandoning all conscious searching for morality, he had proved the morality of the world; he had demonstrated that individual actions must coincide with universal purpose.

Perhaps he confused himself and his contemporaries by defining the Ideal Force or God as the impersonal action of evolution working through industrialism. But his conclusions were the orthodox ones of his American contemporaries who openly avowed their faith in the religion of progress, and for Veblen the mundane force of industrialism operated in the same transcendental way as the spiritual deity of an Ely or a Patten. Industrialism was the force of progress at once in history considered as relativism and in that "History" which was inevitable progress; it was that force which simultaneously lifted the individual out of imperfect society and made him part of the perfect "society." If the mature Veblen no longer spoke in terms of metaphysical idealism, it was only because the ideal had found a perfect vehicle of expression in material forms.

Finally, to complete the religious continuity from Ely to Patten to Veblen, there is the point of individual activism. Ely and Patten urged the individual to exercise his free will; they proved his freedom to choose; then, they affirmed his necessary allegiance to an ideal purpose which predetermined this freedom. Veblen began his argument with his predecessors' conclusion: that the individual must conform to the force that was bringing his salvation. But if all were predetermined, why did Veblen write these massive attacks on the *status quo*? Why did he try to give the individual some standard of judgment by which to condemn the present? Why did he increasingly point out that industrial change was in the nature of a crisis in which civilization might perish? Why did he deliberately associate the values, which he felt should be established, with traditional religious values if he were not interested in inspiring individuals to act creatively to bring about the preordained?

Indeed, there was no reason why the expressly religious prophets of progress who read Veblen should have found in his writings anything but the same overt encouragement of the kind of prophetic Christian doctrine of progress which Richard Ely had made in the 1880s. For a Christian minister like Walter Rauschenbusch, who had discovered Ely in the 1890s, Veblen might stand as a rocklike authority for the intimate relation of industrial crisis and human salvation through religion.[4] As a minister of the gospel who was also aware of the last two decades of economic and sociological writing, Rauschenbusch was perfectly qualified for that task of synthesis which would blend science and revelation into an explicit fighting faith. It would be Rauschenbusch who could find inspiration in mundane methods of induction without the embarrassment of those like Veblen who had to qualify the onward rush of progress with the outward appearance of objective neutrality. Like a virtuoso exercising his skill in counterpoint, Rauschenbusch demonstrated how this complex of dualistic idealism, composed of faith and reason, could be explained in traditional theological language understandable to the average American.

Christianity and the Social Crisis was the title Rauschenbusch gave his first important book in 1907.[5] And the churchman wrote that this social crisis was economic in nature. Industrialism, he began, had destroyed the past and had opened the door to a totally new era in history. Furthermore, this break from the past was not to be defined as mere change or novelty; that would not make this a new era. There had always been change; the record of history was always change. A new period in world history must mean a change from the equilibrium of the past, which had neither seen man escape from the evil of his nature nor completely succumb to it. This, however, was Armaggedon. Mankind must now find either complete salvation or pass completely into the hands of evil powers.[6]

Fortunately, Rauschenbusch argued, the industrial revolution, which had brought the crisis, had also constructed the foundations for a Heavenly City of God on Earth. The constructive elements of the present, its more sensitive means of communication and speeded transportation, blending peoples into one great, friendly community, were made clear by the economists and sociologists. But, warned Rauschenbusch, economic developments alone could not save man. The optimistic picture he had painted was intended to encourage the individual by revealing that the crisis was not merely catastrophic. Yet the crisis was catastrophic if men did not continue to force the new industrial world into a healthy pattern. Untended, the basically good economic trends would disintegrate, causing the total collapse of civilization. If men acted, they would have the material environment on their side. If they passively accepted their fate, industrialism would destroy them. This was the alternative.

Finally Rauschenbusch affirmed, therefore, that it was not the environment which would determine man's future, but it was man's free choice which would determine the shape of his environment. The proper environment would bring out the best in human nature, but human nature must transcend its immediate surroundings to create the ideal material conditions of life. So it was then that the prophet Rauschenbusch announced that mankind desperately needed the inspiration of religious faith that would raise it above itself to wield the control over the future that was necessary to assure total salvation. Only the enthusiasm born of a Christian revival could assure the birth of the new era.[7]

But what was the crisis and what was the Christianity which should inspire men, and how should they act when they understood their task? Writing lines of total despair and magnificent optimism around the concept of cataclysm, Rauschenbusch felt no need to define terms immediately beyond the fact that Christianity, as a faith, was threatened. To know this faith, to grasp its inspiration, was the responsibility of every American, and it was the added responsibility of every Christian minister to open the minds of his contemporaries to the message of Christianity. This message, which would transform the world, was one which could at once lift Americans out of their complacency, teach them to fight to control the future, and also teach them what that future was to be.

In spite of the teachings of the churches throughout history, Rauschenbusch thundered, it had always been the essential purpose of Christianity "to transform human society into the Kingdom of God by regenerating all human relations and reconstituting them in accordance with the will of God." [8] Even before Christ's direct teachings, he continued, the Hebrew prophets had proclaimed the fundamental truth that religion must find expression in ethical conduct and that the perfection of ethical behavior in human society was the highest religious act. God had revealed himself through history, and the study of the historical roots of Christianity then clarified God's message to man.[9]

Here, Rauschenbusch urged, was a point where theology and historical theory merged. The God of the prophets, the God of Christianity, was personal and active, taking interest and working at all times in the world. In short, God had not finished His creation, but was constantly perfecting His work. There was no final revelation to be found in the Bible or in the words or writings of any of the Lord's spokesmen. Each generation must constantly find divine truth for itself. This was the truth which secular historians had also discovered at the beginning of the twentieth century. There was no finished structure of the historical past to be enshrined in perfect exposition in history books. History was changing, growing, and every generation must discover its own past; in a sense, it made its own past.[10]

Theologically, Rauschenbusch was limiting God's omnipotence. His God was personal, present in a creative sense in the world at all times. Obviously, however, this God was not the complete author of the world He was creating. He was creating a moral world out of some kind of recalcitrant material, which must be subdued to the proper purposes. The ideal of perfection had always existed in God's mind, but it had not yet found full expression. Here, then, was the God of Rauschenbusch's contemporaries: the limited, but ultimately triumphant God of F. H. Johnson. He was immanent in that He was working in this world, but He was transcendent in that He could not be defined merely in terms of the world as it existed at any given moment. The ideal purpose existed always outside of time, waiting to find ultimate expression in the world and to stop the flow of history. From the divine aspect, there were then two histories. One was that of mundane appearance, seemingly the record of chance occurrences. The other was progress according to divine will which actually entered into everyday happenings and shaped them into the pattern of progress.

For Rauschenbusch and for his readers, there now appeared the burning question of man's relation to these two histories. If God were not omnipotent, if He still had to overcome and spiritualize the brute matter of the world, was man a part of his natural surroundings and also made up of nonspiritual elements subject to the evolution of God's plan of progress? The traditional Christian viewpoint of man's dual character would seem to support this view. Rauschenbusch, however, rejected the orthodox view of man's inherent sinfulness. As an adherent of evolution as spiritual progress he subscribed to Johnson's thesis that man had evolved out of nonspiritual matter until, at the beginning of written history, he suddenly attained full spirituality. For Rauschenbusch, however, it was enough to ignore the prehistorical state of man and begin his analysis of man's relation to God and the world with the assumption that man's nature was completely good, completely spiritual. Without fear of contradiction, Rauschenbusch wrote: "History is never antiquated, because humanity is always fundamentally the same." [11]

This did not contradict his previous statement that men lived in an ever-changing history because there were the two histories: one of change, and one of permanence. For Rauschenbusch, mankind, at the beginning of written history, was a pure expression of God. The original family group was the model for the perfect society which was the culminating point of progress, of God's effort to spiritualize the world. The Hebrew tribes had lived in anticipation of God's final triumph in their primitive democracy without social caste and with an equal distribution of property. The Hebrew prophets had preached the gospel of the coming social utopia when they emphasized social solidarity based on fraternal love: that sin and salvation were social not individual. The prophets had forecast the ultimate completion of the spiritualization of the world when they had refused to speculate about heaven and had argued that "God must prove His justice here or never." [12]

In essence, then, man was not of this world but of God. As a child of God, he was perfect. But he had been placed on earth as the necessary agent of God's purpose. Here again Rauschenbusch assumed the limitation of divine power. Matter could not be made to express the ideal without the activity of mankind. This was the realm of human freedom and responsibility. Men were creators and they alone made the final choice to carry out God's will or to allow the imperfect earth to remain unsanctified.

Humanity, the expression of God on this planet, necessarily shared in the two histories. As part of the ideal, mankind transcended its environment and lived in the realm of divine history with unchanging principles of progress. It had the potential for perfection, but it had to build the environment for the full fruition of this potential. It was, therefore, committed to mundane history which was characterized by meaningless relativism except insofar as man managed to force this history to conform to history as progress and perfection.

Unfortunately, according to Rauschenbusch's explanation of the divine drama, mankind, like its creator, was not powerful enough immediately to transform the material environment. Humanity, indeed, was so weak that it was influenced by its amoral surroundings. To an extent, Rauschenbusch retreated from his assertion of the absolute goodness of human nature. Or rather, he insisted that man had two natures: one, the exalted, enduring spiritual core given by God, and the other, plastic, susceptible to manipulation by brute externals. This situation set the stage for what so far had been the tragedy of human history — the suppression of the human potential by the imperfections added to man's historical character.

Although all men five thousand years ago were innately perfect, historically, they were far from being the proper agents of God. Above all, they had not yet reached self-conscious comprehension of their own nature or their relation to God. Gradually, however, the Lord began to make men aware of themselves and their destiny through his chosen people, the Jews. Through the centuries before Christ, a succession of prophets explained the sanctity of the group and its responsibility to carry out God's mission on earth. But, in its very emphasis on the Jewish group, this religion failed to express the truth of the fraternity of all men in the eyes of the Father; it was a narrow and nationalistic faith which erred not only in denying God to all men, but also in not emphasizing the religious importance and role of the individual.[13]

Then this national religion of the Jews, directed toward the salvation of the group in this world, was shattered by foreign conquerors. In one sense, this was advantageous to the progress of understanding the true faith. The possibility of national fulfillment was destroyed and the Jews, for the first time, turned to personal religion. This gain, however, was balanced by a serious reversal. The impossibility of a perfected mundane Jewish community drove the newer Hebrew prophets to shift the goal of salvation from an immediate factual future to a far-off utopian dream. With the focus and magnet for immediate ethical reform removed, ceremonialism increased, making ritual more important than practice.[14]

This was the debilitating situation of religious thought when God caused His son Jesus to be born into the world. For Rauschenbusch, whose major philosophical presuppositions rested on the assumption of the divinity of all men, Jesus was not all important in history as the son of God, but as the first man. It was Jesus who first realized what man's potentiality and responsibility were. It was he who first fully explained what the Fatherhood of God and the brotherhood of man meant — that love is the key to God's relation to man and also that of man to man. It was Jesus who transcended his Jewish background and made the Jewish national faith universal while he, at the same time, returned it from other worldly speculation to the business of this world. It was Jesus who argued that salvation must be individual and yet fully integrated with the inherent gregariousness of humanity; the individual must save himself; he must do this by saving his society, and his society included all men. It was Jesus who said that mankind must accept the responsibility of its own salvation without direct intervention from heaven. It was he who added that this salvation must be accomplished according to the doctrine of love, without bloodshed and violence.[15]

It was Jesus, above all, who realized that salvation would be accomplished slowly and gradually without any divine catastrophe and that this salvation would eventually culminate in the establishment of the Kingdom of God on Earth. Jesus, indeed, according to Rauschenbusch, was the first evolutionist. He grasped that the process of progress, or spiritualization, worked slowly through something like organic development as higher and more ideal forms rose above the nonethical brute stuff of this world. Accordingly, Jesus was the constant attacker of all established law and religious ceremonialism. The institutions of any period expressed man's past progress, but it was his destiny to strive forward and upward and to make his institutions conform to the transcendental ideal which constantly inspired him. The past, the given, the orthodox, must always be outdated until the Kingdom was reached. Until that time, men must be guided by the living faith, not by its temporary, mundane trappings.[16]

But temporarily, this world with its history overcame man's potentiality as it had found perfect expression in the teachings of Jesus. Men had the fatal weakness that part of their natures was shaped by custom which they could not overcome. A series of false ideas and attitudes, carried along by the inertia of history, perverted or diverted the message of Jesus. Out of the Jewish past came the idea of millennialism, the hope of the immediate return of Christ. With it marched the equally vicious fallacy of other worldliness, the belief that this world would end and the Second Coming would mean escape to heaven. From the Greek environment in which Christianity took root, were added the debilitating doctrines of extreme individ-

ualism and hostility to the state; and worst of all, the lack of awareness that the family was the social cell, the model of the perfect
society in miniature. Slowly, Christianity was twisted by the Greco-
Roman environment reinforced by Jewish millennialism into a
doctrine of asceticism which found its ultimate expression in monas-
ticism. The Christian, interested above all in his individual soul,
would abandon the corruption of the Roman Empire to await the
imminent end of the world.[17]

Consequently, since the majority of men must live in this world,
the Church, led astray by its best men who had rejected their
responsibility to society, fell into the hands of the secular traditions
of the Empire. This meant that the Church quickly lost its initial
democratic organization and was modeled after the authoritarianism
of the secular government. Still further, the Church leaders, who
were no longer motivated by the ideal of social regeneration and
who could not follow an impossible asceticism, surrendered themselves to those who controlled secular life for the benefit of their own
selfish interest.[18]

Here, Rauschenbusch declared to his Christian readers, here was
the history of the Christianity you had been taught to believe followed the inspiration of Christ. What passed for Christianity in the
twentieth century bore almost no relation to the truths preached by
Jesus. And it was time for a religious awakening that would return
the Church to its proper task of reforming the world according to
Christ's doctrine of love. Rejoice and take heart, he urged the faithful, in this effort of reformation, for "The sadness of the failure . . .
is turned into brightest hopefulness if we note that all the causes
which have hitherto neutralized the social efficiency of Christianity
have strangely disappeared or weakened in modern life." [19]

First, and of greatest importance, the majority was no longer
ground under heel, but had risen through democracy to a command-
ing place in society and government. Inherently, democracy, with its
fraternalism, was the secular parallel of the Christian doctrine of
brotherly love. In many ways, democracy had opened the door for
greater freedom of discussion, greater agitation against the corrupt
minority that tried to suppress progress and utilized an equally

corrupt church in its conservative aims. Democracy, too, was based on a faith in human ability in this world, and so it had turned men away from the notion of an immediate catastrophic millennium. Furthermore, democracy, in its self-confidence, had lost the primitive fear and distrust of the state; it was willing to use governmental machinery for reform. Democratic self-confidence had already begun to force the doctrines of the Church away from asceticism, ceremonialism, and dogmatism; democracy was committed to a faith in experimentation for the most efficient ways of controlling the social and physical environment. And finally, democracy had at hand the perfect tool for reform: social science which revealed the course of human progress.[20]

For the first time since Christ, men had grasped the truth of evolution and history. They had learned, therefore, that the world, natural and social, had been constantly changing and "that the present system of social organization, as it superseded others, may be displaced by something better." Evolution and historical relativism had melted the conservative defense of the *status quo*; they had proved the possibility of reform. Coupled with this intellectual revolution was the development of sociology, economics, and political science, which provided the reformers with the laws of social development on which to build their new society. Now Rauschenbusch related his doctrine of the two histories to social science. The sociologist, the economist, could see that the history which man was living and had lived was ephemeral; he could also see beneath this meaningless multiplicity to the laws of that history which was progress. Looking at the past orderly working of God in the world, he could predict what the next step of progress was to be.

If Rauschenbusch believed that the historical trend of democracy was progress and that men had the intellectual tools to bring about adjustment to the future development of progress, why was it necessary to have a religious revival? On what logical grounds could he return to his harsh warning of crisis — that "We are standing at the turning of the ways. We are actors in a great historical drama. It rests upon us to decide if a new era is to dawn in the transformation of the world into the kingdom of God, or if Western Civilization is to descend to the graveyard of dead civilizations and God will have to try once more." [21]

The crisis was here, Rauschenbusch urged, because the industrial revolution, which had created the wealth and broken the stability of classes so that democracy could emerge, was now at work destroying democracy. Industrialism, in breaking up the old provincial class-bound world, had made possible the intimate association between all men that could make for worldwide fraternity. Disastrously, however, this economic change had taken place within a framework of older traditions that were corrupting it. The institution of private property had survived out of the past to allow a single class of rich to appropriate now the greatest share of the new wealth and to use that wealth to entrench themselves against possible reform. Slowly but surely, they were gaining control of the total economy and, eventually, would also dominate all of society.

With their organized selfishness, they would destroy the possibility of universal fraternity and true Christianity. The people, the common people, must rise up to take conscious control of the economy, to bend its material forces into the creation of the foundations for the cooperative commonwealth. But, without a religious revival, humanity would remain a prisoner of those who controlled the wealth and the communications of society, those who created values for the common man. Inspiration was needed to give the individual perspective beyond his immediate society. This was why, without a religious revival, it would be impossible to use the tools of social science for progress. The laws of the future could be predicted, but they would not come into being automatically; they would have to be established by human effort. And men could not do this through the exercise of reason. Since every man was part of his society, since he owed allegiance to the *status quo*, he was not capable of transcending the present to participate in the future unless he was inspired by religion.

"No man can help the people until he is himself free from the spell which the present order has cast over our moral judgment. . . . The men of faith are the living spirits, the channels by which new truth and power from God enter humanity." [22]

In spite of this crisis, however, when one looked at the present in a different light, every element of the situation provided reassuring evidence to Rauschenbusch that his contemporaries would transcend their society and escape its embodiment of the irrelevancies of the past. God had never ceased to work for his final purpose; the centuries between Jesus and the present had carried humanity far along the path of salvation. More than at any previous time in history, this generation questioned the sanctity of the *status quo*. Industrialism had snapped much of the continuity with the past and had set men free to think for themselves. Science, embodied in social disciplines like economics and sociology, had brought men to examine the rationality of institutions. These were the fundamental conditions that prepared individuals to open their minds and hearts to the transcendent word of God and to commit themselves to the establishment of the divine vision that was given to them. Daringly, Rauschenbusch brought his book to a climax with these hopeful lines: "Perhaps these nineteen centuries of Christian influence have been a long preliminary stage of growth, and now the flower and fruit are almost here." [23]

His next book, *Christianity and the Social Order*, was based on the belief that his hope had become a certainty.[24] Rauschenbusch then wrote, with full elation, this preface in 1912: "When 'Christianity and the Social Crisis' was published in 1907, I thought I had said all that God had given me to say on our social problems. . . . But meanwhile the social awakening of our nation set in like an equinoctial gale in March. . . ." The mystery of spiritual inspiration and regeneration had occurred in the hearts of the majority of Americans. "This," he proclaimed, "is religious energy, rising from the depth of that infinite spiritual life in which we all live and move and have our being. This is God." [25]

Yet it was not mysterious that America and the civilized world should be swept into utopia at this moment. There were the clear lines of God's evolutionary progress shaping mundane history through the last several centuries, blending conditions to create a pattern that could serve as a final springboard for humanity to transcend imperfect history for the fulfillment of the perfection of divine history. The Reformation had broken the power of Rome to keep men's creative spiritual energies from finding expression in this world. The Enlightenment of the eighteenth century had given men democracy and science. Democracy meant a collective self-consciousness and understanding of their own instincts and needs by the common people. This, in turn, brought the masses to demand a good life for themselves in terms of the social message of Jesus. Democracy had also given the people the educational background necessary to visualize science as the directive power to fulfill social needs. With unbounded enthusiasm, Rauschenbusch drove on to the conclusion that "The largest and hardest part of the work of Christianizing the social order has been done." [26]

A summary of the major institutions that marked the modern world, born during the Enlightenment, demonstrated clearly the overwhelming degree to which life had come into harmony with the ethical convictions of Jesus. The family, the basic social cell, was marked by cooperation, love, equality, and respect for the individual, and these traits would also ultimately define society. Slowly, the perfection of the family had spread out to the rest of society under the driving impetus of historical change since the Reformation. The churches, freed from the weight of false historical tradition embodied by the medieval papacy, could become truly Christianized. As individual churches were no longer associated with the authoritarianism of empire, this structure was democratized. Standing as the representatives of individual congregations, they became much more responsive to the changing earthly needs of each generation. They relearned, therefore, the last message of Jesus: service in the world. And as this service was associated with human needs rather than institutional dignity, they regained the fundamental message of love.[27]

Spontaneously, out of the new world of life and growth and hope, a world which encouraged men to think in terms of experimentation and fulfillment of potentialities, also came a new philosophy of education — freedom. Learning that life lay in the future rather than in the past, men no longer accepted education as a tyranny, as an acceptance of blindly held aristocratic principles of obedience

241

and conformity. Democratic forms fostered democratic education which returned, as the spirit of experimentation, to strengthen the whole basis of democracy. Then, finally, with the revolutions at the end of the eighteenth century, democracy began to conquer politics. Fundamentally, Rauschenbusch argued, politics was democratized. Everyone accepted the theory that the majority must rule its own affairs through its political institutions. Furthermore, he continued, adequate governmental techniques had been worked out for this purpose. But he also admitted that politics in practice was not democratic. This, however, was not the fault of political theory or political institutions; it was to be attributed to the economy with which politics was connected.[28]

The economy of capitalism, declared Rauschenbusch, was the only institutional aspect of American life that was not Christianized. It was the final citadel of historical imperfection which would be swept away by the current religious revival. Even now, in the full sweep of his optimism, Rauschenbusch continued the warning of his first book: unless the revival were carried to the successful conclusion of converting capitalism to Christianity, capitalism would destroy Christianity.

Western man, he wrote, should be grateful to capitalism for creating so much of the necessary material environment for the Heavenly Kingdom. It was capitalism which made possible the industrial revolution. The enterprise of capitalists had begun large-scale cooperative economic endeavors; the enterprise of capitalists had linked science to business in the fruitful marriage of technology and theory, so that constant invention and material progress became the mark of our society. This was the constructive and necessary history of capitalism. Nevertheless, Rauschenbusch added, as he continued a direct parallel of Veblen's historical analysis of capitalism, the capitalist, using cooperative methods of organization and applied technology, had remained a businessman. As a businessman, he had had no real interest in service to the community. His only real interest had been profit; his was a purely selfish outlook, rationalized by a theory of the benevolence of competition. There was never anything rational in his development of large-scale factories or in his use of practical inventions. When it was profitable to organize, to build, to become more efficient, he did those things; but when it was profitable to destroy or impair the efficiency of production, then he would follow the interests of self rather than society.

Inevitably, this antisocial competitive urge for material gain was negating the constructive work of capitalism. Competition was an unnatural human attitude in direct conflict with man's propensity for cooperation. Since all institutions were built from the economic base, they could not avoid contamination by the economic focus and attitudes of society. Competition would inevitably be carried into every aspect of life so that even in the family, brother competed with brother; in education, student with student; in religion, church with church; and in politics, social group with social group. Truly, it had to be reiterated that Christianity and cooperation must convert capitalism or be destroyed by it.[29]

Yet history was working against capitalism and for Christianity in this battle for total triumph or total defeat. Rauschenbusch concurred with Veblen's belief that the logic of industrialism was against the spirit of business. The businessman depended for profit upon the techniques of large-scale organization and scientific, technological advance. Slowly but inexorably, these institutions habituated all of the community to the rationality of efficient production.

While even the capitalists were learning to live in a new world of cooperation, it was the laboring class which had first felt the full influence of the new economic structures. The first full expression of the ethics of the cooperative commonwealth, then, was given by the fast-growing labor movement. Since God's will must find embodiment in this world as it worked for a final fulfillment in His Kingdom here, since it must be carried to victory by men, the labor movement was to be seen as the last great divinely material agency for the triumph of the cooperative commonwealth.

But the triumph of the laboring class in forging the utopia would not require destruction or negation of any existing classes or institutions except that of monopoly capitalism. Labor which had, at first, leaned toward doctrinaire socialism was returning to the path of moderation. Abandoned and attacked by the traditional church,

243

labor had proclaimed the heresy of material socialism, denying the guidance of God. With the transformation of the churches to social Christianity, however, labor realized the necessary spiritual basis of society. Similarly, the first stirrings of labor had been met with stern repression by the possessing middle class, and labor had naturally talked of class warfare. As the middle-class church reformed itself, however, it pointed the direction for the mass of middle-class citizens. In North America, the labor movement had become the progressive movement. While labor might supply the weight and energy for the achievement of the Christian commonwealth, the American middle class would now provide the leadership. There was no danger from uncivilized labor in America, Rauschenbusch reassured his middle-class readers, because the laboring men were, after all, "tools in the hands of the Almighty," and one might add, tools in the hands of the middle class.

After all, the militant Rauschenbusch had qualified his extremely radical terminology. He had written that capitalism was but a limited stage of economic evolution, standing between primitive communism and the communism of the concluding historical era of industrial communism. Now he explained that communism was but a translation of the more gentle era of cooperation defined by Ely. Basically, Ely was prepared to retain private property and individual enterprise. Only where capitalism became monopoly enterprise should the community control it. This, it turned out, was what Rauschenbusch also meant by communism.[30]

This was crisis, but an eminently respectable middle-class crisis. Rauschenbusch wrote that it was a matter of individual choice and will whether Christianity should triumph. This was the grandeur of human freedom and responsibility. To strengthen the resolve and bolster the morale of the middle class, Rauschenbusch could only promise that both profane and divine history were on the side of the righteous. Industrialism had constructed the material foundations of the Heavenly City by bringing prosperity, by bringing men together in cities and factories, by bringing about a worldwide community through new means of transportation and communication, by educating men in the habits of cooperation and brotherly love. Beyond this, industrialism had broken the cake of custom so that modern man developed a sense of history, an understanding that institutions had changed and could be changed. The greater freedom of mind also brought about the use of the scientific method in social life, so that men charted with accuracy the laws of social growth and could predict with scientific precision what the future would be like. This was the armory of weapons, drawn from profane history, to use in the crisis.

Of infinitely greater importance was the divine gift of inspiration directly from God. Each step in progress was recorded in history and society. Each succeeding environment in the course of time shaped its inhabitants that much closer to the ideal. Always, however, until the Heavenly City was established, the real fell short of the ideal; always men learned incomplete moral lessons from tradition and the immediate society; always, if there were to be progress, the individual must transcend the present and the past to learn God's will; always the inspired individual had the power to mold mundane history and society to a still closer approach to perfection. And now, at the beginning of the second decade of the twentieth century, God had provided inspiration to a large group of individuals to visualize the completed outline of heaven on earth; God had provided the inspiration to see the task through. This was the climax and triumph of the religion of progress when worldly history should be absorbed totally by the divine history of progress, and imperfect society should become the perfection of the ideal society.

The World as History

AMERICAN life had turned a corner in the 1890s; this is a major watershed in our history. It was a turning in economic and social areas accompanied by tremendous dislocations. Standing near mid-century, we can look back and say that here the industrial evolution accelerated to the point of producing revolutionary ramifications in the total fabric of society. We can look back over this half-century and see a unity, a unity of continuing revolution. We can look into the future and predict continued revolution.

Similarly, in the realm of ideas, by the 1890s, America had entered a new era. Much of the old complacency associated with the Enlightenment had disappeared. But, in perspective, one can see less unity in ideas during the passing decades from 1890 to the present, than in the material world of permanent revolution. We know that the nineteenth century witnessed the steady influx of machine power to provide the foundation for the new departure in the twentieth century. What is much less certain is that the influx of new ideas in the nineteenth century provided the foundation for a twentieth-century climate of opinion when that of the eighteenth century was destroyed.

And was the eighteenth-century climate of opinion truly destroyed? Can one make the analogy that a new way of economic life must find an equal parallel in a new way of intellectual life? Or, indeed, has even the material world of the twentieth century escaped a legacy from the past? Of one thing we can be sure, however, science did not control the American mind from 1900 to 1950, just as it does

246

not control the present. There was no steady, logical erosion of eighteenth-century concepts culminating in the emergence of a new outlook in 1890 or 1900 or 1910. When progress and its primitivistic implications were truly challenged, they were confronted with the brute strength of historical events. If there is a modern climate of opinion, sharply differentiated from the past, it is the intellectual world of men like Carl Becker who were left to wander intellectually and spiritually alone when the world they had known disintegrated so suddenly. This is the world of experiment, not of carefully reasoned, objective conclusion. But this is not the realm in which most men have dwelt and do dwell as they continue their allegiance to traditional attitudes. Yet the world of fragmentation and doubt has greatly influenced our modern outlook. Much of the apathy or confusion of the modern American thinker can be related to the disintegration of the myth of absolute progress.

We have been told by the liberal historians like Goldman, Aaron, and White that young men and women failed to answer the challenge of totalitarian political theory that came after 1920 because they were the prisoners of a debilitating philosophical relativism. Relativism, born of excessive dependence on a scientific version of evolution, made it difficult for them to write about democracy with eloquence or conviction. But to the degree that the progressives of this book are representative of pre-World War I liberalism, it is understandable why the men of that generation and of the younger generation that followed them had difficulty in reacting with decision against the serious ideological challenges that confronted them after World War I. Social theories were so constructed as to leave their possessors in utter bewilderment once their basic premises were demolished — for they were insulated from the world of reality by the very belief that they were realistic because they used the terminology of pragmatism and historicism. Convinced of the soundness of their philosophy, they drifted along the smooth utopian routes they had imposed on the roughness, the contradictions, the problems of their America.

Postulating a perfect human nature, to reach full expression through the new forms of industrialism, the reformers had no obligation to search into the actual conditions of the America or the world of 1910 for the nexus of historical development which had made liberalism possible and which ensured its future. Given the purity of this vision, they could shun the historical record; they had to avoid the bumbling confusion of life for fear that it might obscure the clarity and truth of that vision. And so they could have no vital interest in the day-by-day struggles of liberalism, they could not be bothered with a pragmatic appreciation of methods needed to defend liberal gains or extend them; the ordained, the inevitable, victory of liberalism made superfluous everyday political, social, and economic organizations.

This was the point of no return for many progressives when World War I struck; their entire picture of the world was smashed. The historical record is clear that the war crushed a great deal of romanticism within liberal ranks. Yet the sudden deflation of progressive utopianism has not been related to the problem of explaining the failure of the young people of the 1920s to find principles and ideals to guide their thinking, a failure that has continued to plague liberalism through succeeding years. It is certain that the youth of the 1920s must have looked with something more than skepticism at theories like those of the believers in progress; the weaving of sound liberal sentiments within the framework of an impossible blueprint of social development would make it difficult for the older men to communicate in a constructive manner with the younger. The legacy of inevitable progress and its collapse were, then, a debilitating relativism and an inability to define and to distinguish the respective natures of the individual and society — the very essentials for meaningful political and social theory. Values were to be accepted as the threads of a progressive cosmos, and the individual and society were reciprocal aspects of the mundane expression of that cosmos. What was left when that cosmos no longer existed?

Another recent historical writer, Daniel Boorstin, in contradiction to the liberal historians, has declared in his book *The Genius of American Politics* that Americans need not be concerned with their lack of political theory in the twentieth century. It is to our credit, he believes, that we have never had a political theory. Such theories, his argument runs, are the products of man's desire to alter his institutional environment. But, for Boorstin, "The belief that man could change his institutions at will and that from such changes utopia would flow was perhaps the most basic of the romantic illusions to dissolve in America." [1] He uses the concepts of Frederick Jackson Turner as an example of why Americans have never needed political theory. Turner was aware that American life had flowed out of the past without interruption or major alteration. He was aware of the "givenness" of American history, the inexorable product of our history and geography. He was aware of what Boorstin calls the "seamlessness" of experience which "comes from sensitivity to the fact that American values arise out of a frontier, that the politics and culture of the city are one thing, those of the country another; that the problems of America may be of one kind, those of Europe of another." [2]

Turner was aware, for Boorstin, that America could have no political theory because there was perfect coincidence between institutional and individual life. Turner was aware then "that the whole American experience has been utopian."

Now it is true, as Henry Nash Smith has demonstrated, that Turner had no political theory because he did believe that the American experience had been utopian. Nor did he believe that man had the power to alter his institutions at will. All he postulated was that perfection had been reached when the savage frontier had stripped innately perfect man of his institutional baggage.

But Turner was not prepared to defend his theory of democracy in the twentieth century, a century into which he lived. How could he? He had postulated democracy as the absence of institutional restraint; he had postulated a frontier that would remove that restraint. In 1893 he declared the frontier to be gone and institutions re-emerging. The logical consequence would be the destruction of democracy.

Other men of his generation had broken from this dilemma while remaining true to Professor Boorstin's definition of America as utopia. The political theory of Herbert Croly, influenced by the ideas of the other men in this book, buttressed anew Turner's definition of democracy as the free individual unhampered by institutional restraint.

Croly and colleagues were not wild-eyed European revolutionaries who believed man could create institutions that would achieve utopia. Rather, like Turner, they postulated a force, industrialism, which would remove from man the burden of tradition, of institutions and of history and which would allow the natural man, perfect and innately utopian creature that he was, to stand forth. True, to accomplish this, they had to alter Turner. The natural man was not complete unto himself, he was social. He also had a limited free will to help the cleansing process of industrialism.

But these were not major modifications. They merely allowed Turner's definition to stand in an industrial society. The key to this continuity is the definition of the social man. He was just as given, just as indescribable, just as ahistorical and metaphysical as Turner's individual, because the society of which these men were a part sprang from within them. It was not a society of history, made up of institutions and traditions; it was from prehistory, existing before those irrational and imperfect obstructions to man's perfection appeared. When industry had destroyed history, natural society would stand forth once more.

If, then, Americans have not written political theory in our century, it is because they cannot relate democracy to a historical world filled with institutions and traditions. Democracy, as it is the legacy of the progressive generation, is still freedom from history. Metaphysical affirmation, not tools of understanding, were given by their elders to the generations that have come of age since 1920; and these are affirmations that do not coincide with the world in which Americans have lived since that time.

Carl Becker has left an autobiographical analysis of the intellectual chasm he helped create for himself and his America. What happened to the historian who had interpreted history as progress and then lost that faith? How would Becker react as the lost individual, who believed his only contact with an outer world was through science, which could not verify the existence of a social world, or through subjective desire, which again did nothing to acquaint the individual with the real social world? What could he say about the relative value of democracy as against totalitarianism?

We know from his presidential address, "Everyman His Own Historian," that he could say nothing in the early 1930s, that he had no basis for action. Modern democracy, wrote Becker, is based on the intellectual precepts of the Enlightenment. When the climate of opinion of the eighteenth century was demonstrated to be ephemeral, then democracy lost its meaning. Indeed there were no standards to make the world meaningful. Once we accepted the world as a process of material change, once we accepted reason as the tool of adjustment to change, then all must be forever meaningless subjectivism. There was no definition of right other than might.

On the other hand, Becker related, an amoral attitude was also encouraged by the tradition of objective science which reacted against this subjectivism. If nothing in the realm of values were true, one could renounce responsibility for morality and make a god of science and its application in the realm of technology. Delineating such men, with the sensitivity of autobiography, Becker wrote, "Fascinated by the delicate precision and sheer power of the devices he has invented, he is disposed to use them for doing whatever by their aid can be done, in the confident expectation that what can be done with such clean efficiency must be worth doing." [3] This moral insensitivity to the moral implications of conduct also led irresistibly then to the enthronement of the doctrine that might makes right.

But what, asked Becker, are the implications of the fact that civilization has always felt the threat of the sophistry of this Machiavellian doctrine, that the most famous exponent of the doctrine of might for might's sake is the figure, Thrasymachus, from classical literature? Is it not true, he asked, that societies in transition always foster doctrines of subjectivism or irresponsible factual knowledge? Must not one, therefore, question the perspective of those who, at this moment, deny man's ability to comprehend meaningful standards of behavior? Granted, he continued, that intelligence is shaped by subconscious desire and emotion, is it, therefore, totally shaped by them? Granted that science provides the only way of experimentally proving specific facts in the face of the control of man's mind by desire and emotion, is experimental science, then, the only method of objective knowledge?

Becker's answer to these two questions was by now, in the late 1930s, an emphatic no. Like the *philosophes*, he affirmed that man had the faculty of reason to complement his subjective nature and his tool of science. Like the *philosophes*, he believed the proper area for the exercise of reason was the historical past. And like the *philosophes*, he now believed that man, using reason, through the study of history, could distinguish fact from illusion in the realm of the humane and rational qualities of human personality. He now believed that the rational study of history could demonstrate that there were certain universal standards of moral behavior because he no longer considered himself or any other man as an isolated individual. When he placed Thrasymachus and Machiavelli in history, he also placed the *philosophes* and Carl Becker in history. Reason was the tool that related man to history not the means to escape from it. Universal human nature was the constant relation of man to his institutions and traditions; as integral parts of society, not self-contained individuals, men had the unending responsibility to make their world moral.

It was true, Becker admitted, that the moral ideals of the *philosophes* reflected an immediate environment. It was true that the ideals of Carl Becker also reflected his environment. And if there were a similarity in the two positions, it could be argued that Becker still reflected the vestiges of the Enlightenment. But what is more important, argued Becker, is the fact that reason can transcend the limitations of immediate environment to come into contact with more universal standards. What is more important than the manner in which the *philosophes* and Becker reflect their immediate environment is the fact that their ideals find sanction in the traditions of all civilized men. While it is true that democracy reflects the concepts of the bourgeoisie, it is a higher truth that democracy is merely one more codification of ideals that are as old as the history of civilization. These ideals, Becker affirmed, ". . . are older and more universal than democracy and do not depend upon it. They have a life of their own apart from any particular social system or type of civilization. They are the values which since the time of Buddha and Confucius, Solomon and . . . Jesus, men have commonly employed to measure the advance or the decline of civilization." [4]

With the caution of qualification, but with the dignity of a man, a moral man, Carl Becker urged on his profession the consideration of this alternative to the subjectivism of both behaviorist and positivistic philosophy. Consider, he asked, the possibility that man lives not only in the world of science and in his own mind but also in the world of history that is tradition preserved and clarified; consider the possibility, then, that the historian deals with facts that are not completely the subject of science or of personal desire. For those of us who must consider the future of whatever is left of our revolutionary century, Becker would add that perhaps we might do well to attempt an understanding of the past and therefore that future, not in terms of watersheds that cut us off from that past or sharply differentiated climates of opinion, but in terms of his final admonition to consider the constant humanity of man throughout time.

NOTES AND INDEX

Notes

Chapter I. A World without History

[1] H. S. Commager, *The American Mind* (New Haven: Yale University Press, 1950), 41.

[2] *Ibid.*, 47.

[3] *Ibid.*, 54.

[4] Carl Becker, *The Heavenly City of the Eighteenth-Century Philosophers* (New Haven: Yale University Press, 1932), 7.

[5] *Ibid.*, 16.

[6] *Ibid.*, 27.

[7] *Ibid.*, 31.

[8] Quoted in Carl Becker, "The Dilemma of Diderot," *Philosophical Review*, XXIV (January 1915), 61.

[9] Becker, *The Heavenly City*, 102.

[10] *Ibid.*, 15.

[11] Ernst Cassirer, *The Philosophy of the Enlightenment* (Boston: Beacon Press, 1955).

[12] Charles Frankel, *The Faith of Reason* (New York: Columbia University Press, 1948).

[13] Arthur O. Lovejoy, *The Great Chain of Being* (Cambridge: Harvard University Press, 1942), 250.

[14] Bert J. Loewenberg, "Darwinism Comes to America, 1859–1900," *Mississippi Valley Historical Review*, XXVIII (December 1941), 339–368.

[15] Sidney Ratner, "Evolution and the Rise of the Scientific Spirit in America," *Philosophy of Science*, III (January 1936), 104–122.

[16] Becker, *The Heavenly City*, 20.

[17] Morton G. White, *Social Thought in America* (New York: Viking, 1949); Daniel Aaron, *Men of Good Hope* (New York: Oxford University Press, 1951); Eric Goldman, *Rendezvous with Destiny* (New York: Alfred A. Knopf, 1952).

[18] Goldman, *op. cit.*, 93–94.

[19] *Ibid.*, 200.

[20] Becker, "Everyman His Own Historian," *American Historical Review*, XXXVII (January 1932), 221–236.

[21] *Ibid.*, 227.

[22] *Ibid.*, 233.

[23] Becker, *The Heavenly City*, 20.

[24] Becker, "The Dilemma of Diderot," 69.

[25] Becker, "Some Aspects of the Influence of Social Problems upon the Study and Writing of History," *American Journal of Sociology*, XVIII (March 1913), 641–675. Phil L. Snyder, in his article "Carl L. Becker and the Great War: A Crisis for a Humane Intelligence," *Western Political Quarterly*, IX (March 1956), 1–11, has analyzed the manner in which the events of World War I helped to corrode Becker's earlier optimism. It was not philosophy alone which presented Becker with his dilemma.

[26] *Ibid.*, 672.

[27] *Ibid.*, 664.

[28] *Ibid.*, 674.

Chapter II. The Heavenly City of the *New Republic*

[1] Herbert Croly, *The Promise of American Life* (New York: Macmillan, 1909). For the founding of the *New Republic*, see Herbert Croly, *Willard Straight* (New York: Macmillan, 1924) and the group of essays on Croly in the *New Republic*, LXIII (July 16, 1930), 243–271, and Goldman, *Rendezvous with Destiny*.

[2] Quoted in Goldman, 232.

[3] *New Republic*, V (November 6, 1915), 6.

[4] *Ibid.*, III (May 29, 1915), 95–97.

[5] *Ibid.* See the *New Republic* during the fall of 1914 and winter of 1914–1915.

[6] Quoted from Robert M. Lovett, *All Our Years* (New York: Viking, 1948), 173.

[7] *New Republic*, I (December 12, 1914), 7.

[8] *Ibid.*, I (December 12, 1914), 7.

[9] *Ibid.*, III (July 10, 1915), 242.

[10] *Ibid.*, III (May 22, 1915), 56.

[11] *Ibid.*, V (November 20, 1915), 58; VI (March 11, 1916), 144.

[12] *Ibid.*, V (November 6, 1915), 6.

[13] *Ibid.*, VII (June 3, 1916), 108.

[14] *Ibid.*, VII (June 24, 1916), 182.

[15] *Ibid.*, VII (July 1, 1916), 212.

[16] *Ibid.*, VIII (September 9, 1916), 129.

[17] *Ibid.*, IX (November 25, 1916), 81–82.

[18] *Ibid.*, IX (December 16, 1916), 168.

[19] *Ibid.*, IX (December 30, 1916), 230.

[20] *Ibid.*, IX (January 20, 1917), 311–313.

[21] *Ibid.*, X (February 3, 1917), Cover.

[22] *Ibid.*, 3–4.

[23] *Ibid.*, X (April 7, 1917), 280.

[24] *Ibid.*, X (April 21, 1917), 336–338.

[25] *Ibid.*, X (March 31, 1917), 249–250.

[26] *Ibid.*, XVII (November 16, 1918), 58.

Chapter III. Herbert Croly: The Progressive Road to Political Utopia

[1] Goldman, *Rendezvous with Destiny*, 192–193.

[2] See Goldman, Aaron, and John Chamberlain, *Farewell to Reform* (New

Notes

York: Liveright, 1932); the issue of the *New Republic* devoted to the memory of Croly, *New Republic*, LXVIII (July 16, 1930), 243–271; and *Dictionary of American Biography*, XXI, 209–210.

[3] Croly, *The Promise of American Life*, Chapter I.

[4] *Ibid.*

[5] *Ibid.*, 117–126.

[6] *Ibid.*, 141–154.

[7] *Ibid.*, 16–26.

[8] *Ibid.*, 207–214 and 279–288.

[9] *Ibid.*, 212.

[10] *Ibid.*, 2.

[11] *Ibid.*, 454.

[12] *Ibid.*, 21.

[13] For the Hegelian influence on American thought at the end of the nineteenth century, see Merle Curti, *The Social Ideas of American Educators* (New York: Scribner, 1934); Fay Berger Karpf, *American Social Psychology* (New York: McGraw-Hill, 1932); and Frances Harmon, *The Social Philosophy of the St. Louis Hegelians* (New York: privately printed, 1943).

[14] Croly, *Progressive Democracy* (New York: Macmillan, 1914).

[15] Croly, *The Promise*, 453.

[16] Croly, *Progressive Democracy*, 1–2.

[17] *Ibid.*, 41, 153–154.

[18] *Ibid.*, 168.

[19] *Ibid.*, see the analysis in Chapter VIII.

[20] *Ibid.*, 177.

[21] *Ibid.*, Chapter IX.

[22] *Ibid.*, 38, 154.

[23] *Ibid.*, 215–216.

[24] *Ibid.*, 311.

[25] *Ibid.* Chapters XIII through XVI deal with Croly's ideas on the role of the executive and legislature.

[26] *Ibid.*, 217. The analysis of the administrator is in Chapter XVII.

Chapter IV. James Mark Baldwin: The Social Psychology of the Natural Man

[1] G. S. Brett, *A History of Psychology* (London: Allen, 1921); Karpf, *American Social Psychology*; James Mark Baldwin, *Between Two Wars* (Boston: Stratford, 1926); and Vahan D. Sewny, *The Social Theory of James Mark Baldwin* (New York: Kings Crown Press, 1945).

[2] Quoted in Brett, III, 38.

[3] James Mark Baldwin, *Darwin and the Humanities* (Baltimore: Review, 1909), 48.

[4] Baldwin, *Social and Ethical Interpretations in Mental Development* (New York: Macmillan, 1906), 166–167.

[5] Baldwin, *Darwin and the Humanities*, 61.

[6] Baldwin, *Development and Evolution* (New York: Macmillan, 1902), 305.

[7] Baldwin, *Darwin and the Humanities*, 83.

[8] *Ibid.*, 85.

[9] H. W. Schneider, *History of American Philosophy* (New York: Columbia University Press, 1946), 240–246, 370–372.

[10] F. J. Teggart, *Theory of History* (New Haven: Yale University Press, 1925), Chapter VII, "The Idea of Progress and the Foundations of the Comparative Method."

[11] William C. Lehmann, *Adam Ferguson and the Beginnings of Modern Sociology* (New York: Columbia University Press, 1930); Gladys Bryson, *Man and Society* (Princeton: Princeton University Press, 1945); and Lois Whitney, *Primitivism and the Idea of Progress* (Baltimore: Johns Hopkins, 1934).

[12] Bryson, *Man and Society*, 45.

[13] Adam Ferguson, *Civil Liberty*, quoted in Bryson, *Man and Society*, 51–52.

[14] Adam Ferguson, *Principles of Moral and Political Science*, quoted in Whitney, *Primitivism and the Idea of Progress*, 151.

[15] Baldwin, *Social and Ethical Interpretations in Mental Development*, 201.

[16] *Ibid.*, 40–65. *The Individual and Society* (Boston: Richard Badger, 1911), 13–32.

[17] Baldwin, *Social and Ethical Interpretations in Mental Development*, 521–522.

[18] *Ibid.*, 27.

[19] Baldwin, *The Individual and Society*, 46. *The Genetic Theory of Reality* (New York: Putnam, 1915), 19.

[20] Baldwin, *The Individual and Society*, 36–50.

[21] *Ibid.*, 124–127. *Social and Ethical Interpretations in Mental Development*, 163ff.

[22] *The Individual and Society*, 118ff.

[23] *Ibid.*, 136–144.

[24] Baldwin, *Social and Ethical Interpretations in Mental Development*, 303–329.

[25] Baldwin, *The Individual and Society*, 69.

[26] Baldwin, *Social and Ethical Interpretations in Mental Development*, 567.

[27] Baldwin, *The Individual and Society*, 46.

[28] Baldwin, *The Genetic Theory of Reality*, 39.

[29] *Ibid.*, 22–39.

[30] *Ibid.*, 217–308.

[31] *Ibid.*, 267.

[32] *Ibid.*, 114.

[33] *Ibid.*, 117.

Chapter V. Charles H. Cooley: The Transcendentalism of Social Science

[1] Edward C. Jandy, *Charles Horton Cooley* (New York: Dryden, 1942).

[2] Charles H. Cooley, Journals (University of Michigan Library).

[3] Journal, 1882.

[4] Journal 16 (1903), 46.

[5] Journal 16 (1902), 18.

[6] Journal 11 (1896), 37.

[7] Journal 12 (1897), 50.

[8] Journal 11 (1896), 57. *Sociological Theory and Social Research* (New York: Henry Holt, 1930), 297.

[9] For the German influence on Cooley, see Jandy, *op. cit.*, and Richard Dewey's chapter on Cooley in *An Introduction to the History of Sociology* (Chicago: University of Chicago Press, 1948).

Notes

[10] Cooley, "The Process of Social Change," *Political Science Quarterly*, XII (March 1897), 63–87.

[11] Cooley, *Human Nature and the Social Order* (New York: Scribner, 1922).

[12] *Ibid.*, 118–119.

[13] Cooley, *Social Organization* (New York: Scribner, 1913), 97.

[14] *Ibid.*, 320.

[15] Cooley, "The Institutional Character of Pecuniary Valuation," *American Journal of Sociology*, XVIII (January 1913), 543–555; "The Sphere of Pecuniary Valuation," *American Journal of Sociology*, XIX (September 1913), 188–203; and "The Progress of Pecuniary Valuation," *Quarterly Journal of Economics*, XXX (November 1913), 1–21.

[16] Cooley, *Social Process* (New York: Scribner, 1920), 391.

[17] Cooley, *Social Organization*, 47.

[18] *Ibid.*

[19] *Ibid.*, 23–24.

[20] *Ibid.*, 28.

[21] Journal 17 (1903), 9; Journal 16 (1902), 118.

[22] Cooley, "Process of Social Change," 71.

[23] Cooley, *Social Organization*, 90.

[24] *Ibid.*, 118.

[25] *Ibid.*

[26] Cooley, *Sociological Theory and Social Research*, 258.

[27] Cooley, *Social Process*, 42.

[28] *Ibid.*, 400, 395, 401.

[29] *Ibid.*, 413.

[30] Journal 11 (1896), 55.

[31] Journal 15 (1902), 68.

[32] Cooley, *Social Process*, 418.

[33] *Ibid.*, 109.

[34] *Ibid.*, 103.

Chapter VI. F. H. Johnson and H. D. Lloyd: Immanent God and Creative Man

[1] Daniel Day Williams, *The Andover Liberals* (New York: Kings Crown, 1941).

[2] Johnson is discussed in Stow Persons' essay, "Evolution and Theology in America," in *Evolutionary Thought in America* and in Herbert W. Schneider, "Evolution and Theology in America," *Journal of the History of Ideas*, VI (January 1945), 3–18.

[3] F. H. Johnson, "Theistic Evolution," *Andover Review*, I (April 1884), 371.

[4] F. H. Johnson, "The Evolution of Conscience," *Andover Review*, II (December 1884), 535.

[5] F. H. Johnson, "Mechanical Evolution," *Andover Review*, I (June 1884), 631–649; "The Evolution of Conscience," *Andover Review*, II (December 1884), 529–548.

[6] Johnson, "The Evolution of Conscience," 546.

[7] *Ibid.*, 530.

[8] Johnson, "What Is Reality," *Andover Review*, XI (March 1889), 225–240.

[9] Johnson, "The Answer of Life," *Andover Review*, XII (July 1889), 89.

[10] Johnson, "Pantheistic Theism," *Andover Review*, XIII (June 1890), 644.

[11] Johnson, "The Thing-in-Itself," *Andover Review*, XII (September 1889), 235.

[12] Johnson, "Pantheistic Theism," 638.

[13] For a full discussion of Abbott, see Persons, *Free Religion* (New Haven: Yale University Press, 1947).

[14] *Ibid.*, 108.

[15] *Ibid.*, 140.

[16] For a discussion of Ward, see Richard Hofstadter, *Social Darwinism in America* (Philadelphia: University of Pennsylvania Press, 1945) and Samuel Chugerman, *Lester Frank Ward* (Durham: Duke University Press, 1939).

[17] See Chugerman, 82–96.

[18] Lester F. Ward, *Pure Sociology* (New York: Macmillan, 1907), 56–57.

[19] Ward, *Applied Sociology* (Boston: Ginn, 1906), 89–90.

[20] The facts of Lloyd's background are to be found in Caroline Lloyd, *Henry Demarest Lloyd* (New York: Putnam, 1912), and interpretations of his career in C. M. Destler, *American Radicalism* (New London: Conn. College Book Shop, 1946) and Daniel Aaron, *Men of Good Hope.*

[21] Lloyd, *Man the Social Creator* (New York: Doubleday, Page, 1906), 118, 119.

[22] Lloyd, *Lords of Industry* (New York: Putnam, 1910), 147.

[23] Lloyd, *Wealth vs. Commonwealth* (New York: Harper, 1894), 497.

[24] Lloyd Transcript Papers (Wisconsin Historical Society Library), Small Notebook B (1881), 14. Card notes, 146.

[25] Lloyd, *Man the Social Creator*, 220–221.

[26] *Ibid.*, 174.

[27] Lloyd, *Man the Social Creator*, 44.

[28] Lloyd Papers. Transcript Card notes 3. Small notebook F (1883), 66.

[29] Lloyd, *Man the Social Creator*, 67.

[30] Lloyd Papers. Transcript Notebook 13 (1888), 341.

[31] Lloyd Papers. Notebook 18 (1890), 487.

[32] Lloyd Papers. Transcript Notebook 12 (November 1888), 330.

[33] Lloyd, *Man the Social Creator*, 179.

[34] *Ibid.*, 135.

[35] Lloyd, *Man the Social Creator*, 12.

[36] *Ibid.*, 16, 94.

[37] Lloyd Papers. Transcript Notebook 11 (1902), 51.

[38] Lloyd, *Man the Social Creator*, 10.

[39] *Ibid.*, 100–177.

[40] *Ibid.*, 153–177.

Chapter VII. Richard T. Ely: The Economist as Christian and Prophet

[1] See Joseph Dorfman, *The Economic Mind in American Civilization* (New York: Viking, 1949), Vol. III, Chapter IX.

[2] The details of Ely's life are to be found in Richard T. Ely, *Ground under Our Feet* (New York: Macmillan, 1938) and John R. Everett, *Religion in Economics* (New York: Kings Crown, 1946).

[3] Ely, *The Past and Present of Political Economy* (Baltimore: Johns Hopkins, 1884).

[4] *Ibid.*, 12–13.

Notes

[5] *Ibid.*, 46–47.

[6] This analysis is found in Ely's *Studies in the Evolution of Industrial Society* (New York: Macmillan, 1913), 398–408.

[7] *Ibid.*, 403.

[8] Ely, "Fundamental Beliefs in My Social Philosophy," *Forum*, XVIII (October 1894). *The Social Aspects of Christianity* (New York: Thomas Crowell, 1889), 122.

[9] Ely, *The Social Aspects of Christianity*, 119.

[10] Ely, *The Social Law of Service* (New York: Methodist Book Concern, 1896), Chapter VII.

[11] *Ibid.*, 145–146.

[12] *Ibid.*, Chapter VII. *Socialism and Social Reform* (New York: Thomas Crowell, 1894), 50–55.

[13] Ely, *Studies in the Evolution of Industrial Society*, 26.

[14] Quoted in John R. Everett, *Religion in Economics* (New York: Kings Crown, 1946), 83.

[15] Ely, *Socialism and Social Reform*, 50–55.

[16] For Ely's view of conservative leadership, see his "Fundamental Beliefs in My Social Philosophy," 183.

[17] Ely, *Socialism and Social Reform*, 206–214.

[18] Ely, *The Social Aspects of Christianity*, 53.

[19] Ely, *The Social Law of Service*, Chapter V.

[20] Ely, *The Social Aspects of Christianity*, 12–17.

Chapter VIII. Simon Patten: The Economist as Biologist and Prophet

[1] "Memorial Addresses on the Life and Service of Simon N. Patten," *Annals of the American Academy of Political and Social Science* (May 1923), 333–367, and Rexford G. Tugwell, "Notes on the Life and Work of Simon Nelson Patten," *Journal of Political Economy*, XXXI (April 1923), 153–208.

[2] Patten, *The Premises of Political Economy* (Philadelphia: Lippincott, 1885).

[3] *Ibid.*, 75–76.

[4] *Ibid.*, 66–75.

[5] Patten, *Essays in Economic Theory*, ed. by Rexford Tugwell (New York: Alfred A. Knopf, 1924), 28.

[6] *Ibid.*, 137–140.

[7] Patten, *The Premises of Political Economy*, 92.

[8] Patten, *Essays in Economic Theory*, 189.

[9] Patten, "The Failure of Biologic Sociology," *Annals of the American Academy of Political and Social Science*, IV (May 1894), 923.

[10] Patten, "The Theory of Social Forces," Supplement to the *Annals of the American Academy of Political and Social Science* (January 1896), 5.

[11] *Ibid.*, 52–55.

[12] *Ibid.*, 78.

[13] Patten, *The Development of English Thought* (New York: Macmillan, 1899).

[14] *Ibid.*, 1–14.

[15] *Ibid.*, 17.

[16] *Ibid.*, 21–37.

[17] *Ibid.*, 27–30.

[18] *Ibid.*, 30–32, 185–186.
[19] *Ibid.*, 369.
[20] *Ibid.*, 391–392.
[21] Patten, *Heredity and Social Progress* (New York: Macmillan, 1903).
[22] *Ibid.*, 24–27.
[23] *Ibid.*, 183.
[24] *Ibid.*, 139.
[25] Patten, *The New Basis of Civilization* (New York: Macmillan, 1907).
[26] *Ibid.*, 39.
[27] *Ibid.*, 91, 114.
[28] Patten, *The Social Basis of Religion* (New York: Macmillan, 1911).
[29] *Ibid.*, 196.
[30] *Ibid.*, xiii–xiv.
[31] *Ibid.*, ix–xi.
[32] *Ibid.*, 151–153.
[33] *Ibid.*, 10.
[34] *Ibid.*, 39.
[35] *Ibid.*, 70–71.
[36] *Ibid.*, 229.

Chapter IX. Thorstein Veblen: The Economist as Scientist and Prophet

[1] Joseph Dorfman, *Thorstein Veblen and His America* (New York: Viking, 1947).

[2] Thorstein Veblen, "Why Is Economics Not an Evolutionary Science?" *Quarterly Journal of Economics*, XII (July 1898), reprinted in *The Place of Science in Modern Civilisation* (New York: Huebsch, 1919).

[3] *Ibid.*, 61.

[4] Veblen, "The Preconceptions of Economic Science," *Quarterly Journal of Economics*, XIII (January 1899; July 1899; February 1900), reprinted in *The Place of Science in Modern Civilisation.*

[5] *Ibid.*, 73.

[6] Veblen, "The Place of Science in Modern Civilisation," *American Journal of Sociology*, XI (March 1906), reprinted in *The Place of Science in Modern Civilisation.*

[7] *Ibid.*, 5.

[8] *Ibid.*, 11.

[9] *Ibid.*, 21.

[10] *Ibid.*, 25–26.

[11] Veblen, *The Instinct of Workmanship* (New York: Macmillan, 1914).

[12] Veblen, "Some Neglected Points in the Theory of Socialism," *Annals of the American Academy of Political and Social Science*, II (1892), reprinted in *The Place of Science in Modern Civilisation.*

[13] *Ibid.*, 406–408.

[14] Veblen, "The Socialist Economics of Karl Marx and His Followers," *Quarterly Journal of Economics*, XX (August 1906), reprinted in *The Place of Science in Modern Civilisation*, 410.

[15] *Ibid.*, 416–417.

[16] *Ibid.*, 22.

[17] Veblen, *The Theory of the Leisure Class* (New York: Modern Library, 1934).

Notes

[18] *Ibid.*, 236–245.
[19] *Ibid.*, 1–2.
[20] *Ibid.*, 204.
[21] Veblen, *The Theory of Business Enterprise* (New York: Scribner, 1904).
[22] *Ibid.*, 308ff.
[23] *Ibid.*, 14.
[24] *Ibid.*, 72ff.
[25] *Ibid.*, 375.
[26] *Ibid.*, 66–67.
[27] *Ibid.*, 374.
[28] *Ibid.*, 358.
[29] *Ibid.*, 358.
[30] Veblen, *The Instinct of Workmanship*, 36.
[31] See the analysis of Arthur K. Davis in his "Sociological Elements in Veblen's Economic Theory," *Journal of Political Economy*, III (1945), and David Riesman, *Thorstein Veblen* (New York: Scribner, 1953), Chapter II.
[32] Veblen, *The Instinct of Workmanship*, 49, 50.
[33] Veblen, "Christian Morals and the Competitive System," *International Journal of Ethics*, XX (January 1910), reprinted in *Essays in Our Changing Order*, ed. by Leon Ardzrooni (New York: Viking, 1934).
[34] *Ibid.*, 209.
[35] *Ibid.*, 218.
[36] For instance, Veblen mentioned the possibility of a revival of barbaric qualities in his *The Theory of Business Enterprise*. However, it was a possibility that did not fit the logic of his arguments on social causation and social discipline.

Chapter X. Walter Rauschenbusch: Prophet

[1] Veblen, "Kant's Critique of Judgment," *Journal of Speculative Philosophy*, XVIII (July 1884), reprinted in *Essays in Our Changing Order*.
[2] *Ibid.*, 185.
[3] *Ibid.*, 193.
[4] Vernon P. Bodein, *The Social Gospel of Walter Rauschenbusch* (New Haven: Yale University Press, 1944).
[5] Walter Rauschenbusch, *Christianity and the Social Crisis* (New York: Macmillan, 1907).
[6] *Ibid.*, xi–xii.
[7] *Ibid.*
[8] *Ibid.*, xiii.
[9] *Ibid.*, 1–3.
[10] *Ibid.*, 45.
[11] *Ibid.*, 1.
[12] *Ibid.*, 17.
[13] *Ibid.*, 27ff.
[14] *Ibid.*
[15] *Ibid.*, 45ff.
[16] *Ibid.*, 60ff.
[17] *Ibid.*, 100ff.
[18] *Ibid.*, 149ff.
[19] *Ibid.*, 201.
[20] *Ibid.*, 209.
[21] *Ibid.*, 210.

[22] *Ibid.*, 349, 352.
[23] *Ibid.*, 422.
[24] Rauschenbusch, *Christianity and the Social Order* (New York: Macmillan, 1912).
[25] *Ibid.*, vii, 6.
[26] *Ibid.*, 124.
[27] *Ibid.*, 136ff.
[28] *Ibid.*, 150.
[29] *Ibid.*, 3.
[30] *Ibid.*, 341.

Chapter XI. The World as History

[1] Daniel Boorstin, *The Genius of American Politics* (Chicago: University of Chicago Press, 1953), 173.
[2] *Ibid.*, 175.
[3] Carl Becker, "Some Generalities That Still Glitter," contained in the collection of essays *New Liberties for Old* (New Haven: Yale University Press, 1941), 140.
[4] *Ibid.*, 149.

Index

Aaron, Daniel, 247; on relativism in American thought, 16–17
Abbot, Francis, 133, 134
Andover Review, 127, 132, 133
Aristotelian evolution: Baldwin and, 85–89; Cooley and, 114–118; Lloyd and, 148–149; Ely and, 168; Patten and, 189–191; Veblen and, 223–225
Aristotle, 98, 103, 117, 118, 129, 148, 159, 166, 167, 188, 189, 193

Baldwin, James Mark, 78–102, 103, 104, 109, 111, 112, 113, 114, 115, 116, 119, 121, 125, 126, 127, 129, 138, 145, 150, 151, 171, 188; and physical science, 78–81, 83–84; rejects determinism, 80–83; on Darwinian evolution, 80–82; finds Spencer inadequate, 80–83; rejects William James, 84, 100; and pragmatic approach to evolution and progress, 84, 99; and limitation of relativism, 84–85; and theory of social science, 84–89; Calvinist background of, 85; on Aristotelian evolution, 85–89; on Hegel, 89–93; and primitivism, 90–98; and theory of historical stages, 94–98; on Comte, 98–99; and millennialism, 98–102; on relation of science to faith, 100–102; and theory of history as moral progress, 101–102; and religion of progress, 101–102
Becker, Carl, 103, 158, 200, 201, 213, 247, 250–251; and science, 5–10, 18–34, 251–253; on climates of opinion, 5–11; on relativism, 9–10, 18–

19, 251–253; on twentieth century, 14–15; on progress, 23–25; on morality, 26–30; "Everyman His Own Historian," 30–32; rejection of subjectivism, 252–253
Bentham, Jeremiah, 212
Bluntschli, Johann, 160
Boorstin, Daniel, 248–249
Bryson, Gladys, 87

Cairnes, John, 204, 206
Calvinism: and Baldwin, 85; and Lloyd, 138–139; and Ely, 160–161; and Patten, 174–175; and Veblen, 199–200
Cassirer, Ernst, 15; theory of nominalism in the eighteenth century, 11–12
Christianity, 7, 8, 113, 116, 133, 160, 185, 186, 191, 192, 227, 230–245; Cooley and, 116–118; Johnson and, 127–132; Ely and, 171–173; Patten and, 192–198; Veblen and, 225–227; historical analysis by Rauschenbusch, 232–238; Rauschenbusch on Christian basis of modern society, 240–245
Commager, Henry S., 4, 15
Comte, Auguste, 78, 81, 98, 99, 101, 125, 135, 179, 194
Cooley, Charles, 103–124, 125, 126, 127, 138, 139, 145, 150, 151, 171, 224; and transcendentalism, 104–107; rejects determinism, 105–110; and physical science, 106–109; and pragmatic approach to evolution and progress, 107–109, 113–114; and

Index

American thought, 16–17; description of Croly, 55

Green, Thomas Hill, 165, 166, 167

Hanna, Mark, 68

Hegel, George F. W., 79–81, 89, 90, 91, 92, 93, 95, 99, 103, 111, 120, 125, 126, 130, 194, 212

Historical relativism, *see* History

History: Commager's view of *1890s*, 3–5; Becker on, 5–10, 18–20, 23–25, 250–253; *New Republic* and, 52–54; and millennialism, 52–54; Croly and, 57, 61–65, 75–77; historical crisis, 57, 114, 139–140, 168–170, 219–223, 230–231; historical context, 61–65; as moral progress, 75–77, 101–102, 122–124, 129–132, 153–154, 171–173, 198, 225–227, 238–240; historical stages, 94–98; Baldwin and, 94–98, 101–102; Cooley and, 113–114, 115–116, 122–124; historical relativism, 113–114, 142–143, 161–163, 175–180, 201–206, 232–233; ahistorical society, 115–116, 144–150, 167–168, 181–185, 190–192, 207–209, 214–219, 223–227, 233–235; Johnson and, 129–132; Lloyd and, 139–140, 142–143, 144–150, 153–154; Ely and, 161–163, 167–168, 168–170, 171–173; Patten and, 175–180, 181–185, 190–192, 198; Veblen and, 201–206, 207–209, 214–219, 219–223, 223–227; Rauschenbusch and, 230–231, 232–233, 233–235, 238–240; *1920* as a turning point in, 247–248; Boorstin on American history, 248–249

Hume, David, 6

Industrialism: Commager on, 2–4; as revolutionary force, 3–4, 57–60; and war, 41–42; *New Republic* and, 41–42, 43–44, 52–53; and established society, 43–44, 52–53; Croly and, 57–60; Cooley and, 113–114, 117–118; industrial crisis, 113–114, 139–142, 161–165, 168–170, 183–185, 218–222, 230–240; industrial society, 117–118, 150–156, 168–173, 190–198, 222–225, 240–245; Lloyd and, 139–142, 150–156; Ely and,

161–165, 168–173; Patten and, 183–185, 190–198; Veblen and, 218–222, 222–225; Rauschenbusch and, 230–240, 240–245; and the modern political crisis, 246–250. *See also* Labor

James, William, 84, 99, 193

Johnson, Francis H., 125–134, 233; and Darwinian evolution, 127–129; finds Spencer inadequate, 127–128; rejection of determinism, 127–129; and physical science, 127–129; and Christianity, 127–132; and theory of history as moral progress, 129–132; and pragmatic approach, 130–132; and evolution and progress, 130–131; and limitation of relativism, 131–133; and transcendental evolution, 131–132

Kant, Immanuel, 228–229

Knies, Karl, 160

Labor: *New Republic* and organization of, 42–44; Croly on specialization of, 59; Lloyd and, 152–156; movement for reform, 152–156, 170–173, 243–245; disappearance of laboring class, 153; Ely and, 170–173; middle-class leadership for, 170–173, 183–185, 243–245; Patten and, 183–185, 190–191; laboring man and natural man, 190–191, 208, 217–225; Veblen and, 208, 217–225; middle-class corruption of labor, 217; Rauschenbusch and, 243–245. *See also* Industrialism

Lamarck, J. B. P. A. de M., 81, 187

Lieber, Francis, 139

Lippmann, Walter, 35

Lloyd, Henry D., 138–156, 157, 158, 159, 170–171; rejection of Calvinism, 138–139; and theory of historical crisis, 139–140; and theory of industrial crisis, 139–142; rejection of determinism, 141–146; and theory of historical relativism, 142–143; and theory of social science, 142, 154; and pragmatic approach, 142–143, 146–148; and evolution and progress, 142–143; and physical sci-

Index

Baldwin and, 84, 99, 100; of William James, 84, 99, 193; Cooley and, 107–109, 113–114, 115–124; Johnson and, 130–132; Lloyd and, 142–143, 146–148; and economics, 160–164, 175–178, 196–197, 201–206; Ely and, 166–173; Patten and, 175–180, 193–198; Veblen and, 201–206, 207, 208–209, 214–215, 223–227; Rauschenbusch and, 233–234; Boorstin on American political theory and, 248–249

Primitivism: and the Enlightenment, 7–10; and progressivism, 23–26; and the *New Republic*, 52–54; and Croly, 58–59, 76–77; and Greek philosophy, 85–86; and Scottish philosophy, 86–89; and Baldwin, 90–98; and Cooley, 115–118; and Lloyd, 148–152; and Ely, 167–169; and Patten, 179–180, 189–192; and Veblen, 202–204, 207–208, 214–219, 223–227; and Rauschenbusch, 233–235

Progress: Becker on, 23–25; Croly on, 68–73, 75–77; pragmatic approach to, 68–73, 84, 99, 107–109, 113–114, 130–131, 142–143, 232–233; religion of, 70, 101–102, 122–124, 144–145, 195–198; history as moral progress, 75–77, 101–102, 122–124, 129–132, 153–154, 171–173, 225–227, 238–240; Baldwin on, 84, 99, 101–102; Cooley on, 107–109, 113, 114, 122–124; Johnson on, 129–132; Lloyd on, 142–143, 144–145, 153–154; Ely on, 171–173; Patten on, 195–198; Rauschenbusch on, 232–233, 238–240; Veblen on, 225–227

Ratner, Sidney, 15

Rauschenbusch, Walter, 228–245; theory of historical crisis, 230–231; theory of industrial crisis, 230–240; rejection of determinism, 231–233; historical analysis of Christianity, 232–238; pragmatic approach to progress, 232–233; theory of historical relativism, 232–233; on physical science, 232–235; and primitivism, 233–235; limitation of pragmatic approach, 233–234; limitation of

relativism, 233–245; and evolution, 236–238; theory of history as moral progress, 238–240; theory of social science, 238; and millennialism, 239–241; on relation of science to faith, 239–240; on Christian basis of modern society, 240–245; theory of industrial society, 240–245; theory of importance of labor for reform, 243–245; theory of middle-class leadership for labor, 243–245

Reed, John, quoted, 35

Relativism: Commager on, 4; Becker on, 9–10, 18–19, 251–253; and the *philosophes*, 11; Cassirer on, 11–12; Frankel on, 12; Lovejoy on, 12–13; Loewenberg on, 13–14; White, Aaron, and Goldman on, 16–17; and the modern historian, 24–25; and the *New Republic*, 52–54; rejection of determinism, 68–72, 80–83, 105–110, 127–129, 141–146, 160–165, 201–212, 231–233; Croly and, 75; limitation of, 75, 84–85, 114–118, 131–133, 133–134, 135–138, 147–152, 166–170, 190–198, 214–227, 233–245; Baldwin and, 84–85; Cooley and, 114–118; Johnson and, 131–133; Abbot and, 133–134; Ward and, 135–138; Lloyd and, 147–152; Ely and, 166–170; economic, 175–186; biological, 186–190; Patten and, 190–198; Veblen and, 214–227; Rauschenbusch and, 233–245; and modern political thought, 247–253. *See also* History, Science

Ricardo, David, 175–176

Roosevelt, Theodore, 35

Schaeffle, Albert, 109–110

Science: and modern historiography, 4–6; in twentieth century, 4–6; Becker and, 5–10, 18–34, 251–253; in eighteenth century, 7–13; Cassirer on, 11–12; Lovejoy on, 12–13; Loewenberg on, 13–14; Aaron, Goldman, and White on, 16–17; and relativism, 16–17, 251–253; importance for *New Republic*, 52–54; Croly and, 61–62, 69–71, 75–77; physical, 61–62, 78–83, 106–109,

271